FINDING
SUZY

ABOUT THE AUTHOR

David Videcette is a former Scotland Yard investigator with expertise in counterterrorism and organised crime. He is the author of the Jake Flannagan crime thrillers based on true events.

Website: www.davidvidecette.com

FINDING SUZY

THE HUNT FOR MISSING ESTATE AGENT SUZY LAMPLUGH AND 'MR KIPPER'

DAVID VIDECETTE

Finding Suzy
Published by Videcette Limited

Copyright © Videcette Limited 2021

Ebook ISBN: 978-0-9934263-6-0
Paperback ISBN: 978-0-9934263-7-7
Hardback ISBN 978-0-9934263-8-4

Copy-editing and typesetting by
Ten Thousand | Editing + Book Design
www.tenthousand.co.uk

Find out more about the author and his upcoming titles at:
www.DavidVidecette.com/about-david

DISCLAIMER

The book you are about to read is a work of non-fiction depicting actual events as recollection and notes permit and/or can be verified by research. Certain names and details have been changed for legal reasons and to respect privacy.

PROLOGUE

'There has not been a single trace of her. Nothing. Just as though she has been erased by a rubber.'

(Diana Lamplugh)

Approximately 2,500 people go missing in the UK every single year and are never seen or heard from again.

They vanish into thin air.

For their families, it's as if their loved one has simply been erased.

On the last Monday in July 1986, 25-year-old estate agent Suzy Lamplugh became one of the 2,500. She disappeared in a smart London suburb, ostensibly whilst out conducting a house viewing. For Suzy, it was completely out of character.

She was reported missing by her estate agency branch manager. A police investigation began in earnest almost immediately, but after just over a year, it was closed – having developed few, if any, leads worthy of mention.

Police investigators focused on a man in a suit, often described as 'a suave businessman', who was reportedly seen with a woman outside the house Suzy was believed to be showing on the day of her disappearance.

In 1993, Suzy was officially declared dead by a court in Wales. It was the seventh anniversary of her disappearance. The court accepted that Suzy likely died on the day she went missing; her death certificate records 28 July 1986 as the day of her death.

No crime scene was ever located; her body never recovered.

At the turn of the millennium, fourteen years after Suzy's disappearance and following pressure from Suzy's mother, the case was reopened by a second team of police investigators.

Diana Lamplugh had alleged, amongst other things, that the original police team had failed to investigate a key suspect in the case. A review and subsequent reinvestigation led police to officially name this man at a press conference in 2002 but concluded there was insufficient evidence to prosecute him. It was an unprecedented move by the police, and it led to the man, a convicted murderer and rapist called John Cannan, complaining he had been 'tried and convicted in the media' with no chance of defending himself.

What happened to Suzy's body? Why was no crime scene ever found? And, ultimately, if the police had the right man, why couldn't they find the evidence to prove it?

There were so many questions left unanswered, not just around why someone would take Suzy, but how? People who knew her well simply couldn't understand it. If she'd been abducted, as the police were suggesting, how could someone have whisked her away without causing a fuss or being spotted in broad daylight?

'She was no mug, and she could certainly look after herself,' was how one former boyfriend described Suzy to me.

With more than three decades having passed since the day Suzy vanished, was it possible for me to uncover the mystery of what really happened to her, when multiple police investigation teams had failed?

Uncovering the truth would take me more than five years, cost tens of thousands of pounds of my own money, involve tracing and speaking with more than a hundred people, and conducting over a hundred hours of detailed interviews.

You need to forget everything you thought you knew about Suzy's story.

People don't just vanish without a trace.

1

My police radio had crackled into life as I clipped the battery into place: 'Is there a unit that's free to deal please? A caller claims to have found what he thinks is someone's arm sticking through a pile of soil and rubbish on the railway embankment behind their house.'

The 999 operator had tried to keep the man talking. She'd sensed his stress and anxiety immediately and was trying to despatch someone from the station as quickly as possible.

Had it not been for the rings on the body's cold fingers, the dying sunlight of the day dancing and glinting off the metallic surfaces, the caller would have probably mistaken the hand sticking from the undergrowth for twigs. What remained of the flesh was blackened and covered in a putrid mould.

He'd hoped the pungent sulphurous smell pervading the garden would be something simple to resolve – perhaps a pile of rubbish or a dead animal. But that evening, as the sun paint-ed the sky in dusky reds and oranges, and the smell of decay and decomposition finally became too much to bear, it had beckoned him to explore an area over the back fence, at the rear of his house.

In the undergrowth, on the railway embankment, he found a mound of earth teeming with flies and beetle larvae.

The earth was stained and discoloured by rich nutrients as they drained from a rotting corpse.

In a panic, he had rushed back over the fence and into his house to call 999.

2

I was never much of a cricket fan, but my parents were. I remember their excitement when the first Test got underway between England and New Zealand at Lord's Cricket Ground on Thursday, 24 July 1986. It was just a day after much of the nation had been transfixed by the royal wedding between Prince Andrew and Sarah Ferguson.

It was a nerve-wracking summer. The Chernobyl nuclear reactor disaster had left us all wondering if we'd die from cancer or radiation poisoning. The explosion had released more radioactive material into the atmosphere than the atomic bombings of both Hiroshima and Nagasaki. My mother even suggested the New Zealand Test might be the last one we'd ever see.

When I look back now at that cricket match, I can almost taste the pineapple, orange and grapefruit of the Quatro fizzy drink we were allowed as a treat as I watched the bowlers take the wickets and the batsmen make the runs. But three decades on, analysis of the weather became my focus, not the scorecard. By the fourth day of the Test, Monday, 28 July, play in London was curtailed by bad light and rain. This would be just one of the thousands of things which helped to inform my research as I pieced together the mystery of Suzy's case.

The mundanity of that last Monday morning now seems surreal. Sitting in the small kitchen of her top-floor, two-bedroom Putney flat in her dressing gown, Suzy drank instant coffee from her favourite mug as the radio played.

It was 8 a.m. and according to the news bulletin, the Queen and the Prime Minister had fallen out. 'High level sources from within Buckingham Palace have suggested that Margaret

4

Thatcher's policies are "uncaring"...' announced the radio news presenter.

As Suzy finished her instant coffee, Nick Bryant, Suzy's lodger, emerged from his bedroom to say he was leaving for the office. It was the start of an average working day, which was to turn into anything but.

Suzy asked Nick if he'd left the ironing board up for her in the lounge, and he assured her he had. The headlines gave way to the jazz piano of a track by Bruce Hornsby and the Range as Nick said his goodbyes on the way out.

After ironing her chosen work clothes for the day, believed to be a peach blouse, grey skirt and dark blazer, Suzy dressed, locked her flat door and left for work in her company car.

Putney was an up-and-coming area, best known as the starting point of the annual University Boat Race along the Thames. It epitomised Suzy's life: glamorous, fun, energetic and full of promise about the future.

In the nine months leading up to her disappearance, Suzy had been employed as a negotiator for the Fulham branch of Sturgis & Son estate agency. It was a role her colleagues told me she had been successful at, and one which they believed she'd enjoyed.

She had a reputation for being good with clients. It was a skill she'd learned in her former career as a beauty therapist. In the twelve months prior to May 1984, Suzy had worked the transatlantic route between Southampton and New York, as a beautician on board Cunard's luxury cruise liners. But the work had been infrequent, often leaving her high and dry and living off her parents, Paul and Diana Lamplugh, which inevitably caused some conflict between them.

Some of those who'd known Suzy, and kindly agreed to be interviewed, described her to me along the lines of: 'prim and proper', 'conservative' and 'well spoken' – exactly how her parents had hoped to bring her up. However, others who'd known her well would claim she was 'no shrinking violet', or she'd 'frequently use bad language', 'do way too much to excess' and revel in 'outrageous, politically incorrect banter.'

But that was Suzy – a conundrum.

Even when it came down to the very issue of defining her name, Suzy was a riddle. Family members and close friends would call her 'Suze'. On board the ship she'd insist loudly in a plummy Richmond accent that her name was 'Susannah with an "H"'. As a result, she quickly became known by staff and crew as simply 'H'. Her parents had in fact officially registered her birth in Cheltenham in 1961 as 'Susanna', without an 'H' – a version which, by all accounts, she detested. But in 1986, at the time of her disappearance, she was referred to by much of the media as 'Susie' or 'Suzie'.

For the sake of argument, in this book I will use the modern spelling of 'Suzy'.

During the mid-eighties, back on dry land, with her sailing days behind her, Suzy would work at various London hotels as a beautician. Now in her own Putney flat, bought with a sum of money left by her grandmother and a mortgage, she was nevertheless finding it increasingly difficult to reconcile her upbringing with her glamorous, eighties, girl-about-town lifestyle.

Whilst outwardly worshipping as Anglicans in their later years, her parents, Paul and Diana Lamplugh both had strict Wesleyan Methodist backgrounds, which inevitably impacted on Suzy's behaviour. She would not smoke in front of her parents. Any of her partners lucky enough to be introduced to them would be advised not to attempt such a thing either; the Wesleyan faith preaches against the use of tobacco. Suzy would also instruct boyfriends to remove any jewellery, such as ear piercings, before entering her parents' presence. Some boyfriends even spoke of how they had been expected to rise from their chair when Diana Lamplugh entered a room.

After her mother admitted to intentionally breaking up both her first serious relationship and one of her sister's relationships, because she did not approve of either of the boys they were dating, Suzy surely must have wrestled with the thorny issue of whether it was just easier to keep her private life private?

What *was* certain, in the run-up to her disappearance: Suzy was juggling a very busy lifestyle.

Following a frantic weekend in which she had organised theatre tickets and an overnight stay at Le Meridien hotel in Piccadilly as a special present for her mother's fiftieth birthday, she'd worked a Saturday shift at the estate agency, attended a twenty-first birthday party with friends on Saturday night in Surrey, gone windsurfing on the south coast with her boyfriend and friends on the Sunday morning, before, it was said, finally catching up with her parents on the Sunday night.

On the day of her disappearance, Suzy left home around 8.30 a.m., got into her company car, and drove the short distance to her office. The ten-minute drive took her north over the River Thames via Bazalgette's Putney Bridge and into the wine bars, hair salons and vegetarian restaurants of Fulham – a pleasant middle-class suburb for those who couldn't quite afford a home in Chelsea.

Suzy parked her work car – a nearly new, white Ford Fiesta – in a side street close to the Sturgis estate agency and breezed into the glass-fronted, Fulham Road branch.

Life in the office that morning was as most other Mondays – hectic and bustling. Viewings over the weekend had led to numerous offers coming in from prospective house buyers. Outside, it was surprisingly dark and overcast, but without the ominous rumble of thunder.

At 12.40 p.m., Suzy left her office, alone – her handbag remaining at her desk in the front window. Taking her purse and car key with her, she walked out of the office – and vanished.

Suzy's work desk diary held a 12.45 p.m. appointment to show a 'Mr Kipper' around a property that had only recently been taken on by Sturgis, Fulham. The three-storey terraced house on the market for £128,000 was located at 37 Shorrolds Road, just half a mile from the office – a mere three-minute drive away.

She never returned.

By around 3.30 p.m. that afternoon, Suzy's work colleagues had begun to wonder where she was. Was she taking a long unauthorised lunch somewhere? Had she become ill and gone home? Or had an accident befallen her?

They began to make phone calls to friends and family in order to ascertain her whereabouts, but no one had heard from her. At 6.45 p.m., Suzy was formally reported missing to police by her boss, Mark Gurdon, after she had failed to attend a viewing listed in her work diary for 6 p.m.

It had been at least six hours since anyone in the office had seen her.

3

As the street lights flickered into life, PC Christopher Dollery happened across the first tangible piece of evidence which suggested Suzy had been the victim of a crime. He'd discovered her company car – unlocked, awkwardly parked and abandoned at the side of a residential road not far from Fulham Football Club.

Inside the white Ford Fiesta was Suzy's purse, containing her bank card and fifteen pounds. The keys to the car were missing.

PC Dollery had been acting on the instructions of Duty Inspector Thompson, who, on hearing of the circumstances of the missing woman from the local control room some hours earlier, had sensed there was something seriously wrong. He had wasted no time in circulating the registration number of Suzy's missing Ford Fiesta to his team, ordering them to be on the lookout for the vehicle in the Fulham area. He'd also engaged the Criminal Investigation Department and asked two local detectives to begin an investigation.

The two detectives engaged from CID were DCs Mick Jones and Steve Hill. They had attempted to make contact with a known boyfriend, Adam Leegood, who'd been mentioned in the missing person report by Suzy's work colleagues. But Leegood was not at home.

DCs Jones and Hill had then visited Suzy's parents at their home in the leafy suburb of East Sheen, but Diana and Paul Lamplugh could shed no light on what might have happened to their daughter.

Eventually, the police had decided upon breaking into Suzy's flat in Disraeli Road, Putney, just to check she wasn't inside. But they could find nothing they deemed suspicious, and there was no sign of Suzy.

With the registration number of Suzy's missing Ford Fiesta now in circulation to Fulham officers on the ground, PC Dollery had spotted the missing car just before he was due to clock off from his shift, helpfully right under a street lamp.

But the car was located in a different part of Fulham to the address listed in Suzy's desk diary for a 12.45 p.m. 'Mr Kipper' viewing appointment. PC Dollery had discovered it in Stevenage Road, more than a mile from the property she was supposed to be showing that day at 37 Shorrolds Road.

Why was Suzy's car here?

The mystery deepened.

4

A four-storey, red-brick building constructed in 1931, Fulham police station's only real claim to fame was that it had featured in the very first episode of *Minder*, a British comedy-drama series about London's criminal underworld. But on the last Tuesday in July 1986, this normally quiet, divisional station was to become a hive of news media activity as a press conference was called to appeal for the public's help in the Suzy Lamplugh case.

Apart from the royal wedding and the opening of the Commonwealth Games in Edinburgh the previous week, there had been little exciting domestic news to speak of but plenty of column inches and airtime to fill. The red-top tabloids in particular were now keen to get the story on the attractive, young estate agent and her mysterious disappearance.

Det. Supt Nick Carter, the senior investigating officer, had only been assigned to Suzy's case that morning at around 7 a.m. Just six months away from retirement after a thirty-year career in the police, the only thing Carter lacked was time to play with.

While it had been less than twenty-four hours since Suzy had been reported missing to police, at least one newspaper had already started covering the story. *The London Standard*, as it was called at the time, had published a piece about Suzy's disappearance in an early Tuesday edition. From the timings and content, it was clear to me that someone very close to the case had leaked it to the press almost as soon as the CID had been handed the job the night before.

By Tuesday morning, few, if any, investigative lines had yet been followed, but Carter was keen to harness the frenzied media. It was Carter's view, and that of those around him, that if there was any chance of finding Suzy alive, the police needed to act quickly and get the public to help. He'd decided on a press conference in the station's small canteen – the only room capable of holding the number of journalists who flocked there, hunting for a story.

With so many journalists and reporters covering the case, researching and reconstructing what unfolded that day was relatively easy. Making sense of it all was the hard part.

Alongside Carter in the hastily assembled police canteen-cum-conference room were Suzy's parents, Paul and Diana Lamplugh.

Paul had rushed there in work attire: a shirt, tie and smart jacket. Diana Lamplugh had been at home when she'd received the call. She'd had time to do her make-up and wore a casual summer dress.

With them was Adam Leegood, Suzy's boyfriend, in a pale polo shirt and light-coloured chinos. He'd spent most of the previous night at Fulham police station being questioned by detectives. The police, convinced these sorts of crimes were normally perpetrated by the nearest and dearest, had attempted to exert some pressure on him to see what they could find out. It's not clear at whose behest Adam was attending the press conference, though his appearance was supported by Suzy's parents.

Carter outlined what little information the police had been able to scramble together in the case thus far.

Suzy left her office at about 12.45 yesterday lunchtime. And in her diary is an appointment to meet a client outside number 37 Shorrolds Road. We have a witness who says that he saw a fair-haired lady and this man leaving the property at about ten past one. And that is the last time she has been seen. Suzy was wearing a grey skirt, a peach-coloured blouse and a dark jacket. She was wearing small stiletto-heeled shoes.

We're appealing for anyone. Did you see her and this man in the Fulham area? And did you see her white, Ford Fiesta car?[1]

Following Carter's brief interpretation of events, journalists now fired numerous questions at the panel, all of which were patiently answered as the press scribbled notes into their pads. Members of the media still had a requirement to fulfil their word counts and obtain decent sound bites – an objective made all the more difficult after they'd received such a scant police briefing.

'How worried are you?' asked one reporter.

'It does not look good,' Carter replied toward the voice from the corner. 'We are gravely concerned for her safety. The longer it goes on without finding Suzy, the worse it will be.'

'Who is this "Mr Kipper"?' another voice shouted, referring to the entry in Suzy's diary.

Carter smiled awkwardly. 'We assume it is a false name.'

'Tell us about Suzy – has she done this before?'

'She is hardworking and conscientious,' Carter responded, the smile now gone. 'She's not the kind of girl who would just wander off without letting anybody know…'

But Diana came to the rescue by outlining her version of events. 'I have absolutely no doubt she has been abducted,' she said, matter-of-factly. 'Suzy would *never* have gone away of her own accord.'

And although there was no evidence to suggest it, Diana provided her desired outcome. 'We are hoping she may have been driven off in a car and then taken miles away.'

Adam supported this idea. 'I'm hoping against hope she will turn up unharmed in some remote spot,' he offered.

Paul was less certain. 'None of us can understand what has happened,' he said, 'but she must have been taken away against her will.'

Adam agreed that it was highly unlikely that she had gone off of her own accord. 'Her purse was left in the car and her

---

1. Source: LBC/IRN, 29 July 1986, Copyright Global Radio UK Ltd. Reproduced with permission.

handbag in the office... I believe she is being held against her will.'

'I'm sure Suzy would have put up a struggle,' Diana advanced, 'unless whoever took her had a weapon. She's a very fit girl who loved wind-surfing and all sports.'

And Adam agreed. 'She is a very sporty girl. If she had been involved in any struggle, then I think she would have been able to give a good account of herself.'

Diana provided an alternative theory. 'Maybe she doesn't know what's happened to her because she's been hit on the head or something? If she had a knock on the head and was dumped, she may be wandering around in a daze.'

The hot canteen packed full of journalists spilled out into the yard of Fulham police station as Diana and Paul Lamplugh shared more thoughts about their daughter's nature.

'She's a super outgoing girl. The sort of girl with no hang-ups or worries. She's straightforward. She's lovely to look at. We love her very much,' Paul Lamplugh began.

'And she was in very good form on Sunday evening when we saw her last. She was perfectly okay, and I know she would not have missed my birthday tomorrow. She's very full of life,' Diana concluded.

'I've known her for about a year and she had no worries that I know of. She was a perfectly happy girl. She is very conscientious, sensible and level-headed,' Adam provided.

As a lone female worker, the media was keen to know if Suzy had ever expressed any worries about her job?

Paul shook his head. 'Surprisingly not, no. She didn't. She never gave us the slightest intimation that she was worried about it in any way.'

'It was a very ordinary job. Actually, it'd never occurred to us that it could be dangerous until...' Diana fell silent, perhaps not knowing the words to ascribe to what had happened, but nonetheless reinforcing the idea that Suzy had disappeared as a result of her estate agency work.

If the press seemed surprised that Carter was allowing them so much space to ask what they wanted, Carter was just happy there were so many journalists covering the story. Besides, he knew nothing concrete at this stage of the investigation. What more could he add?

With Diana and Paul apparently willing to answer anything and everything they were asked and with no police intervention, the question on every reporter's lips was about what *could* have happened.

There was a pause before Paul replied. 'We are totally sure that she has been taken. She's been abducted,' he said, reconfirming Diana's earlier narrative.

'Against her will,' Diana added hastily.

'You read about horrific cases involving women, and you can't help fearing the worst,' said Adam.

Perhaps their emotions were getting the better of them. Yet emotion was exactly what the press wanted – the Lamplughs were already well on their way to becoming media personalities recognised up and down the country.

Paul tidied up what they were trying to say. 'She couldn't possibly have gone off of her own accord,' he said, reiterating Diana's earlier point.

Diana continued. 'And she wouldn't have left her car unlocked with her purse in the passenger side. She's very efficient and straightforward. It's an automatic reaction to her to leave her car locked up and take the purse with her.'

'Totally out of—' Paul agreed, but then stopped himself from talking over Diana.

'It's quite out of character... She could only have been taken. I'm just praying she's being taken by somebody who will then just let her go,' Diana finished off.

'We just want her back,' said Paul.

There was silence.

'We're hoping that somebody will recognise her photograph in the paper and will come forward with information which will help the police in confidence,' Paul said, trying to sound more upbeat.

Adam added, 'We are optimistic. We have to believe she'll be found.'

But perhaps Adam and Paul's optimism didn't add much to this great lead story? With Suzy's purse untouched in the car and no evident robbery or carjacking, the media wanted to know what the motive might have been.

'Well…' Diana began to answer and then hesitated, 'I can only imagine she's been kidnapped. She was a very attractive girl. She was beautiful. She *is* beautiful,' she finally said, confirming her worst fears, all in that one last sentence.

5

'And lastly tonight,' the male newsreader rounded off the late-night news bulletin, 'house-to-house enquiries in Fulham, a search of parks and cemeteries by District Support Units and a fleet of police divers scouring the Thames have revealed nothing in the hunt for the missing estate agent Susanna Lamplugh this week. Police say they have now received 800 calls from the public. The final movements of the 25-year-old will be reconstructed by the Met on Monday, as their search continues for the woman estate agent who's thought to have been abducted by a man posing as a house buyer. That's all the news for this evening; I'll be back for the Sunday bulletin.'

Television was about to shut down for the night. Although Suzy's disappearance had been a constant in the headlines all week, twenty-four-hour broadcasting was still at least a year away for many viewers.

Diana Lamplugh's fiftieth birthday on the previous Wednesday had passed without much celebration. She'd spent the day attempting to get as much press coverage as possible by visiting radio stations and doing interviews. Later she'd held a press conference in the rear garden of her home.

The police had just released an artist's impression of a man they believed to be the mysterious 'Mr Kipper'. It had been created from a rough description provided by a neighbour called Harry Riglin, who lived next door to the house for sale in Shorrolds Road, the address written in Suzy's work desk diary. The neighbour had recalled seeing a man. The pencil-drawn sketch was of a well-groomed, smartly dressed man with dark,

17

swept-back hair. One could imagine Suzy standing talking to such a man regarding the property for sale. It all added to the intrigue, and the media couldn't get enough of it.

Scotland Yard had called the public response 'very pleasing'.

But under the surface, cracks were beginning to show. Fulham's CID department was trying its best to follow up on reported public sightings of a well-dressed man, whilst struggling with the volume of press interest and the flow of information. Suzy's parents had already sought legal advice about the police investigation and its progress, and had contacted Sir David Napley, an eminent lawyer, described by the media as 'solicitor to the stars'.

Of course, Suzy's case was not the only one the police station was handling. While Fulham wasn't exactly the busiest division in the Met, there was crime there, just like anywhere else.

Besides general assault and thefts, the division was helping in the hunt for the Thames towpath rapist. They were the lead team in a huge fraud investigation involving employees of the Blue Circle cement works at Hurlingham Wharf, and this alone had led to the arrest of scores of people in the days following Suzy's disappearance. They were also helping to solve the rape and murder of a local pensioner in her ground-floor flat, which had taken place on the very day of Prince Andrew and Sarah Ferguson's marriage. The victim had had her hair done especially for the occasion of the royal wedding. A suspect in that case had been arrested on the very day Suzy had gone missing. He would subsequently be found guilty of the murder of seven elderly people and suspected in the murder of at least four more.

These other investigations couldn't just be dropped because they didn't excite the media in the same way that Suzy's case did.

6

The seven-day anniversary of Suzy's disappearance coincided with the Queen Mother's eighty-sixth birthday. Virtually every member of the Royal family was at Clarence House, the Queen Mother's central London home, to enjoy a summer garden party.

The Prince of Wales drove himself there in his prized, vintage Aston Martin DB6 Volante. Diana, Princess of Wales, wore a wide-shouldered, drop-waist red dress, with matching red tights and red shoes. And a crowd of more than 2,000 gathered at the gates of Clarence House in the hope of catching a glimpse of the Royal family together. There was even a surprise appearance from newlyweds the Duke and Duchess of York. It should have been one of the highlights of every photojournalist's summer.

Yet the pomp and glamour of Clarence House barely got much of a mention in the local media. The focus of the news was on events four miles upriver in Fulham.

London was transfixed by the mystery of the missing young lady wearing small stilettos, a grey skirt, and a peach work blouse as she drove a nearly new Ford Fiesta.

During the first week of the investigation, even before the police had properly interviewed some of the witnesses, TV news networks had agreed with the police that they would film and air a reconstruction of Suzy's last known movements.

The press had jockeyed for position outside the Sturgis estate agency on the busy Fulham Road, just as the Queen Mother's garden party was getting underway. Rather than push the glitz and glamour of the royal birthday party, the forthcoming televised reconstruction had been trailed by TV networks all weekend – testimony to just how big Suzy's story had become in such a short space of time.

The reconstruction began with a very blonde Suzy lookalike doing her best to re-enact what the police believed to be Suzy's final moments in the office. She was sitting in a grey, fabric office chair at a dark wooden desk in the estate agency's front window.

Holding the receiver of her desk phone in one hand, the blonde lookalike flicked through the pages of the large office appointment book with the other, asking the potential buyer which house they wanted to view.

Suzy's role was not played by an actress but a police officer.

WPC Long, as she was known at the time, was part of the original investigation team and had been chosen because of the vague physical similarities – the two women were about the same age, height and weight.

The reconstruction continued with the 'Suzy' lookalike taking a key from a board at the rear of the estate agency before getting into her white Ford Fiesta and making her way to the property for sale.

A suspicious-looking businessman in a dark suit lurked at the front door of 37 Shorrolds Road, awaiting 'Suzy's' arrival. The sinister character of 'Mr Kipper' was played by a dark-haired police officer called DC Ball. This was the infamous 'house for sale' listed in Suzy's diary which the police were now telling the public she had shown the infamous 'Mr Kipper' around.

WPC Long let 'Mr Kipper' into the property and then followed him in, removing the key from the lock in the front door as she did so.

The press vied for position on the narrow pavement as they waited for the murder mystery characters to exit the terraced house.

The police officers were then shown standing directly in the middle of the road, deep in discussion and looking up at the house appraisingly.

With the Suzy lookalike driving, the two stand-ins then abandoned Suzy's white Ford Fiesta in Stevenage Road, in the same spot that the car had been found the previous Monday at 10 p.m. by PC Dollery.

Photographs of the police re-enactment would be all over the following morning's newspapers.

Det. Supt Nick Carter had organised a mobile command and control unit to be delivered to the quiet street in which Suzy's car had been abandoned. The control unit was so big, it had needed a lorry to tow it there. The whole thing was designed to attract as much attention as possible.

Carter said he hoped the reconstruction might help uncover a crucial local witness going about their normal routine exactly one week later. Yet afterwards, police admitted they had drawn a blank. They'd received a thousand calls in total over the past seven days, but Suzy's whereabouts and fate remained a mystery. They had received no useful information whatsoever. One officer on the case said it was as if she'd been abducted by a UFO, another that she'd vanished into thin air.

Despite all the pantomime and the best intentions of the police to grab public attention, ultimately, by the time the case was closed in 1987, just three things had been established:

Suzy left the office at some point before 1 p.m. that lunchtime.

Her car was discovered at 10 p.m. that night.

She had disappeared.

7

I was early for my shift. It was very warm, despite being 9.30 p.m. at night, though being the height of summer, darkness had only just fallen.

I didn't actually start for another half hour, but this was my only chance to catch up on the intelligence briefings in the tiny coffee room of the police station, before I started work. At twenty-five, I was fairly new to 'The Job', as we affectionately referred to working in the police. My second summer outside of training school meant I was still learning the ropes as a constable in the small South London police station I'd been sent to after my initial training.

I'd selected a police radio from the communal cupboard and plugged a fresh battery into the archaic thing. Radios weren't a personal issue piece of equipment at the time; they were a shared resource. They were never very good, and it was hit and miss as to whether you got one that actually worked the first time. The forty-year-old system was due to be upgraded sometime soon, or so they kept promising us.

Despite being fairly fresh into the role, I was already learning never to expect too much from the organisation, or for it to actually do what it said it was going to do. 'The Job' was like a lazy dinosaur – it was rooted in tradition, protocols and procedures from way back, which made it virtually unable to change when the conditions dictated. It would just plod along as it always had, and it expected, somehow, things would be alright. It didn't matter, for example, that we were getting beaten up and injured every day in the street because we couldn't

22

call for backup when the forty-year-old radios didn't work. We were simply expected to put up with it, adapt and somehow overcome. And for the most part, we normally did.

There was a hiss of static as the radio battery slid into place, before that ominous call about the putrid body on the railway embankment at the end of the garden.

Had I expected it to be Suzy? It was almost ten years to the very day she'd disappeared...

No.

The moment I heard that call on the radio, I had a very good idea whose body it would be on the railway embankment, and it wasn't Suzy's.

Fifteen-year-old Joanne Eddison, the eldest of four children, had failed to return home from school one Tuesday afternoon in May 1996, nine weeks beforehand. She'd disappeared just two days before her sixteenth birthday.

When I'd heard the broadcast on the radio, asking for someone to go and help the gentleman in his garden, I'd feared the worst. Joanne had lived in Eastcombe Avenue, the very road where the railway embankment was. My stomach lurched.

It was my team that had taken the missing person report when Joanne had failed to come home from school. Her worried parents had called the police in the early part of the evening. I'd originally been assigned to go and take the initial missing person report, but en route, I'd become involved in another incident, witnessing a drug deal and making an arrest. Sent in my place were two officers from my team who had vastly more experience than I, with almost forty-five years' service between them.

The two officers met with Joanne's parents, who were out of their minds with worry. They explained nothing like this had ever happened before; Joanne had never disappeared without explanation. She'd been looking forward to celebrating her sixteenth birthday in just a couple of days.

But there was something else. Her parents were insistent her disappearance must somehow be linked to a boy from her school, a boy who lived in their street, several houses up the road. Fifteen-year-old Liam Tovell had been causing trouble for Joanne and had hit her in school the previous week.

A few days later, in an effort to trace her, my colleagues spoke with Joanne's friends. They too had their suspicions Liam might somehow be involved in her disappearance.

My colleagues had interviewed Liam on the night Joanne had gone missing. Joanne's parents had insisted that they do so. Both of my colleagues described Liam as 'a bit odd'. They were also told by Liam's mother that he had been acting strangely that day; he'd washed all of his school clothes before she'd returned home from work, a household chore he'd never done before.

Perhaps the officers should have been hearing alarm bells ringing in their heads?

Perhaps. But while they felt his behaviour and actions that day were strange, neither felt there was enough evidence to arrest him nor to search his house.

They duly left – updating the missing person report with what they'd established – probably believing their suspicions were wrong and ill-founded. Someone else would pick up the investigation and make the relevant connections?

But unlike Suzy's case, the CID didn't take the investigation on, not that night. It was classed as a simple missing person case. Despite the unusual circumstances of Joanne not returning home, there was no evidence of any actual crime having taken place, and with no crime scene or any witnesses, the local CID refused to carry out any of the enquiries with Joanne's friends and family.

The uniform team at the small station I worked at led the investigation into Joanne's disappearance, and I helped over the following days and weeks. In many ways our efforts were similar to the effort mustered back in 1986 for Suzy. The world didn't stop. There were other things going on, and unless a crime was immediately identified, it was considered recognised practice not to place dedicated teams on missing persons cases straight away.

Although there was a major investigation pool engaged on Suzy's case, the reality was that this pool of officers was also dealing with several other cases at the same time. Just as in Joanne's case, the team consisted of officers who normally answered 999 calls and investigated low-level crime, progressing the cases as much as possible, with scant information to go on.

Much like Suzy, Joanne had seemingly just vanished into thin air. She had been seen leaving school that day. But she had never arrived home. Where the cases differed, however, was in terms of the gulf in press and media coverage and resultant national public interest.

As the weeks passed, the search for Joanne intensified and Liam remained on our radar. He was someone slightly odd in the investigation, but no one was prepared to actually accuse him of anything, and no one was prepared to obtain a warrant to search his home or garden.

Some weeks after Joanne had gone missing, another allegation of assault was made against Liam. Again, another classmate had claimed Liam had lashed out at him at school, in much the same way Joanne's parents had claimed he'd hit their daughter. I was sent to interview Liam with one of the original officers who'd reported Joanne missing.

As we tried to interview Liam in his living room about the allegation made against him, his mother – an attractive, smart and professional lady who was decidedly house proud – fussed around us, making us tea and handing us plates of biscuits. But when we asked him about the incident at school, he claimed he was just defending himself – the other boy was at fault.

The case of assault had to be dropped due to a lack of evidence.

After several weeks it was accepted that Joanne had likely been murdered, and eventually it was agreed the case would be passed to the CID, who then passed it on to a homicide team – they would review everything we'd done. They ordered a search of the railway embankments and waste ground near Joanne's home.

Nothing was found.

I felt sick to my stomach as I thought about all of this, on my way to speak to the gentleman who'd called to tell us about an arm sticking out of the railway embankment.

Nine long weeks had passed since Joanne's disappearance.

On my arrival at the spot in Eastcombe Avenue, I realised the caller had been right: it was indeed a dead body. It was the badly decomposed remains of Joanne Eddison, lying virtually behind Liam's house. We quickly identified her from the rings on her fingers. An officer went to speak with Joanne's parents to confirm this and deliver the news that her body had been found, just 100 yards away from their home.

Liam was arrested and taken to the police station.

I was posted to stand guard over Joanne's body until we could organise a forensics team to recover her and collect any evidence that may be on or around her, although that wouldn't be until the morning. Her parents now knew their daughter was dead and lying beneath a pile of rubbish at the back of what was very likely the killer's house.

As soon as Joanne's father heard, he clawed his way through the undergrowth and trees at the back of the houses to try and dig his dead daughter out of the ground with his bare hands. I had to stop him.

'You can't just leave her there in the ground! It's inhuman – that's my daughter. I just want to take her home. Let me take her home. You can't leave her lying there!' he screamed into my face, his spittle settling on my cheeks and lips. His eyes filled with tears as he bristled with pain and anger.

How do you reason with a man in this state and stop him? They'd never taught me how to handle anything like this at police training school. I seriously considered simply letting him dig her out with his bare hands. If it would make him feel better, who was I to stop him? It was his daughter after all.

But somehow I managed to convince him, and myself, there was only one right way to do this. I assured him I was doing the best I could for Joanne. It was now my job to preserve as much evidence at the crime scene as I could. By stopping him doing what he wanted, I was doing the best for Joanne.

'Justice will be done, I promise, but you need to let us do our job,' was what I kept saying to her father.

8

'It is a matter of great regret for us all at the Metropolitan Police that significant opportunities were missed during the original inquiry. If these had been grasped, it may have led us to a prosecution many years ago. But that did not happen...' said Deputy Assistant Commissioner Bill Griffiths, a balding and bespectacled man, as he gave a pronouncement on the Lamplugh case from the dais of Scotland Yard's auditorium.

The auditorium wasn't somewhere the press often visited. But today they were here in their droves, filling the hundred or so seats. Having recently been upgraded from a sixties-style briefing room, it was probably now the best space in the building. It felt more like a small cinema, complete with deep blue fabric walls, acoustic panels, projectors and surround sound. This was a major announcement on a high-profile case and there was no expense spared – the Met wanted to placate all of those present.

Smarting from their failures in the Stephen Lawrence case, the Met were desperately trying to recover from their 'institutionally racist' tag following a scathing report by Sir William Macpherson into the failed murder investigation in South London.

Today there would be yet another scramble to recover from criticism, levelled by yet another family, of yet another murder victim.

Despite the agitation and restlessness of both the press and the guests sitting on the stage alongside him, Griffiths, the lead for London's murder teams, gave a sombre address in his dark suit and striped tie.

A number of failed murder cases from the eighties and nineties were still causing the Met severe embarrassment, and Suzy's case was one of them. Griffiths would have the unenviable task of steering the Met's newly formed, full-time murder teams to achieve successful convictions where they could showcase their investigative skills. Today, however, he had to publicly explain, to the Lamplughs' satisfaction, why nobody had been put behind bars in Suzy's case.

'John Cannan has been interviewed twice by police in connection with Suzy's murder since his arrest. He has not been eliminated from our inquiries as a suspect. As this investigation has progressed, more and more questions about his involvement remain unanswered. He's the only suspect. We've the benefit of cutting-edge technology. Every piece of forensic evidence has been revisited and re-examined,' he continued.

It sounded more like a press briefing after an unsuccessful prosecution, reminiscent of those on the steps of the Old Bailey under the watchful eye of Lady Justice, where the prosecution had missed a conviction by a whisker. But in this case there had been no court appearance and none of the evidence, which the police claimed to have found, had been tested at trial.

In fact, many weeks before this press conference, the Crown Prosecution Service had told the police that there was insufficient evidence to proceed with any case against Cannan.

The CPS had engaged with Queen's Counsel, the most senior of legal advocates at the bar, to provide them with advice on the evidence the police had recovered. And the advice was firmly against any criminal proceedings. The police could not prosecute. Insiders on the ground said this was no surprise – the submitted file had been weak at best.

But none of this seemed to have stopped the Met from ploughing on with an unprecedented announcement in the hushed auditorium.

Griffiths continued in his conciliatory tone. 'The detailed investigation of the last few years has demonstrated to us what a lovely person Suzy was and that it was a matter of great misfortune that, apparently through her work as an estate agent, she was stalked and murdered. Although we have not lost hope that Suzy's body will eventually be discovered, we greatly regret that we have not been able to find her so far.'

This press conference was to be the culmination of two years of police work.

In the years following her daughter's disappearance, Diana Lamplugh had repeatedly claimed John Cannan was Suzy's killer. Numerous senior investigating officers had told her time and again there was no evidence against this man, but it hadn't stopped the stories in the media from becoming bigger, bolder and wilder as time had gone on.

Finally, after fourteen years, the stars had aligned for Paul and Diana. With a change of police commissioner and the investigative failings in the Stephen Lawrence case flung open for all to see, the Met had softened their stance on reopening inactive cases. When an 'anonymous prison source' had contacted Diana toward the end of 1999, intense media pressure had led to Scotland Yard launching a review of Suzy's case. DCI Shaun Sawyer commissioned an internal report to be written by DCI Barry Webb. It would become known as the Phoebus Report. Within months, John Cannan, by then a convicted murderer and a serving prisoner, had been arrested.

The body deposition site suggested by Diana's secret anonymous source was Norton Army Barracks, a former military installation in Worcestershire, which police had searched in December 2000. Despite no remains having been found, and no charges being laid, all of that police activity had eventually led to this day.

Today the police were officially naming Cannan as the chief and only suspect in their case, in front of an ensemble of the press and media in the Yard's newly decorated auditorium.

Sitting alongside Griffiths were Paul and Diana Lamplugh, eager to have their say. After all, it had been them that had pushed and pushed for this moment for many years.

Paul read out a pre-prepared statement. 'Until the new investigating team was appointed, we were frustrated that the investigation was static, and we have indeed been most disturbed to know how many opportunities have been missed in the past. We are greatly distressed and indeed considerably angered that after all these years it is still not possible to prosecute the person we, and the police, believe murdered Suzy. It is greatly distressing that Suzy's body has not been found, nor do we know how she was killed… The least the offender can do now is tell us where the body is.'

Despite having wanted the police to publicly name Cannan for many years, it was apparent to some present that Diana's behaviour on this big day was noticeably strange. One unnamed journalist stated that during the press conference, Diana was markedly terse with reporters during the question-and-answer session. Perhaps the agony of waiting for this day had taken its toll.

The press conference covered a wide range of excuses for the failings in Suzy's investigation. The Met said that they now dealt with missing people and murder inquiries very differently to the way they had done in 1986. They suggested the original investigation team had not been able to access information technology; that there should have been more resources available to deal with the huge public and media interest; that they should have investigated sex offenders who had recently been released from local prisons, of which Cannan was one – and that they should have considered him as a suspect.

Officers on the original investigation were even accused of 'falling out' with the Lamplugh family. But as the day wore on, retired Det. Supt Nick Carter and former DI Pete Johnstone hit back at this criticism of them and their original investigation, releasing their own statements, and sounding rather bemused by the claims.

During the original investigation in 1986 and 1987, their relations with the Lamplughs had been amicable, they claimed, and that the Lamplugh family were happy enough with them and their work to attend the retirement parties for Carter in 1987 and Johnstone in 1999.

My research backed this up. I'd found evidence that Diana had even invited members of the original investigation team to Paul Lamplugh's sixtieth birthday party in May 1991. Back then, she'd confessed how the police officers had become part of their lives and had suffered just as much trauma as the family. Both Nick Carter and Pete Johnstone even went on to work on charitable projects that were set up and funded as a result of Suzy's disappearance and the Suzy Lamplugh Trust.

It was all rather odd.

Other bizarre alleged anomalies were provided by the police at the press conference as to why the case had never been solved. The new investigation team claimed that back in 1986, the police had circulated the wrong photo of Suzy Lamplugh with long brunette hair. They claimed this was a serious mistake that should not have happened, because Suzy had had her hair cut and highlighted blonde before her disappearance.

However, my research showed this claim wasn't wholly correct. Although Suzy had indeed changed her hairstyle many times during her twenties, the police in 1986 had stated from the outset that they were looking for a blonde woman. She'd been listed as blonde on the entry in the *Police Gazette*. She'd been described as fair-haired by Det. Supt Nick Carter in his urgent Fulham police station media appeal, within twenty-four hours of Suzy's disappearance, and she was described as blonde on the 'Appeal for Assistance' posters, alongside an accurate photo with her hair in a choppy highlighted do at a party. The police had even entered the details of Suzy's most recent hairdo into their investigation files – £18.50 for a cut and highlights on Friday, 25 July 1986.

In this instance, the police investigation in July 1986 seemed to have got all of that right. So where had this idea of a mistake around Suzy's hair colour come from?

Within forty-eight hours of Suzy's disappearance, in her desperation to find her daughter, Diana Lamplugh had unleashed her own portfolio of additional photographs on Fleet Street. These images showed Suzy at various life stages, and with various different hairstyles. At the time of their distribution, Diana had asked a close friend if they thought Suzy would have liked the generous selection of pictures in the paper of her – she hadn't known which ones to choose.

Many of the photos Diana released were blurry holiday snaps, and some of the images showed Suzy with dark hair. But one professional set of photographic prints in particular was very striking and became ubiquitous in the media's coverage of the case. It was a collection of shots taken during a Lamplugh family portrait session at a London studio. Against a plain pale background, Suzy is shown in close up, wearing a silky blue outfit and sporting longer, darker hair. Because of the clarity of the professional head and shoulders shots, they would become the 'go to' images for many picture editors and be reprinted again and again across the media. Diana would later admit in print that she had had no 'recent portrait pictures' of Suzy at the time of her disappearance.

My own research has borne this out. Trawling through press archives, I obtained original photographic prints of Suzy with shorter blonder hair that carried the caption 'Issued by Scotland Yard' on the reverse. The prints of Suzy I managed to obtain with longer, darker hair did not appear to carry this tag.

Many years later, Diana agreed that the photographs of her daughter with long dark hair were from an earlier time period and showed a younger Suzy, but the photos of Suzy with a shorter, highlighted hairstyle had been taken much nearer to when her daughter disappeared, showing a likeness much closer to how she looked at the time.

Yet, by the time the investigation had outgrown its Fulham base and a major investigation room (MIR) had finally been set up at Kensington police station, a police whiteboard photographed in September 1986 would carry a description of Suzy as: 'hair: dark brown, shoulder-length, highlighted'. Upon it was pinned one of Diana's prized portfolio shots of Suzy with long dark hair, next to other more recent shots. Evidently, by this point, there was confusion within the MIR itself as to Suzy's appearance. She couldn't possibly have looked like *all* of these photos at the exact time of her disappearance.

At the 2002 press conference, the police team explained that this photographic mix-up was entirely their own fault; that they had hampered their own investigation, confused witnesses and made them discount sightings. The police were beating themselves up about an issue that wasn't entirely of their own making. After all, it was Diana who had initially released the dark-haired images directly to the newspapers, whilst the police had initially been describing her daughter as blonde to the media. Yet it was an issue that the police should have recognised and addressed early on in their investigation and one which had come back to haunt them. Who had been in control of this investigation?

The proceedings grew stranger and stranger – but more was yet to come.

DCI Shaun Sawyer then announced that the 1986 police team had failed to follow up a written note they'd received from Paul and Diana. The Lamplughs claimed that they had passed a note to the police explaining that their daughter had been pursued by a 'businessman from Bristol' but that this had never been investigated.

This, again, was not entirely true. The police *had* investigated the intel.

My research uncovered that the information stemmed right back to a conversation Suzy had once had with one of her beauty clients in 1984 – two years before she disappeared.

In 1984, Suzy was working as a beautician in a salon called Joan Price's Face Place. She'd mentioned to one of her clients at the time that she was seeing a married man aged thirty-eight. The man allegedly went home to the West Country at weekends, but during the week, he lived in an expensive apartment in London and sometimes cooked superb meals for Suzy there.

Not long after Suzy's disappearance, this 1984 information had been supplied to the police – but it was already two years out of date. The investigation team double-checked the information and indexed it on new cards in the incident room, but no links in the case could be found to the West Country. A long list of car owners in Bristol was even compiled from central computer licensing records – but not a single one of them could be linked to Suzy.

When police asked Suzy's peer group about this titbit from her 1984 private life, nobody else was aware of this particular man. In summer 1986, Diana Lamplugh was even asked about the potential of this lead. Her reply had been that she was certain this man was not real – Suzy would have been far too busy to be dating a married man.

Over the years, police had returned numerous times to this low-grade piece of intel, yet each time, following consideration, it had been dropped.

But now, at the press conference in 2002, police were claiming that not only had this link *never* been considered, but that John Cannan must be the 'married businessman from Bristol'.

Yet whichever way you looked at it, this just was not possible.

In 1984, Cannan was not married, and he was just turning thirty, rather than thirty-eight. Hailing from Sutton Coldfield, his speech was still peppered with elements of a Brummie twang – which would have stood out in Fulham and could not conceivably have been mistaken as being from the West Country.

But more than all of this, in 1984, under no circumstances could Cannan have been the 'businessman' with whom Suzy was having a relationship.

Why?

Because in 1984, he was incarcerated full-time in prison.

Had the new investigation team failed to check this information? Been misled by those who wanted the case reopened? Or both?

Immediately after the 2002 press conference had taken place, Cannan's solicitor, Matthew Claughton, complained bitterly that, despite previous assurances from the CPS that he would be kept informed of events, he had no knowledge that this police press conference was even going to take place.

'Because we had no prior knowledge of this announcement, we were effectively denied the opportunity of responding at that time on his behalf. John Cannan is absolutely devastated at the way in which he has been treated by the police. He has, to all intents and purposes, been tried and convicted by the media,' Mr Claughton's statement read. 'The press conference announcement was the first we knew of the formal decision that *no charges* were to be brought against John Cannan.'

So if the police had ultimately failed to bring this case to court, because the CPS said there was insufficient evidence to charge a man, even after a two-year-long investigation with no expense spared, why this sudden rush to hold a huge press conference and create a blaze of publicity announcing that nothing was to be done?

9

14 March 2018
30 years, 7 months, 14 days missing

The sun was trying its best to brighten a bitterly cold March day in the heart of London, though it was losing the battle with the north wind's icy fingers. They cut right through the fibres of my clothes and grabbed at my skin beneath. It was the sort of day you wish you'd decided not to venture out, but today was a must.

Arriving early, I hoped we'd find enough space in the crowded coffee shop to carry out our interview. I'd already spent eighteen months analysing Suzy's case, along with Caroline, a colleague whom I'd previously worked with on a series of thrillers based around my life in the police. My fictional writing had started as a catharsis, but while the writing had certainly helped me, there were some demons that simply would not leave; they were ever present, haunting me most days. Ultimately, it was why we were here in the coffee shop on this dreadfully cold day.

Despite the promise of justice I'd made to Joanne's father on finding his daughter's body, justice would never really be done, not in my eyes. Joanne was probably strangled, and that's exactly what the prosecutor told the court, but the delay in finding Joanne's body had meant that cause of death could not be established.

Liam had stayed silent during his police interviews, waiting until he arrived at the door of the courtroom to claim that Joanne's death was an accident, that he'd accidentally hit her on the head with a snooker cue, killing her. The months that she'd lain concealed and undiscovered in the ground on the railway embankment meant the prosecution couldn't prove otherwise. The prosecution had to accept his account, despite claiming he may 'have got away with murder'.

A young woman lost her life.

Joanne's family lost a much-loved daughter and sister.

Liam spent less than seven years in prison.

Most days the ghosts and demons that haunted me were never very far away. Flashbacks, unpleasant feelings, depression – they were all common to me. Joanne was one of the ghosts. Deep down I knew that there was nothing I could do to change the outcome in Joanne's case. It was too late. But maybe I could for Suzy – and maybe then Joanne's ghost would leave me alone?

Today's interview venue wasn't ideal, but it was the only place our interviewee would agree to meet us. Located at the foot of a famous skyscraper, it was a coffee shop by day and a bar by night. The counter was stocked with expensive spirits and bottled beer; the walls covered in street art.

We found a spare table next to a multicoloured mural of a woman staring down at us, peeled off our coats and scarves, and laid claim to it.

'I'm looking forward to meeting him,' Caroline said, frowning as she positioned her chair carefully at the table.

I hoped we'd chosen a quiet corner because this was to be an important milestone. After months of research, today would mark the very first witness interview conducted in our reinvestigation into Suzy's case.

Back in July 1986, Adam Leegood had been a 27-year-old reinsurance broker. He'd known Suzy for almost a year but had only been dating her for a few months when Diana and Paul Lamplugh had thrust him into the limelight after the sudden and unexpected disappearance of their daughter.

Adam was a natural starting point as far as our interviews were concerned. Firstly it's where the police had wanted to start their own investigation on the day Suzy had gone missing. More than that, Adam had been easy to locate; I'd already realised that some of the witnesses in Suzy's case would likely be almost impossible to find. And quietly I hoped Adam might be someone who could put us in contact with others, or at least point me in the right direction of where people lived now, more than three decades on.

10

14 March 2018
30 years, 7 months, 14 days missing

From our research, we'd established that Adam Leegood was open to talking about Suzy and their time spent together. It was another reason why I'd not been hesitant about contacting him and persuading him to meet with us.

Caroline and I had read, listened to and watched every piece of media we could get our hands on which had featured Adam over the past three decades – even down to his instructional work videos. Where appropriate, he'd always seemed willing to answer questions about how he felt about her disappearance, what sort of person Suzy was, what he thought might have befallen her, and how she might have reacted to an abduction.

In 1986, it had taken the police some time to conclusively eliminate Adam from their investigation. But once they had concluded Adam was not 'Mr Kipper', the police stopped trying to comprehend his relationship with Suzy. They seemed to care even less about how the relationship was being presented in the media.

The best demonstration of the strangeness of their courtship was evidenced by what the police uncovered when they tried to understand what Suzy had been doing over the weekend prior to her disappearance.

The police believed that 'Mr Kipper' must be responsible for whatever had happened to Suzy. Thus, by unmasking this person, they'd solve the case.

None of the other estate agency staff had ever seen or heard of a 'Mr Kipper', and none of the normal upfront paperwork in the estate agency's files, which would have held his contact details for the appointment, had been completed by Suzy.

The initial investigation team therefore hypothesised that this appointment might have appeared in Suzy's diary at some point over the weekend of 26–27 July. Perhaps it was when Suzy had worked a Saturday shift at Sturgis estate agency.

With no alternative explanation, and no one in the office ever having seen or spoken to a 'Mr Kipper' themselves, the police would later say that that weekend was their best guess as to when the mysterious man, whoever he was, had most likely made his appointment with Suzy. But did he come into the office, or was it someone that Suzy had met over the course of the weekend before she went missing?

Suzy worked a shift in the Fulham branch of Sturgis estate agency that Saturday, but the investigation found she may have clocked out of work a little early. With bags already packed, she had been whisked off by a female friend for a weekend away to celebrate the twenty-first birthday of a friend in Surrey. It seems that Adam wasn't invited to the party and Suzy was in no mood to make sure he was present. This was despite the couple having not seen each other much over the course of the previous few weeks due to Adam being away on holiday in Tenerife.

After partying until the early hours and crashing overnight at her friend's parents' house in Surrey, on Sunday afternoon, Suzy and friends headed for the south coast for a spot of wind-surfing. Later that afternoon, Adam Leegood is said to have joined them at the beach in Worthing.

Suzy windsurfed for a while, but despite plenty of daylight hours left and her boyfriend's recent arrival, she soon packed up to head home. And she didn't wait with Adam at the beach. Instead, at around 5.30 p.m., Suzy returned to London in her female friend's car, leaving Adam Leegood in Worthing. He then made his own way back to London alone.

Suzy and Adam were said to have made loose arrangements to see each other later that Sunday evening, provided that they were both back in London by 8 p.m. Yet they didn't. That moment at the beach was the very last time Adam said he actually saw Suzy in person before her disappearance.

Although Suzy had indeed arrived back in London by about 8 p.m., it appears she didn't wait to see Adam. Instead, she went to see her mother and father. Diana Lamplugh claims that Suzy came to see her and Paul at their home in East Sheen. Why would Suzy have done this rather than see her brand-new boyfriend, freshly tanned and recently returned from holiday?

It was perhaps something as mundane as washing. We'd discovered Suzy didn't have a washing machine at home, and that she was no fan of launderettes. So, with a weekend bag full of dirty washing, this was perhaps why she'd gone to see her parents that evening. I'd found numerous pieces of information to support this. It was something that I intended on asking her father about, when eventually I got to meet him.

And it was during this research into why Suzy hadn't met with Adam, in our attempt to understand what their relationship actually was, that Caroline and I had found something rather strange. Something that the police had missed; something they'd missed because they didn't feel there was a need to understand Suzy and Adam's relationship. After all, Adam had an alibi and couldn't be 'Mr Kipper'.

In an open letter to her missing daughter, Diana Lamplugh would later write that she believed Suzy had left their East Sheen home that Sunday night at around 9 p.m., en route to see the boyfriend she'd missed so much:

> I gather you went on to see Adam when you left us and then went back to your flat where you spent a couple of hours just chatting to your flatmate, Nick. It sounded a friendly, fun end to a super weekend, and all was normal when you went back to work on Monday.

But our research suggested that this wasn't correct. The last time Adam had seen Suzy in person was at the beach in Worthing that Sunday afternoon. He had merely spoken to her on the phone that night. They'd chatted briefly at around 10.15 p.m., and in fact, this was the last time he ever spoke with her.

So why did Suzy's parents think that she'd gone to see Adam? And where had the information that she'd spent a couple of hours talking to her lodger come from, to be relayed back to Diana? Was this what Suzy had told Adam she had been doing that evening during their final 10.15 p.m. phone call?

More importantly, if Suzy wasn't truthful with her mother, father and Adam about where she was going that Sunday night, why was that?

Where had she gone that Sunday night? Who was she with? And was it connected to what happened the following day?

11

'He's not due for another half an hour. Do you fancy a coffee before he gets here?' I asked Caroline over the loud music as the warmth returned to my fingers.

The swanky café was starting to fill with smart suits carrying expensive-looking satchels, gleaming laptops and briefcases overflowing with paperwork. It perhaps explained why Adam Leegood wanted to meet us here – familiar, easy, safe.

'Sure.' Caroline nodded. 'We'll need to decide on the game plan for the meeting.'

This was the first investigative interview I'd ever done with Caroline by my side. I was sure she envisaged us playing out some sort of good cop/bad cop scene from *Cagney and Lacey* as we grilled him.

Caroline, a tall, no-nonsense brunette, was slightly younger than me. In her mid-forties, she hailed from Yorkshire, but now lived down south with her husband and two young children. Caroline was the most inquisitive researcher I'd ever met. Once she set her sights on understanding something, nothing would shake her from it.

I was still wondering if our foray was wise, but having convinced Caroline we'd be able to have a positive impact on Suzy's case, we'd moved too far down the track to leave it alone now.

'Let's just play it by ear. Let me do the talking,' I cautioned, trying to manage Caroline's expectations. 'Witness interviews are never very dramatic or as intense as they appear in TV dramas, especially not about events that have taken place more than thirty years ago.'

'Oh, okay.' Caroline looked a little dispirited.

'I'll go and grab some coffee,' I said, trying to cheer her up.

As I headed to buy the refreshments, Adam walked straight through the door and into my path.

He was early. This was a good sign – he must have really wanted to get involved.

Over six feet tall, with a full head of greying hair, Adam had retained his athletic build and was easily recognisable, even from the thirty-year-old photos I'd seen of him. Caroline had described him as 'slightly jaded but still dishy for late fifties' when she'd watched him in a corporate video. This wouldn't have been my choice of words, but several women in the coffee shop eyed the distinguished-looking man as he walked in, so she wasn't alone in these thoughts.

I introduced myself and we shook hands.

We passed pleasantries and remarked on the cold weather as we stood in the queue before ordering. Adam declined the offer of a slice of cake but accepted an organic cappuccino served in a suspiciously small cup and saucer.

We made our way to the table, and I introduced Caroline.

I began by outlining our aim: to find Suzy. Although it was our intention to write a book, we wouldn't do so unless, and until, we could show where she might be. Adam nodded as I spoke.

'The police started with you, as they often do in these sorts of cases, believing the nearest and dearest are their best suspects,' I said, opening our interview.

'I was on the periphery of their investigation,' Adam interrupted me, shaking his head. 'I had a cast-iron alibi.'

The police had spent several hours questioning Adam after Suzy had gone missing. Ultimately, he had been completely eliminated from their inquiry.

'How did they treat you, the police, on the night?'

'The police treated me fine,' he said abruptly.

I was off to a bad start, a very bad start. Adam was already being defensive. I hadn't meant it to sound as if we thought he was involved in Suzy's disappearance; I was just trying to get the conversation started.

'Are you still in touch with Suzy's family?' I changed tack, hoping to diffuse things.

'I'm still in touch with Tamsin Lamplugh.'

Tamsin was the middle sister of the family. There were four siblings: Richard was the eldest, followed by Suzy, Tamsin and then Lizzie, the youngest.

'It must have been hard on the family?' I asked.

Adam nodded but said nothing.

'Suzy's mother and father did quite a lot of work with the media – do you think that helped the police investigation or not?' I tried again to break the ice with him.

'They were just trying to keep Suzy in the news, that's all,' Adam said flatly, as if he felt I was now having a swipe at Diana and Paul. I wasn't – I was simply trying to get him to talk.

He sat back in his chair, folded his arms and looked at me. He hadn't touched the thimbleful of coffee on the table in front of him.

'One of the things that we hope to do, at some stage, is talk to the family. Perhaps we should talk to Tamsin and you could help us with that?' I asked.

'You should contact her yourselves,' Adam replied, his face taut.

I was getting on his nerves, I could tell. It didn't matter what I said.

As if reading my mind, Caroline stepped in and asked what he thought of the second police investigation team which had relooked at Suzy's case at the turn of the millennium.

Adam relaxed slightly and unfolded his arms. I was happy for Caroline to take the lead – he seemed more comfortable talking to her.

Speaking directly to Caroline, he said that he felt the police had named the right man in the end. It couldn't have been anyone else. It made sense to him that John Cannan had killed Suzy, and he felt Diana had been right about it all along.

'Let's talk about the last time you saw Suzy...' I asked, taking charge of the questions again, 'Sunday afternoon at the beach in Worthing?'

Adam looked across at me. The muscles in his jaw appeared to tighten.

He hadn't posed a single question since he'd arrived. Didn't he want to know anything about what we were doing, or why we felt that we might be able to help find Suzy?

'Was anything bothering Suzy that day?' I asked him.

Adam shook his head.

'That was the last time you saw her, wasn't it?'

'Yes,' Adam agreed.

'You were perhaps going to meet up again that night, back in London, but you didn't?'

'That's correct. I spoke to her on the phone about 10.15 p.m.'

'Was there a reason why you didn't see her again that night?'

'I think she went to see her mother and father – that's why we didn't meet up.'

'Can you remember if she called you or you called her?'

'I can't, no. I just remember speaking to her on the phone.'

'I ask only because we aren't sure where she was for some of that evening.' I paused, letting the statement hang in the air.

Adam stayed silent.

'Did you ever read anything about her that upset you?' I asked, wondering if he suspected she was out with someone else that night.

Adam rubbed his nose and looked at me, his jaw clenched again. Suzy's private life had been quite complicated, it seemed. The police claimed to have found several people who alleged that Suzy was about to dump Adam, finishing their relationship. They'd also uncovered information that suggested she had been seeing one of Adam's friends while he'd been away in Tenerife.

'There were quite a lot of things in the press back then, not all of them true,' he replied.

'No, of course,' I agreed, which brought me nicely onto my next question.

I was curious about a documentary Adam had previously appeared in, where he'd described his last big night out with Suzy, which took place on the evening of Friday, 25 July 1986.

He'd mentioned that they'd been out to a restaurant close to Suzy's flat in Putney and then visited the pub next door for a drink. In an unusual turn of events, Adam explained that he thought someone had taken 'a chequebook, a diary, some cards and a couple of other things' from Suzy's bag whilst they were in the pub together that night. Adam described it as an unfortunate finale to their otherwise pleasant night out.

Watching it back, Caroline and I had both remarked on how Adam appeared to enjoy the limelight in front of the camera. It was a total contrast to how he seemed today.

Aside from the allegation of theft from Suzy's bag, which was oddly absent from almost anything else we'd ever seen on the case, Adam made no mention of the fact he'd been out of the country on holiday in the Canary Islands in the run-up to that night. Their Friday evening together would have meant a big reunion after a length of time apart? Yet he described it as just a regular night spent discussing what they'd been up to that week and their upcoming plans for the weekend.

Neither the alleged theft from Suzy's bag in the pub nor their reunification on this romantic night out seemed run of the mill to me. I wondered, given what had happened at the beach on Sunday, whether Suzy had in fact indicated in some way that she was about to end their relationship? I needed to ask him about it.

'Can I ask about the last night out you had with Suzy, which I think was the Friday night before she went missing?'

Adam remained silent.

'You went to a restaurant, for a meal with Suzy, on that Friday,' I continued. 'Mossop's restaurant on Upper Richmond Road in Putney, round the corner from her flat.'

'That's right.'

'It's not there any longer, but it was next to a pub, the Prince of Wales. The pub is still there,' I said.

Adam nodded.

'Did you go to that pub very often?'

'I've never spent any time in the Prince of Wales pub,' he replied.

'Are you sure?' I asked. His response was baffling. He'd said something completely different on the documentary we'd watched.

'I'm sure. There were far nicer pubs down on the river which we would go to. We never ever went in there,' he responded.

I pressed him further. 'But what about Suzy's chequebook being stolen from her bag?'

'Never happened.'

I looked across at Caroline. She raised her eyebrows. We knew the police had recovered Suzy's lost property from the Prince of Wales pub. They'd taken possession of it in the days after Suzy had been reported as missing.

'We never spent any time in the Prince of Wales pub,' Adam said again, curtly, into the silence between Caroline and me.

'Have *you* ever been in the Prince of Wales pub, Adam?' I asked, confused.

'No, I've never been in there,' Adam snapped back, his expression stern.

He sounded riled. This was peculiar. I needed to diffuse the situation and calm him down, but as I took a deep breath to do so, our meeting came to an abrupt halt.

Adam stood up, dragged his coat off the back of the chair and exclaimed, 'You're *never* going to find her, and you're *never* going to find anything out!'

Around us, the clatter of cups and chat fell away. Patrons peered over to see what the commotion was about as Adam stormed off toward the exit without saying another word or looking back, his small coffee going cold on the table in front of us, untouched.

Sitting motionless in my seat, I watched as he departed and the noise level returned to normal. An interview that had taken months to organise was over within minutes. There was no point in trying to chase after and placate him. We'd had our chance, and we were unlikely to get another one.

'So much for these witness interviews not being dramatic,' Caroline quipped. 'That was our first one and he flew off the handle!'

I didn't respond.

'What was all that about?' Caroline asked in shock.

I shook my head and shrugged – I was at a bit of a loss.

I picked up my slice of carrot cake and took a bite from it. I'd been out of the police for several years. I was a civilian now. Maybe I'd lost my touch, forgotten how to interview people? Maybe working on this case was a stupid and naïve idea?

'He was really angry with you. I think it was when you asked if he could introduce you to Suzy's family,' Caroline suggested, trying to analyse what had gone wrong as crumbs dropped onto my suit.

'He certainly was angry,' was all I could muster through my mouthful of cake.

I'd interviewed thousands of people in my police career, and in the main, these things were a fairly straightforward affair. Rarely did they finish so spectacularly as this. But I'd misjudged how to deal with Adam, as his spectacular exit from our interview demonstrated. I'd falsely believed that I understood who he was, and what he was about. He simply wasn't as straightforward as I'd expected.

'I don't think the problem was connected to me asking if he could put us in contact with Suzy's family,' I said finally, putting my plate down and wiping my mouth with a serviette.

'No?'

'No, it was because I was asking about his last big night out with Suzy.'

'Okay...' replied Caroline, not sounding wholly convinced.

'There's something very odd about that Friday night. He's completely contradicted what he said in that old interview,' I concluded as I picked up Adam's untouched coffee and took a sip to wash down the carrot cake.

'Why would he contradict himself?'

'I don't know,' I sighed. None of it seemed to make any sense.

'Maybe all Adam has been doing all these years is some sort of posthumous noble cover, because Suzy was seeing someone behind his back?' Caroline suggested.

I nodded. 'Maybe...'

12

I'd not been able to sleep much. Sitting in the half darkness of the living room in my South London home, I watched as the purple alliums cast long shadows in the early morning light. The sun crept slowly upward.

The voice of Adam Leegood screamed in my head – 'You're never going to find her, and you're never going to find anything out!' – as the scene in the coffee shop played over and over.

Our interview with Adam hadn't exactly gone according to plan. For a while afterwards, I'd questioned whether we should carry on investigating Suzy's case. I wondered whether causing that sort of anger and upset was worth it. Yet, there was something hugely significant in his outburst.

Our research had been spot on. We were asking the right questions, even if Adam didn't like them. Within minutes of our first interview, we'd exposed something that seemed important. Whatever *had* or *had not* happened on that Friday night when Suzy had been out with Adam Leegood, could it be connected to Suzy's disappearance? We just needed to get to the bottom of whatever had caused his outburst.

In the weeks since that interview, Caroline and I had devoted all of our spare time to trying to track down the other witnesses in Suzy's case. I was convinced there'd be other revelations, perhaps even other tantrums indicating where we needed to focus our attention. But progress was slow; no one had spoken to most of the witnesses since 1986, and no one really knew where they were.

We'd painstakingly tracked down and poured over every piece of information we could obtain, much of it pre-internet.

This had meant physically visiting the institutions that held the material on the case, obtaining the relevant access and trawling through documents until we found anything that might mention Suzy, her family or the investigation. While it was time-consuming, it was a treasure trove of information.

Primarily we'd used our extensive research to develop a timeline of events, especially in terms of what the police had communicated to the public and when they had announced a change of tack. You could document how the case had evolved in the weeks and months following Suzy's disappearance and almost chart the police's thinking as their investigation unfolded.

We'd also gained a fairly long list of witnesses, many of whom had previously spoken in the public domain, and it was these people we now needed to trace. But for most of them, all we had was a name and an age. For some, we had a profession and perhaps a rough idea of where they'd once lived in 1986.

Somehow, using just this information, we had to try to find them in the present day. It was a laborious process, but using the skills I'd learned in tracking criminals and terrorists, I was confident it was possible, even if it took dozens and dozens of hours of work just to find one original witness. The worst part was that we wouldn't be totally sure we'd zeroed in on the right person until we knocked on their door and spoke to them face to face.

I wondered if there was a way of streamlining this, a short-cut – it would likely save us several months, perhaps even years of work. But there was only one place that held all the information we needed to shortcut the process of finding people: the police.

The original paper case files held the details of the original witnesses in Suzy's investigation. Although the Freedom of Information Act covered a wide range of government information, there were a number of exemptions, and criminal investigations were one of those, especially the details of living individuals. However, with Suzy's case being more than thirty years old, this placed it into a historical record category, and I wondered if there was new case law that meant some parts of these files would be exempt.

I'd made contact with old colleagues from my time on the Anti-Terrorist Branch, some of whom had since gone to work on the homicide teams. Perhaps they knew the best way in for someone writing a factual book about the Lamplugh case. I asked around to see if anyone knew who I should speak to.

Although a search in 2010 in the West Country for Suzy's body meant the case had been made live again only eight years previously, this dig had been based on old intel. No new investigative activity had been done on the case since 2002. Perhaps I could use the Freedom of Information Act to access some of the information in the files. Or maybe I could build a working relationship with someone in the police in order to share what we'd found out?

One friend suggested that I speak to the Murder Review Group. And, as luck would have it, a contact of a contact was about to take up a civilian job in the review group in just three weeks' time. DCI Graeme Gwyn was retiring from the police and moving over to a civilian role. He had an informal drinks do lined up to celebrate.

'Why don't you come along?' suggested my friend. 'We can have a beer or two together. I'll introduce you to him, and you can have a chat with him about it?'

'As long as he doesn't mind me turning up?'

'I'll mention it to him. I'm sure he'll be fine – you're former police and a mate of mine.'

'Great, sounds good. Please don't mention which case I'm interested in just yet. I just want to have a general conversation with him, nothing specific right now…'

'No worries, mate. I'll drop you a text with the venue and time on it.'

13

The news headlines were all about the meeting between Donald Trump and Kim Jong-un in Singapore, but the story I was more interested in came lower down the pecking order.

Suzy's father, Paul Lamplugh, had passed away aged eighty-seven. Both of Suzy's parents had now died without ever knowing the truth about what had ultimately befallen their daughter. It was desperately sad.

Not long before his death, Paul had said that he had pretty much lost all hope of discovering what had happened to his daughter but that the older he got, the more he missed her.

Perhaps selfishly, I also saw his death as a missed opportunity for any reinvestigation. Although Paul had been interviewed many times, I'd still wanted to talk to him but had been put off from contacting him, or anyone in the Lamplugh family for that matter, by the disastrous meeting we'd had with Adam Leegood.

I figured it would be easier in the first instance to speak with witnesses for whom the case was less emotive but who had been closer to the events on the ground as they'd happened.

Paul and Diana Lamplugh had married in October 1958. It was to be a union that would last nearly fifty-three years, until Diana's death in 2011, and one that would produce four children. Paul and Diana met in Cheltenham but eventually settled in a flat in London because of Paul's work.

Paul had always wanted to be a solicitor and had worked extensively within the legal profession to which he had always aspired. Around the time of Suzy's disappearance, he became secretary of the Law Society's Ethics and Guidance Committee, before taking early retirement in February 1987; his focus thereafter became the Suzy Lamplugh Trust.

When the Lamplughs first arrived in London, Diana had briefly worked in an administrative role at the BBC, though it was a job she would not hold for long. Aged twenty-two and married for just a few months, she fell pregnant with the couple's first child, Richard, forcing her to leave her position with the BBC shortly afterwards. By 1962, Diana was a housewife with three children, all under the age of three. Richard, the eldest, was born in 1960, Suzy followed in 1961, and Tamsin in 1962. The youngest, Lizzie, would not be born until 1970.

But the ever ambitious Diana wasn't content with being a housewife. Despite the demands of four little ones, she openly admitted that she was determined to find time to do things that interested her more than childcare and household chores. Eventually, she would start a business with a friend, promoting a workout called Slimnastics. She would be heavily involved in starting local, at-home fitness groups and helping to formulate several books on health and well-being.

But there was a lot of pressure in the family home, signified by an incident that Diana described in great detail in two of her books. After one never-ending rainy day stuck all alone at home with three children under five, Paul had returned from his work and an argument had ensued between the married couple. The argument was over some onion soup Diana had made for dinner. Paul had said it was too salty, so Diana had picked up a soup plate, full of soup, and smashed it over Paul's head, causing a nasty cut which left a large scar.

Alongside her growing family, Diana's business also expanded, and it was decided they needed more space, so the family moved from their small flat to a house in East Sheen. This prosperous and leafy part of Richmond would be where Suzy would spend her formative years. And it was here that you could start to see the differences between Suzy and her siblings, and the similarities between Suzy and her mother.

Suzy's disappearance, and the vacuum created when the police couldn't establish what had happened to her, reignited the intense spirited nature of Diana Lamplugh. She was determined to expose the truth. The personal crusade to establish the fate of her daughter would eventually turn both her and Paul Lamplugh into household names.

On 4 December 1986 they launched the Suzy Lamplugh Trust – initially a vehicle to keep their daughter's name in the press, but which would become a charity which campaigned for more self-awareness and ran safety courses for people at work. It would earn them both OBEs and Diana would soon be on first-name terms with the Home Secretary.

14

Blackheath village was always a popular venue with the police for office drinks. Just a few miles away, the state-of-the-art police building at the base of Lewisham Hill housed everything from horses to homicide teams.

The Crown pub had begun life as a stop on the Roman road from London to Dover. Sitting right in the heart of the village, it was still an oasis for weary travellers. Its country pub feel meant it was one of the best places for a drink for some miles around – and the din as I entered attested to its popularity.

'Dave…' my friend greeted me with an extended hand as I walked into the bar area.

'Sorry I'm late.'

He laughed. 'Don't worry, I don't think anyone noticed.'

He was right. There were about thirty people at this do, and I recognised barely a handful of the faces. Had I really been gone that long? Had new people come through that quickly? Once upon a time I'd have recognised most of the officers there. I'd only been out of the police for a few years, and already I felt like an outsider at these sorts of functions.

'Let me get you a drink and introduce you to Graeme,' he said, leading me to the bar.

DCI Graeme Gwyn from the Met's Homicide and Major Crime Command was about to retire after thirty-two years as an officer. He would soon take up a civilian role in the Murder Review Group. He'd been in the police around the same length of time as Suzy had been missing.

'Are you Dave?' a tall man with an open face asked as he shook my hand. I actually hated being called Dave, but it was what some of my friends always called me, despite me telling them otherwise. But being stuffy about my name right now wouldn't be conducive to getting off on the right foot.

'I am. Are you Graeme?'

'Yes…' He smiled at me.

'Congratulations on your police retirement,' I replied, shaking his hand. 'When is it you start your new job?'

'I've got a lot of annual leave and rest days to take; I've got to use that up, so I don't actually start my new role until early August.'

'Okay…' I wondered where I'd be with this investigation by mid-August. It sounded like the earliest time we'd possibly now get to talk to him on a professional basis.

'I've been told you've been looking into the Lamplugh case?' Graeme asked.

I shot my friend standing at the bar a look. I'd specifically told him not to mention which case it was that I was working on.

'What work have you done on it so far?' Graeme interjected. Had he spotted the look on my face too?

'Mainly research, at the moment…' I turned my attention back to Graeme. 'I didn't want to get into specifics about the case at this stage; I just wanted to have a hypothetical conversation with you.'

'It's fine, we can do that and have a chat over coffee another time.'

Coffee another day sounded like a good idea. I didn't really want to speak about my research at the moment, not in the pub with all this noise. And besides, I wasn't really sure what I knew. Was anything that we'd found out so far any different from what the police already had in their files?

'What have you found out?' Graeme was intrigued; he'd skipped any small talk.

'Not much, not yet. We've uncovered some inconsistencies and oddities.'

He frowned. 'We?'

'I work with a researcher – there's two of us.'

'Okay, what made you start looking at it?' Graeme asked between sips of beer.

'I started looking at it around the thirtieth anniversary of her disappearance. I can't understand why they've never found her body, and why they've never found the evidence to convict the man they've accused of killing her.'

He nodded as I spoke. 'You don't think it's John Cannan, then?' He knew about the case, and it seemed to me to be more than just a passing interest.

I wondered how much he'd looked into this before our conversation.

'I don't,' I heard myself saying.

Our research thus far suggested that Cannan had been linked to Suzy's case purely by the press. At this stage it appeared to be nothing to do with any actual evidence, and everything to do with pure media speculation.

And the media stories had come at an auspicious time for the Lamplugh investigation.

Back in August 1987, as the original police investigation had entered its thirteenth month, the new senior investigating officer, Det. Supt Malcolm Hackett, conceded they'd made little or no progress on the Lamplugh case. It couldn't run indefinitely. They'd pursued hundreds of avenues of enquiry hoping to find something useful and spent an awful lot of money visiting different parts of the world, but each time they'd been met by a dead end.

Officers from the Area Major Investigation Pool were desperately needed to work on other murders. Hackett, already grappling with the brutal shooting of a car park attendant at the same time as Suzy's case, simply couldn't spread himself and his team far enough.

The police were also being stretched by the Notting Hill Carnival.

Diana Lamplugh stated, 'The police team who were looking for Suzy were based in Notting Hill. They were preparing for the Notting Hill Carnival (though I got the impression that they were perhaps getting ready for a riot a long time before the event!).'

And indeed, the August 1987 carnival ended in unrest.

With more than 800 reported offences, 250 arrests, the murder of a stallholder and the stabbing of a female police officer in the back, the event culminated with police in riot gear patrolling the streets. The carnival faced an uncertain future.

For Hackett, the Notting Hill murder case was now a priority. Stallholder Michael Galvin had been stabbed to death by a gang of youths, following an alleged dispute over a can of soft drink. The 'cola can' murder received considerable publicity at the time, necessitating officers and resources to investigate it. It was one of the reasons that the Lamplugh investigation had to be brought to a close.

However, despite a conviction, the Notting Hill murder case was found to be unsafe and that conviction was eventually overturned during the 1990s. The key prosecution witness was found to have lied – only arriving at the carnival two hours *after* the murder had taken place – and he was imprisoned for perjury while the previously convicted man walked free. The Notting Hill murder case would ultimately end in disaster and chaos.

In the meantime, DI Pete Johnstone was told to complete the outstanding incident room actions and wrap up the Lamplugh case by 23 October 1987.

But on 8 October, just as the first leaves of autumn began to litter the ground, events took a surprising turn when 29-year-old newlywed Shirley Banks, an attractive, strawberry-blonde sales manager at a workwear factory in Bristol, disappeared, ostensibly whilst out shopping in the city's Broadmead shopping centre.

The media began linking the two cases.

On 13 October, the *Daily Express* carried a story about Shirley Banks' disappearance. Within it, the article mentioned Suzy by name:

Police obviously mindful of the mysterious disappearance of estate agent Suzy Lamplugh, said: 'There is speculation that she might have been abducted, but there is nothing to suggest that yet.'

While there were no links to the Suzy Lamplugh case, press and public conjecture were rife.

Previously, when there had been talk of the police investigation being wound down, the Lamplughs had sought help from their eminent legal advisor, Sir David Napley, and the case had remained open. Yet, this time round, by 23 October 1987, as planned, the Lamplugh investigation was closed.

Diana protested furiously to the police. She was desperate to find out what had happened to Suzy, as any parent would be, and she wasn't about to give up without a fight. So, armed with new advice from Sir David Napley and details of Shirley Banks' disappearance as ammunition, she attempted to dissuade the police from dropping the investigation.

Despite her best efforts, the police stood their ground, and the case remained closed.

The case file was listed as 'non-active'. The index cards from the incident room were moved to a storage room in an annexe at Hammersmith police station.

But there had barely been time for the first layer of dust to settle on the tops of the cardboard boxes when, less than a week after the Met had officially closed Suzy's investigation, something remarkable happened. The Banks and Lamplugh cases would become intertwined.

On the afternoon of Thursday, 29 October 1987, John Cannan, a 33-year-old who originally hailed from the Sutton Coldfield area, was arrested for an attempted robbery in Leamington Spa, Warwickshire, ninety-five miles north-west of London.

When police searched Cannan's car they found a briefcase, and inside the briefcase, they found a tax disc belonging to Shirley Banks' car. A later search of Cannan's new home in the Clifton area of Bristol revealed Banks' orange Mini Clubman in a garage. It was now painted blue, bearing false number plates.

News of the arrest caused quite a stir in London.

Police in Bristol released a photo of John Cannan to the press, ostensibly in an attempt to locate Shirley Banks, asking for the public's help.

Within days, the *News of the World* had printed details of Cannan's previous conviction for rape. Following criminal charges for offences relating to Shirley Banks, on Sunday, 1 November 1987, the media began suggesting Cannan's photo looked like the artist's impression of 'Mr Kipper' and that he had a string of professional, upwardly mobile girlfriends.

Using the platform created through the Lamplugh Trust and with the help of the Lamplughs' legal advisor, Sir David Napley, Diana made direct contact with Deputy Assistant Commissioner Paul Condon on 1 November 1987. Contrarily, it was Diana who was informing Condon of the arrest in the Banks case, and she used it to urge him to reopen the investigation into Suzy's disappearance.

Diana was adamant Cannan resembled the artist's impression of 'Mr Kipper'. She also pressed his apparent penchant for professional women whom he spent time surveilling and stalking before eventually killing.

The Lamplughs were armed with more than enough information about Cannan to overcome DAC Paul Condon's arguments. Although he refused to reopen Suzy's case, he conceded that two police officers would be sent from the Met to the West Country to enquire what evidence there was to link Cannan to Suzy's case.

Whilst the Lamplugh's intervention to ensure Cannan was viewed as a potential suspect was done purely to keep the Suzy investigation open, it wasn't entirely without its merits.

The officers found that Cannan had previously been convicted of rape, as the *News of the World* had suggested. And he had been placed on rehabilitative day release from Wormwood Scrubs prison in Hammersmith, London at the time of Suzy's disappearance.

Wormwood Scrubs prison is about five miles from where Suzy worked in Fulham at Sturgis estate agency. The day release meant Cannan was free to move around during working hours, outside the prison. Each night at 11 p.m., he had to observe a curfew and be back at the bail hostel and in his room, where he would sleep each night. He would not be able to leave again until 7 a.m. The hostel was located just outside the main gates of the prison. Any breach of these conditions meant he would be sent back to prison to serve the remainder of his sentence. The purpose of the day release was to enable him to take a job and slowly reintegrate back into society.

Geographically, this could have placed Cannan in the same part of London as Suzy, in the months leading up to her disappearance. And as a recently released sex offender, Cannan perhaps should have been on a list under consideration as a person of interest. The Lamplugh investigation however, had never had such a list.

The Met liaised with their counterparts at the Avon and Somerset force, but not a single shred of concrete evidence could be found to link Cannan to Suzy.

The Lamplugh investigation remained closed, and the case remained dormant for eighteen months.

Unlike Suzy, Shirley Banks' body was eventually found, and on 28 April 1989, following a three-week trial, Cannan was convicted of her murder as well as other offences.

Upon Cannan's conviction, several national newspapers ran stories indicating that those behind the scenes believed he could be Suzy's abductor, her murderer; that he was the infamous 'Mr Kipper'. This was strenuously denied by both the Avon and Somerset Police and the Met, with Hackett having record- ed in his decision log: 'No evidence that Cannan committed any offence against Suzy Lamplugh' and 'No evidence of any connection between the Banks and Lamplugh cases'.

'Why not Cannan?' Graeme Gwyn enquired of me, taking a large swig of his pint.

'I just feel as though the original investigation headed in the wrong direction using lots of assumptions, but I can't prove anything at the moment. I guess you could just call it gut feel…'

There was a lot more to the Cannan story, and we hadn't yet got to the bottom of it all. At that moment, what I wasn't prepared to do was talk about what I 'thought' and not what I could 'prove' with a beer in my hand in the pub. That would be foolish.

'Okay…' He took a final swig from his pint before putting it on the bar then took out his mobile phone from his jacket pocket. 'What's your phone number? I'll give you a call when I'm back at work in August.'

We exchanged phone numbers. Graeme shook my hand and went off to speak with a crowd of people whom I didn't know.

I stayed a little while longer. Long enough to finish my pint at least.

I watched as my friend enjoyed some banter with some of the homicide team in the far corner. I didn't feel like interrupting to say my goodbyes. Although my contact had kindly provided me with an introduction to Graeme, I'd given him specific instructions not to share anything about which case I was looking at just yet. Having worked on counterterror investigations, I knew that keeping secrets was important. Unguarded and idle talk often led to unexpected outcomes, especially in the Met.

Loose lips could sink ships.

15

I was at home, browsing the news. The sun was shining; the day ahead looked to be glorious, but the morning's papers were filled with doom and gloom. It was nearly two years since the UK had voted to leave the EU, and we seemed no nearer to reaching a conclusion on anything at all.

Today, Airbus was threatening to pull its investments and defund its factory in Britain if no deal was reached between the EU and Britain in its Brexit negotiations. Airbus were claiming they'd move production of aircraft wings from their British plants to elsewhere in Europe – or even to the US or China.

It all seemed so pointless.

I threw the papers across the room.

The death of Suzy's father had been a wake-up call. None of us were getting any younger, and neither were the witnesses in this case. Suzy would have celebrated her fifty-eighth birthday this year; we had a limited window to track and trace people before living memory was lost in this case forever.

There was only so much you could learn from research. To stand any chance of finding Suzy we needed to do our own interviews, ask our own questions and, as the Irish part of my family would say, *make our own luck*.

The meeting with Graeme Gwyn the previous evening had made me feel uneasy – he'd seemed far too interested in Suzy's case and far too interested in what I was doing.

If I dropped writing my third fictional book, we stopped all the promotional activities on the other two and I cut back on my security work, Caroline and I could devote more time to tracing and interviewing the witnesses in Suzy's case. It would speed everything up, but it would be costly.

I left the house, locked the door and climbed into my car. I had to collect Caroline from the station; we were heading out of London to meet some of Suzy's former work colleagues.

'How'd it go last night with your meeting?' she asked, skipping the pleasantries and getting straight down to business as she jumped into the car.

'I don't know.' I pulled away and headed for the bypass toward the motorway.

'You don't know? I thought you were meeting the bloke from the Murder Review Group? Did something happen?'

'No. It was fine. I met him; he seemed alright. We swapped phone numbers, he said he'd call,' I replied, scowling as I punched the address we were heading for into the satnav.

'You don't sound convinced?'

'My mate told him which case we were looking at.'

'Oh. Okay. Is that a problem?'

I sighed. 'I'd told him not to.'

'Well, we *are* actually looking at it. You were going to have to own up to it at some point. Why's it a problem if the police know which case it is?'

'The timing. We've only spoken to one witness so far. I know what the Met as an organisation is like. You tell one person, and soon everyone knows. Then before long, someone will start worrying the organisation should at least look as if they're doing something themselves.'

'But it would be quite good if they relooked at it afresh?'

'Just as long as they don't warn us off, which they might if they suddenly fancy throwing their weight around.'

'They'll ring and talk to you first though, now they know, surely?'

'No, they'll consider us a couple of amateurs just stabbing around in the dark, without a Scooby-Doo. They'll only speak to us if they think they can get something from us, information they can take and make themselves look better with.'

'They won't, will they?'

I looked across at her as the road straightened out in front of me. 'They're the police, and we aren't. In their heads they hold all the cards, have all the expertise and get to decide exactly how things work on this.'

Caroline didn't reply.

I carried on. 'While *we* see what we're doing as positive, they won't. They'll see us as a potential problem, perhaps even a threat. Because if we do find something, it means that they failed. And they won't want that.'

'I hadn't thought about it like that,' Caroline conceded.

'The best outcome for the Met in this is that we find nothing. They'll want the public to think they've crossed all the Ts and dotted all the Is. But no one has ever critically looked at this case. It's never been reviewed by anyone other than the Met themselves, and no one has ever gone into as much detail as we have.'

'I understand,' she said, nodding.

'I didn't want them knowing what we were doing before we'd actually done it. But that's no longer possible.

'Okay.'

'We'll need to move faster on this, pull out all the stops, put ourselves in the best position possible before I talk to Graeme again.'

16

Despite months of research, learning about Suzy's childhood, her family and friends, and her previous life as a beautician, Suzy's career as an estate agent was the area where we'd unearthed the least information. It was time to address this.

Sturgis & Son estate agency was a busy, successful, family-run firm boasting a dozen branches across central south-west London. By 1987, the company was selling in the region of 1,500 houses a year worth an estimated £200 million.

The Fulham branch, in which Suzy had been employed, occupied a smart corner plot at 654 Fulham Road, about a mile north-east of Putney Bridge. The boxy corner retail unit sat at the intersection with Chesilton Road, its angular eighties frontage a mix of concrete pillars and large plate-glass windows which displayed dozens of properties for sale, pinned on large cream boards.

In 1988, the entire Sturgis & Son chain had been sold to Prudential, and it no longer existed as an entity. The Fulham Road premises was now a branch of the Chesterton estate agent chain.

Suzy's desk had been at the front of the premises, opposite the main door. She was the face of the branch to anyone walking in off the street. The day she went missing had been a busy one in the office. Busier than normal.

The office was normally staffed with a manager; three negotiators, of which Suzy was one; an office junior; and a secretary. But that Monday, one negotiator, David Craddock, was on holiday in the US, and Mark Gurdon, Suzy's boss, was out on a long luncheon with two Sturgis colleagues. David had been replaced with a temporary staff member from an agency – a secretary, to make up the numbers.

The other negotiator in the office that day, Nigel Hindle, had only recently turned twenty-three. When I'd finally tracked him down and spoken to him on the phone, he'd also heard the sad news that Suzy's father had passed away. He agreed with me that the odds of finding Suzy were dwindling with the passage of time, and I discovered he was still in contact with Mark Gurdon. Kindly, they both agreed to meet us and share their memories of that time.

Mark had chosen our meeting place – a sixteenth-century pub-restaurant in the Home Counties. With wooden beams, low ceilings and tartan-covered, wingback chairs pushed into shadowy corners, it was the perfect coaching-inn setting for a murder mystery.

Sitting in a hot and sticky private dining room with the windows fully open to let in some air, we discussed life in the 1980s as the traffic zoomed past along the ancient thorough-fare outside.

Mark was now in his early sixties – a well-dressed, smartly presented man, keen on his gastronomic delights. He kept his dark hair very short. Back in 1986, he'd been a Ford XR3i-driving, 29-year-old with a coiffed-back mane and an upward curve on his career trajectory.

'It was certainly a boom time. Eighty-four to eighty-nine, they were a great five years to be an estate agent,' he reminisced.

He explained that Sturgis clients were often young urban professionals, known as 'yuppies' for short. Whether advertising executives, accountants or brokers, they would often earn bonuses as big as telephone numbers and frequently drove a rather handsome German car to indicate their success in material terms. People worked hard but partied harder. It was a time when the most fashionable parts of London were paved with gold.

'People were certainly earning lots of money and spending it conspicuously,' he said, smiling.

Nigel was several years younger than Mark but equally as well spoken. He'd met Mark in 1984, back when South West London was enjoying rising prosperity and rising house prices.

'As an office, we were selling fifty to sixty houses and flats a month. That's an awful lot. A massive turnover... And we were all terribly busy. We were young, there was lots going on and we had money in our pockets.'

'In relation to estate agents today, we were all earning very decent money,' agreed Mark.

The Fulham back office was supported by an eighteen-year-old office junior, James Calvert, who would photograph the properties and was in charge of printing the sheets of house particulars. There was also a 22-year-old secretary, Stephanie Flower. Both were 'expected to man the phones' which never stopped ringing, according to Mark. But neither were customer-facing members of staff nor did they show properties to buyers.

With David Craddock, one of the four negotiators, on annual leave and the core team one member down, a female temporary secretary from Australia had been hired to ease the workload, but she was limited to office administrative duties only.

Mark Gurdon, the branch manager, went out for a fairly long lunch on the day Suzy went missing, adding to the staffing problems during a particularly frantic day in what was always a busy branch. The Fulham office consistently surpassed all sales forecasts and continued to outperform the property market generally.

Mark explained how the business worked in simple terms: 'A property became available. As the boss, I would go and see it. I would measure it up. I'd come back and tell everybody in the office. They'd then get onto their respective clients who were on our card system, and they'd have ten house-hunters round to look at it and three buyers would offer on it. It was an extraordinary market, but it was what it was.'

I asked Mark and Nigel what their overriding memories were of the day Suzy went missing. Nigel surprised me with his response.

'That morning was a big Monday morning. There had been loads of offers over the weekend and there was always a bit of argy-bargy between the team as to which buyer should get a house. Obviously we'd all make the case for our own client and Mark would have to act like King Herod and say: "No, he's best placed to do the deal, or he's the one that should get it." So there was always a Monday-morning scrum and then everyone would settle down and the week would unfold. But that particular week unfolded slightly differently... Uh... We had a big argument...'

An argument? This was news to us. Nothing we'd seen documented in either the police investigation or in any other format had mentioned this. Mark chipped in claiming he couldn't remember it.

Nigel explained he would sit diagonally across from Suzy, who had the desk nearest the front window. Mark sat at the rear of the office, almost at the back wall. Was this perhaps to explain why Mark hadn't heard the disagreement? Did they want me to believe they'd never discussed this before, in more than thirty years?

Nigel continued. 'Both Suzy and I had a bidder for one property. My abiding memory of that morning was having quite a ding-dong with her about a particular transaction. The two of us both thought we each had the best buyer. It was all quite competitive "live by the sword, die by the sword", but not unfriendly – it was just that sort of sales environment. So, on the day Suzy Lamplugh disappeared, what was my abiding memory? It was just having had this row, about a deal, and then looking back on it, thinking gosh, that's sad really.'

Nigel gazed down at his place setting and fiddled with the cutlery, then continued. 'Little did I know, a couple of hours later, oh my God, she'd walk out of the office and I'd never see her again. It's weird isn't it, how you select little bits? That's my abiding memory of the time.'

There was silence. I contemplated the thought that Nigel's last words with Suzy had been angry ones. Patently, it bothered him, even after three decades.

It puzzled me that he'd never spoken about it before.

As our food arrived, we began talking about what the estate agency team would do for lunch in the Sturgis office all those years ago.

Nigel explained they would frequently eat their lunch sitting at their desks in the office. The team would often buy their own sandwiches from delivery people who catered for the local office staff along Fulham Road.

'It was busy, so you didn't always have time for lunch,' Mark added.

Nigel nodded in agreement. 'Yeah, it wasn't as if you were sitting there chatting. There was always stuff going on. Or we'd have something to eat and a glass of wine in Crocodile Tears next door… Erm, well the boys did. The girls did that slightly less I would say,' he said, laughing.

Crocodile Tears wine bar, with its loud green and yellow frontage, was just a couple of doors down from the estate agency. It was known as a trendy eighties establishment on the ground floor that led, via a spiral staircase, to an even trendier eating place in the basement. Some apparently joked that no crocodile tears were shed by the staff when they handed you the overpriced bill. Nevertheless it was said to be a fairly acceptable eating place thanks to its decent wine and chicken Kievs – and allegedly the most attractive waitstaff in Fulham.

Suzy was last seen at the office at around 12.40 p.m., right in the middle of the busy lunch period.

I asked Mark what he'd been doing for lunch the day she'd disappeared. 'I went out to lunch at Crocodile Tears with my boss and another of the guys who ran one of the other offices. We all used to go to Crocodile Tears. It was a big social place to go.'

It certainly wasn't a place you'd dine alone, exactly as Nigel had already said.

Caroline asked about the subject of keeping the office running during lunch hours generally, and the pair both said that breaks were taken by agreement among the staff, to ensure the office was always manned.

'It was more by sort of collegiate agreement rather than by a codified shop system,' Nigel explained. 'It was just like, okay, you're going out to lunch then, so we'll go out to lunch then. It wasn't formal. It wasn't like, so-and-so are both in between twelve and one, and you can go out between one and two. It wasn't that rigid.'

I'd heard Nigel refer to himself going out for lunch in the plural sense twice in the last few minutes, with the pronoun 'we' – as if he was talking about regularly going out for lunch with someone in the office.

I innocently enquired if he still kept in contact with the secretary, Stephanie Flower, wondering if she'd be able to tell me more about who Nigel went to lunch with.

There was an awkward silence, before Nigel eventually admitted: 'You probably know that Stephanie and I were once boyfriend and girlfriend?'

'This is a subplot,' Nigel continued, 'which is quite amusing in a way. When I first spoke to the police at the time, and gave my version of events about that day, I hadn't told them we were in a relationship. They then spoke to Stephanie, and she'd told the police that she and I were having a relationship. I was later called back in, because I hadn't told them…'

At twenty-two years old, Stephanie Flower was just a year younger than Nigel. Their relationship would last four years in total.

Both Nigel and Stephanie were younger than Suzy, with Stephanie also some way down the hierarchical office pecking order for when she could allegedly take her lunch – yet Nigel was indicating that he and Stephanie would most often lunch together.

Nigel's description of his relationship with Stephanie as being a 'subplot' in Suzy's murder-mystery story intrigued me. In fiction of course, not all subplots are independent of the main plot. He probably meant this as a throwaway comment during our meeting, but it started to gnaw at me. I didn't know why at first, but something about it was far from insignificant. As we finished our lunch, I couldn't shake the feeling I was now left with.

The Monday lunchtime Suzy went missing, the Sturgis office was desperately short of staff. David Craddock was on holiday in California and Mark Gurdon was in Crocodile Tears quaffing wine and eating overpriced food in the trendy basement. Our research had already shown that Stephanie had just left the office, minutes before Suzy herself, and that Suzy had to wait for the Australian temp, to come back into the office before she could go out herself. Comments from Diana Lamplugh also support this, suggesting Suzy should have arranged to meet whoever she was meeting at the office, so the 'receptionist' could have checked him out.

There had been a significant disagreement between Suzy and Nigel that morning, and they were the only two negotiators left in the office. What was more, Nigel may well have been hoping to go out for lunch with his girlfriend Stephanie – or had already left – which is why Suzy had to wait for the temporary secretary to return to the office.

The atmosphere didn't sound very conducive for a 'collegiate agreement' over who was taking lunch at what time. Was Nigel planning a quick getaway to chase after Stephanie, whilst Suzy had to make do with a soggy sandwich at her desk?

This argument between Nigel and Suzy felt raw. It must have been a fiery discussion for him to be holding on to it all these years later. Yet it had never been mentioned in anything I had ever looked at about the case. It seemed as if the police had never been aware of it, let alone considered its relevance.

I finished off the meeting with a final question: 'Did Suzy mention losing her chequebook and diary at all to either of you that Monday morning, before she went missing?'

'No,' was the answer they both gave as they looked at me blankly.

'Did she lose them?' Mark asked.

'Apparently she did…' I then recounted our peculiar conversation in March with Adam Leegood to them.

Nigel shrugged. 'Maybe she told Stephanie about it?'

'Was Adam actually Suzy's boyfriend?' I asked.

Mark nodded. 'As far as we understood, yes.'

'How did you know he was her boyfriend? Were you told this by Suzy, or did you actually meet him?' Caroline followed up.

'Oh no, we knew him. He came to the wine bar after work, when we went, a few times. If we were all going for a drink he'd come and join in…' Nigel responded. 'We'd have barbecues at each other's houses occasionally, and he'd come along.'

I shook my head. 'I still can't work him out…'

'A lot came out afterwards about Suzy's relationships, after she'd gone missing, and maybe we didn't know her as well as we all thought we did,' Mark said flatly.

After the meeting, I dropped Caroline back off at the station and took a slow drive back into central London alone, enjoying the last of the day's sunshine through the open sunroof.

By the time I arrived home, I'd decided we needed to meet with Mark Gurdon again.

17

There was something amiss about that last lunchtime for Suzy in the Sturgis office. The argument with Nigel, and Mark being out on a long lunch at a wine bar – it all seemed so raw, even after all this time. I needed to understand why. The only way I would get to the bottom of it was to speak to everyone I could from the estate agency, even those the police hadn't bothered much with at the time. There was David Craddock, the negotiator who'd been on holiday when Suzy had gone missing, but at the top of my list was Stephanie Flower, the secretary who'd been involved in the 'subplot relationship' with Nigel Hindle.

After much pestering of Mark Gurdon, he eventually provided me with email addresses for the office junior James Calvert, who was living abroad, and David Craddock, who apparently lived somewhere in the south of England – though he said he didn't have physical addresses for either. I fired off emails to both. With little hope of a reply, it felt akin to shouting into a deep dark well.

Both Mark and Nigel claimed they didn't know how to contact Stephanie Flower and could not help with any information that would help me find her. But after some sleepless nights and a lot of hard work, I managed to hunt down an address for her.

Stephanie had moved up north, several hundred miles from London. Given the distance, I'd elected to send her a letter, hoping she'd get in touch by phone. But after a gap of three weeks with no response from her at all, I realised she wasn't going to contact me voluntarily for an interview.

I'd have to go up there and doorstep her.

Doorstepping was something I was familiar with in the police. There's no legal power or duty to compel people to talk to you or to provide statements about what they know or saw – not even the police can make people do that. Some courts have powers of compulsion over the attendance of a witness, but there was very little that could make people actually talk. And it was surprisingly common for witnesses not to want to talk or to refuse to answer any questions. You had to rely on people's good nature, their sense of right and wrong, and the idea justice should be done, and could only be done with their help.

Some witnesses, once you got face to face with them, were straightforward. Others you had to push a little harder to get the information you needed.

Although it was completely legal, and something journalists did all the time to research a story, obtain an interview or a piece to camera, I'd never done it as a civilian before without prior arrangement or agreement.

We had no choice. But, just perhaps, fate was about to lend us a helping hand.

18

If you were to compile a list of Britain's largest missing persons investigations, then besides that of Suzy Lamplugh, I'd wager author Agatha Christie's disappearance would feature near the top.

One Friday, in early December 1926, a furious row erupted between Colonel Archie Christie and his wife, Agatha, over an alleged affair Archie was having. She got into her car and drove away from the family home in Sunningdale, Berkshire at 10 p.m., leaving her daughter and philandering husband at home.

The next day, her Morris Bullnose was found abandoned at the edge of a Surrey chalk pit. Agatha was nowhere to be seen. There were immediate fears for her safety and speculation in the press that she had committed suicide. Surrey Police mounted a large investigation.

However, eleven days later, Christie was found safe and well. She'd checked into the Swan Hotel in Harrogate over 230 miles away, using the surname of her husband's mistress.

Some reports say she was found following a letter to her brother-in-law, others she was recognised by a maid or musician at the hotel. The public reaction was mostly negative, given the huge amount of police resources employed. Many believed it was a publicity stunt for her books. Others speculated she wanted police to believe her husband had killed her and was extracting some sort of revenge for the affair he was having, or the divorce he had allegedly requested. Some say she'd suffered a severe mental-health episode.

As a result, the Swan Hotel in Harrogate would become synonymous with murder mysteries and crime-fiction writing. In 2005, it became the venue of the Harrogate Crime Writing Festival, one of the biggest and best-known crime-fiction festivals in the world. And each summer, the quintessentially English town of Harrogate – once famous for its tea rooms, spa water and gardens – plays host to crime writers and crime-fiction fans who descend on the town to talk about murder, blood, gore and mysterious disappearances at the very hotel where Christie had holed up all those years ago.

As a crime writer, the Harrogate festival is *the* place to network with reviewers, bloggers, agents and publishers, but also to reconnect with readers and fellow authors. Hotels are difficult to come by, so you have to book well in advance – as I had done, believing I'd be there promoting my third crime thriller – which I'd now shelved to concentrate on Suzy.

But now my plans had changed, perhaps I'd have to cancel everything?

Caroline, ever the practical one, had other ideas: 'Why don't we go to the crime-writing festival anyway and use it as a base to see if we can find Stephanie whilst we're up there?' she'd suggested. 'Maybe we can kill two birds with one stone?'

She was right. This might be an opportunity too good to miss.

On the long drive north, we talked virtually non-stop, mulling over the oddities between Nigel's and Mark's recollections.

By the time we arrived in Harrogate, it was quite late. We attended some of the opening night's formalities, checked into a Victorian apartment overlooking the copper-domed Royal Pump Room and ordered a pizza.

The Pump Room now houses the town's museum but was formerly where visitors took the sulphur waters, which they perceived to have medicinal benefits, curing ailments ranging from gout to back pain. It was built to offer guests an all-weather facility where they could take the water pumped on site from a natural spring.

It wasn't this splendid view that had sold me on the large apartment though; rather that it had an allocated parking space. At the time of booking, a car hadn't necessarily been essential, but now transport was a must. And when I had looked at cancelling or amending the booking, I realised quite how rare allocated parking was in the town.

We needed a car. Stephanie's home was some distance from Harrogate, and you could never tell how many times you'd have to bang on the door before someone would actually answer it. Or worse, have to wait it out on the road outside and confront them in a public place to get your interview. The car offered me the same facility as the Pump Room had to the early Victorians – an all-weather facility to wait out the rain.

Our parking space, hidden behind a mini mart selling long-life milk, sponge fingers and vacuum-packed ham was rather small, but I managed to squeeze my car in before locking it up to enjoy the pizza and discuss our plan of attack.

19

We woke early and agreed we'd avoid the morning's scheduled festival activities – finding Stephanie was the priority. Caroline was taking a while to get ready, so I decided to go and retrieve my car from its secluded spot and bring it round to the front, ready to make a quick getaway.

As I was trying to parallel park my car in a stupidly small space outside the front of the mini market – reversing backward and forward and hoping that Caroline would emerge soon – I failed to spot a man step off the pavement in front of me. And suddenly, there he was, virtually laid across the bonnet of my car.

As I focused on his face, which looked familiar, I realised it was Lee Child, the author of the Jack Reacher thrillers, sandwiched between my car and the vehicle in front of me – all six foot four inches of him, scowling and shouting profanities.

I mouthed my apologies through the windscreen to him, but he sauntered off, cursing me, before taking a seat by the Pump Room and lighting a cigarette, apparently needing to compose himself.

As I pondered how injuring Lee Child outside a supermarket at one of the world's largest crime-fiction festivals might affect my future as a writer, Caroline opened the passenger door and jumped in.

'Okay, let's get going!' she said.

I gulped. 'Give me a minute.'

'What are we waiting for? It may come as a surprise to you, but according to a recent survey, the average British woman takes thirty-eight minutes to put their face on – and I'm no different,' she declared.

'No. It's not that,' I replied, shaking my head.

'What then?'

'I just nearly ran over Lee Child. He's sitting over there cursing me,' I replied, pointing at him.

I tried to compose myself enough to attempt the mirror, signal, manoeuvre procedure required to pull away.

Caroline began to giggle as if I'd just told her a joke. The day had started out on a surreal note.

We headed out to hunt for Stephanie.

20

'Can I help you?' the voice said from behind me.

'Hello.' I spun round and did my best impression of appearing to be startled. In my peripheral vision, I'd seen the well-built, fifty-something man in a brightly coloured polo shirt approaching.

I'd left Caroline sitting in the car whilst I took a stroll along the alley that ran behind Stephanie's large Victorian house. I'd wanted to gauge if anyone was home before I knocked. It was an old habit.

As I spun round and stared directly at the man who'd been following me, I recognised his face from my prior research.

'You're Stephanie's husband,' I stated.

'I am...' He frowned and eyed me up and down suspiciously.

'I'm a writer. I'm actually here looking for your wife. I sent her a letter some weeks back...'

I stopped, hoping to get a sign that he knew what I was talking about, but he gave nothing away.

'It was about Suzy Lamplugh,' I continued.

'Well, my wife's at work. And I'm sure if she wanted to speak to you, she would have called,' he said.

'I'm sorry, but this is really important. I'm trying to find out what happened to Suzy Lamplugh, and I have a couple of questions for Stephanie, that's all.'

He didn't reply.

I handed him a business card. 'Please ask her to call me – I really need to talk to her.'

'You need to respect her privacy.'

'Look, I'm in the area for the next few days; I can come back if she wants me to.'

I shook his hand and walked back to the car at the front of the house.

I explained to Caroline how Stephanie's husband had confronted me as I'd attempted to peer over their back wall.

'That worked well then?' she quipped.

'Not exactly.'

'What now then, Sherlock?'

'We can either wait until she comes home, but who knows when that will be? Or we could try and find where she works.'

'You don't think she'll call you?'

'She hasn't so far, and I doubt I've won her husband over.'

'How are we going to find her when we don't know where she works?'

'I have no idea.'

Caroline looked across at me and half smiled. As a northerner, she was on home turf. 'It's *not* London. There are only so many people that live around here. Maybe she's still in the same line of work?'

'You want to go searching round estate agencies for her?' I asked.

'Have you got a better idea?'

'Nope.'

'Then that's what we'll do. I'll help you do the legwork. But you're the expert in getting people talking...'

Perhaps it wasn't such a bad idea after all. Maybe it would demonstrate to Stephanie that we weren't going to give up until she'd spoken with us.

'Maybe by asking after her, the word will get round,' I reasoned. 'Hopefully, she'll ring. Probably completely pissed off, but she might ring...'

21

20 July 2018
31 years, 11 months, 22 days missing

We arrived back in Harrogate late in the evening, the day spent tramping around in the drizzle with nothing to show for it.

Just as I was about to unlock the door to our apartment, my mobile rang. It was Stephanie – our hard work had not been in vain.

She got straight to the point: 'I really don't think I can be of much help – I told the police everything that I knew at the time, which wasn't a lot.'

'I know you weren't actually in the office when Suzy left that day?'

'I wasn't,' she agreed.

'It's just that I spoke to Mark Gurdon and Nigel Hindle…'

'I know; I've just come off the phone to Mark about giving my address away,' Stephanie said bluntly.

'He *didn't* give me your address; in fact he told me he had no way of contacting you at all,' I responded. Why hadn't Mark and Nigel wanted me to speak with Stephanie?

'Hmmm,' Stephanie replied, sounding unconvinced.

'It took me some time to trace you.'

'Okay, but I don't think I can help you, regardless.'

'Do you remember what Suzy was doing in the office before you left?' I tried again.

'She was getting ready to leave the office, I think.'

'Where for?'

'I don't know.'

'Had she been on the phone – perhaps you'd heard her talking on it before she left the office?'

'She had been on the phone, but it's so long ago, I don't really have any recollection of what she was talking about.'

'Was she happy or sad – can you remember that?' I tried to prompt her.

'She seemed alright, as far as I can remember. I can't help much, honestly,' she said, sighing.

'I know it's hard,' I conceded.

'It is. I'm really sorry.'

'Okay. One last thing that's puzzling me is an incident that's supposed to have happened to Suzy on the Friday night before she went missing. She's supposed to have lost her chequebook and diary while she was out with her boyfriend.'

'Okay...' Stephanie said, sounding intrigued.

'Except I'm not sure it happened on Friday night, and I'm trying to work out why her boyfriend is acting really strangely about it.'

'You've interviewed her boyfriend?'

'We have. He was really odd about the whole thing – it doesn't make much sense. Do you know anything about a lost chequebook?'

There was a long pause. For a moment I thought she'd hung up on me.

'I've got a vague recollection about Suzy talking about a lost chequebook,' she said finally, 'but I can't remember if it relates to that Monday morning or another morning. It could have been a different morning.'

'Do you remember her cancelling a lost chequebook with the bank?'

'No. She certainly wasn't cancelling a chequebook, not that I remember. She might have said that she'd lost one, but she wasn't cancelling it.'

'Did you ever talk to the police about this?'

'I've never been asked about it, no.'

'Okay, thank you. I really appreciate you calling me. If I need to speak to you again, can I call you on this number?'

'Of course.'

We said our goodbyes and I hung up.

85

'Well?' Caroline stood with her arms open in expectation.

'She can't remember much…'

'Oh no! After coming all this way and spending all day traipsing round the north of England for her in the drizzle?' Caroline looked disappointed.

'It's not all bad. Mark and Nigel weren't exactly honest with us. Mark was in contact with Stephanie…'

'He said he wasn't,' Caroline hissed.

'I know. Strange.'

'Anything else?'

'Yeah, she vaguely remembers Suzy talking about a lost chequebook.'

'That's progress.'

'Yeah,' I said, pondering how it all fitted together. 'Anyway, we spoke to her, it's a job well done. Let's get ready and go down to The Swan and have a drink. Maybe I can say sorry to Lee Child?'

22

In 1983, at about the time Paul Young's cover of Marvin Gaye's 'Wherever I Lay My Hat' finally launched him to the top of the charts, Suzy's 78-year-old grandmother passed away. The probate was sorted in the early part of the following year, coinciding with Suzy coming ashore from working on the QE2. So, rather than go back and live with her parents, Suzy used the inheritance as a deposit on a property at 49 Disraeli Road in Putney.

The large, three-storey Victorian house, built around 1880, yards from Putney High Street, had been split into three separate flats. Flat C, on the very top floor, had two bedrooms. There had been talk of Suzy moving in with a boyfriend, but the boyfriend had allegedly decided against living in London, preferring a more relaxed lifestyle in the Home Counties – something by all accounts Suzy didn't want. By amicable agreement, the pair parted company, and Suzy proceeded with the purchase of a flat alone.

To help pay the bills, Suzy rented out the second bedroom. At first this was to a female friend of a friend. But this didn't go well; the girl failed to pay her rent and left owing Suzy a sizable chunk of money. Suzy began to put out the feelers for a new tenant.

Nick Bryant, an advertising executive in his mid-twenties, had been lodging in the Putney area, but this agreement was coming to an end. He'd met Suzy through a close friend and took the vacant room in her flat.

Nick was someone likely to have the inside track on Suzy's life – someone who would have known what was really going on. Given the comments from Suzy's work colleagues who felt they hadn't known her as well as they thought they had, I wanted to speak to someone that did; a flatmate would likely know what Suzy was really like.

The sun was beginning to set on a warm summer's evening as I pulled up outside an impressive-looking detached house. The door was answered by a familiar-looking face. After weeks of dead ends and false alarms spent trying to track Nick Bryant down, I was finally staring at Suzy's lodger, whom I'd seen on screen in a 1986 *Crimewatch* reconstruction and in numerous newspaper cuttings.

Tall, slim and well dressed, the years had been kind to Nick Bryant. He led me into a library dominated by a large model yacht on a side table. It was a quiet and relaxing room where you could lose yourself in a good book: light grey woodwork against white walls; seagrass on the floor; a slouchy sofa and an old leather chair.

Nick got out of the blocks first. 'Look, just before you start... this is for your own research, right? Not at all for the newspapers. I've always been very careful... cautious... over the years.'

'It's taken me weeks to find you. It's for my own research – I'm trying to find Suzy, that's all.'

'Have you spoken to anyone in the family?'

'No. I haven't. Her father died in June; it's not a good time to be speaking with the family.'

'I do know that, yes,' he replied. 'To be honest with you, I hardly ever think about what happened; it's really difficult. But recently I've thought about it again, because of Paul's death.'

'Yes, I can imagine.'

'How do you think I can help?'

'At the moment I'm just trying to firm up the background research I've done. I've been working on this for a while now, but talking to people, I get a different feeling about the case to the one the police presented to the press...'

'What do you want to know?'

'Maybe we can start with what Suzy was like?'

'She was good-looking, conventionally very pretty...' Nick sighed. He looked a little wistful at first. Evidently he was very fond of Suzy. He smiled, looked skyward and continued. 'She was gregarious and outgoing. She was sporty. She used to like windsurfing...'

Nick tailed off.

'And she seemed to...' He frowned as he continued. 'She seemed to like male company, and to enjoy it...'

This was an area of Suzy's life which had been the cause of much distress to Diana and Paul Lamplugh. Not only had their daughter gone missing, but they were faced with having to ward off persistent rumours that Suzy's love life was rather fuller than they would have wished it to be.

By 1988 – and following the publication of a book on Suzy's disappearance commissioned by the Lamplughs themselves – there was also friction between the family and the police on the subject. These rumours, stories of numerous relationships, had been printed in the book. And they'd come largely from the police investigation to which the author of the book had been given unprecedented access. This infuriated Diana Lamplugh, who'd demanded the Met say that the stories were simply untrue and without foundation. While Assistant Commissioner Paul Condon duly complied with the request and issued a statement saying, 'Our investigations revealed nothing more than that Suzy was a modern young woman,' it was hardly the outright denial Diana had hoped for.

What's more, Condon's statement seemed only to draw more attention to the issue, with some of the broadsheets then speaking with 'senior unnamed sources' who'd actually worked on the investigation. These sources criticised Condon for becoming involved and said he'd been wrong to issue any statement at all, especially one that contradicted what the investigation team had actually found.

'She did have a boyfriend though, at the time,' Nick added.

'Was that Adam?' I asked.

'Adam Leegood, yes.'

'And did you meet Adam?'

'Yeah, many times…'

'Was that when he'd come round to the flat?'

'Not really, no. I don't remember him coming round to the flat much at all.'

'So you'd only see him socially, in a crowd with others, and not at the flat?'

'Yes, he was kind of friendly with some people that she knew, and when I was living with her, I spent quite a lot of time with her and her friends.'

This made Adam sound as if he was more just part of Suzy's social crowd, someone she saw infrequently, rather than a full-time boyfriend.

'You lived with her for about a year, is that right?'

'Something like that.'

'Was she having any problems with anybody in particular?'

'No, not as far as I remember – I'm sure the police asked me this at the time.'

'There's information in the press which says you were aware of a number of phone calls coming in to the flat, somebody bothering her, sending her flowers?'

There was a long pause. Perhaps this was why he'd asked if I was writing for a newspaper. Perhaps he'd been misquoted in the press.

'I do remember something about flowers,' Nick conceded after what seemed like too long. 'Were there a number of phone calls?' he continued. 'Again, it's so difficult to remember after all this time. There was nothing that made me think there was anything unusual. Have there been any unusual activities? Have things changed in the previous two or three months? Did she seem concerned about anything? These were all things the police asked.'

I nodded in encouragement.

'I do vaguely remember some flowers being delivered, now you come to mention it, shortly before she disappeared,' he said finally.

'And how did she feel about that?'

'Neither ecstatic nor the opposite, as far as I remember – nothing out of the ordinary.'

90

'They weren't from Adam?'

Nick shook his head. 'I don't think so…'

I wondered what had made him think they weren't from Adam.

'Did that surprise you, given Adam was her boyfriend at the time she disappeared?'

Nick looked slightly uncomfortable and shifted around in his seat as he answered. 'I always got the impression that theirs wasn't a particularly serious relationship…'

'Suzy's and Adam's relationship?' I thought back to the Sunday afternoon, when Suzy had left Adam at the beach.

'No. It didn't seem like a serious, monogamous, long-term relationship to me. Not on Suzy's part. He was a good-looking guy, and she was a good-looking girl…' Nick shrugged. 'He wasn't the great love of her life, so if she was seeing somebody else, I wouldn't have been at all surprised, no.'

Nick confirmed everything that I'd thought about Suzy and Adam.

'Not that I think she was particularly promiscuous,' he continued, 'don't get me wrong.'

'It's difficult to understand.' I shook my head.

'What?'

'Why was Adam at that very first police press conference if he wasn't the love of Suzy's life?'

'Adam was the kind of boy that her mother would have approved of. He was a nice, middle-class boy, good-looking, polite. He certainly wouldn't have been someone Diana disapproved of.'

There was some history of Diana interfering in the relationships of both Suzy and her sister, Tamsin, when they were teenagers, splitting them from boys who Diana felt were unsuitable. Was Diana reputation-managing for the purposes of good press, or was there something more behind it?

'How were the police with you?' I asked.

'I tell you, I wasn't super impressed by the police at the time. I was twenty-five years old, and it was my first encounter with the police…'

91

'They treated you badly?'

'No, they treated me perfectly well. It very soon became apparent that I had nothing to do with it. But they were a bit "Keystone Cop-ish" about it all, to be honest with you. It seemed a bit chaotic, but as a 25-year-old you don't know what normal police activity is. It did seem hit and miss.'

Nick had last seen Suzy as he left for work that morning. When he returned home in the early hours of the following morning, having been out with friends in Wimbledon, he found police had broken in to search for Suzy. The door to the flat had been left open; a note asked him to contact Fulham police station.

But Nick, not realising the seriousness of the situation, and being a little worse for wear, didn't contact the police until later on Tuesday. Before the police had even spoken to him, before they knew what he had to say about anything, they'd ploughed ahead with the press conference in the police canteen. It seemed an odd thing to do.

As far as the media were concerned, Adam's appearance alongside Suzy's mother and father at the press conference confirmed a serious relationship. The public-facing narrative around Suzy's private life was dictated right from the start.

Perhaps if the police had spoken to Nick before they'd done the press conference that afternoon, they would have objected to Adam being presented in this way?

I rounded off my questions by asking Nick about the Sunday night before Suzy had gone missing. But Nick claimed he had no recollection of seeing Suzy at all on Sunday evening when she returned from her mother and father's house.

This was odd. In an interview shortly after Suzy had gone missing, Nick had claimed that on the Sunday evening, following her late return from windsurfing, he had stayed up for a couple of hours chatting with her about nothing in particular before going to bed – adding that she had been in good spirits.

However, the article had caused quite a stir for Diana, perhaps because of the implication that Suzy might have gone to bed with Nick. Within a fortnight, Diana had penned a public, open letter to her daughter which suggested Suzy had gone to see her boyfriend Adam that evening, before finally spending some time 'just chatting' platonically to Nick, as any friend or flatmate might do, on her arrival back at their flat.

I decided not to challenge Nick about this discrepancy. It was better to bank it as something we should bear in mind.

The Sunday night before Suzy went missing was becoming more and more interesting.

Who was Suzy with after she'd left her parents at 9 p.m., and where had she gone?

Was she with Nick, or had he been covering for who she was with?

And if she wasn't at home, where had she made the 10.15 p.m. phone call to Adam from?

I'd bide my time and wait and see what else came up. If I then needed to talk to him again, I could. I thanked Nick and left, happy that we were starting to make some real headway in the investigation.

We needed to track down some of the original investigating officers and get some insight on how they saw things.

That would be our next task.

23

At 6.45 p.m. on Monday, 28 July 1986, Suzy's boss, Mark Gurdon, called the police to alert them that his employee was missing. The incident was subsequently escalated to the local Criminal Investigation Department (CID).

Most of the local CID officers worked 8 a.m. to 4 p.m. During evenings and throughout the night, it was staffed by a skeleton crew; the bare minimum available just to offer advice or undertake essential, time-critical enquiries. Outside of normal office hours, others were only called in if absolutely needed.

That evening, there were just two detectives manning the Fulham CID office on the 2–10 p.m. shift, known in the Met as 'late-turn'. These were DC Mick Jones and DC Steve Hill.

Former DC Mick Jones had retired as a police officer but was still working in a civilian role. He kindly agreed to discuss the case and suggested we meet in the basement café at Methodist Central Hall in the heart of Westminster. Despite all my years of working just a stone's throw away at Scotland Yard, I'd never actually been inside.

Methodist Central Hall is an iconic building and a major tourist attraction because of its location directly opposite Westminster Abbey. It had been a meeting point for the suffragette movement, the venue of the first meeting of the United Nations General Assembly in 1946 and a focal point for various famous political rallies. In 1966 it was also the venue for an audacious theft when the football World Cup trophy was stolen.

Though the elaborate baroque-style building is now multi-purpose with art galleries, offices and conference facilities, it had originally been constructed as the headquarters of the Methodist Church of Great Britain, which had occupied the building until the turn of the millennium.

It was a place which I imagined Diana and Paul Lamplugh would have visited many times, given that both of their families held strict Wesleyan Methodist beliefs.

As I walked down the stone staircase and into the large vaulted café, I wondered how Suzy's parents' strict beliefs and their upbringing would have impacted upon Suzy's behaviour. Would she have tried to shield them from her complicated private life in the hope that they'd not be upset with her or for fear of disappointing them?

Paul Lamplugh believed his ancestors were intrinsically involved in the formation of Wesleyan Methodism. For many generations, his middle name, Crosby, had been passed down from father to son to honour Sarah Crosby, a revered Wesleyan Methodist preacher born in 1729, and a possible lover of John Wesley himself. Paul's grandparents could be found listed in old copies of *The Methodist Who's Who*.

If the rumours and suggestions in the media that there had been a large number of lovers in Suzy's life were correct, it would have been something the Wesleyan Church disapproved of.

Their teachings preach that human sexuality is to be expressed only in a monogamous, lifelong relationship between one man and one woman, within the framework of marriage and that this was 'God's plan'.

Few of us would wish to share the full extent of our twenty-something love lives with our parents, though they would perhaps likely be aware to some extent. But for Suzy, that would have been something she could never dream of discussing with the older members of her Wesleyan Methodist family – perhaps something that she was deliberately deceitful about? In fact, there were few aspects of Suzy's exciting eighties lifestyle that any strict Wesleyan Methodist would *not* have had some criticism of, even down to the fashionable way in which she dressed.

I settled into a quiet spot of the refurbished café with a large coffee. Mick, a softly spoken Welshman with the sort of suntan you get after far too many hot foreign holidays, arrived slightly late. We shook hands, and he sat down opposite me, declining the offer of a cup of tea or coffee.

'You were part of Fulham CID back then, is that right?' I asked, trying to break the ice.

He smiled. 'Yes.'

'And the night that Suzy disappeared, you were working with a guy called Steve Hill – do you remember much about it?'

'Steve and I were late-turn, yes. We were just about to go out to do some enquiries, and then the local Inspector, Thompson, came and said, "Listen guys, we've got a misper. Estate agent. Sturgis." I didn't think much of it really. She was an adult.

'We did the ordinary sort of enquiries,' he continued. 'We went and saw the parents. We saw the manager of the estate agent, Mark Gurdon, and then it escalated from there.'

Misper was the police abbreviation for 'missing person'.

During the eighties, adult missing persons were given a very low priority – sometimes even ignored totally. As Mick had inferred, he'd not assigned it much importance at the time. But to me this seemed at odds with how the local police in uniform had dovetailed with the CID. It was curious that Mick was asked to investigate a misper by the local uniformed inspector, because at the time, the CID wouldn't have had anything to do with missing persons. They only dealt with serious crime, and they would often flatly refuse to deal with anything they considered to be minor, such as an adult missing person. It was something that the local uniformed police would have been tasked with.

'You went to Suzy's flat in Disraeli Road, Putney, that night, is that right?'

'We went to the flat. Her dad, Paul, was with us, yes,' Mick agreed.

'And you broke into her flat?'

'We did – we tried to keep her dad away, just in case we found the inevitable, though he wasn't having any of it.'

Mick believed it was a possibility, at that stage, that Suzy might have simply gone home and committed suicide. 'The inevitable' meant a dead body.

'But we found nothing,' he continued. 'Nothing untoward was found in the flat, so we came away. Then, as we were driving back to the police station, we heard over the radio that her car had been discovered in Stevenage Road.'

'Her car was found abandoned?'

'Yes, it was parked in an awkward place, doors unlocked, car seat pushed right back. And it all became very suspicious *from then on.*'

'You said you spoke to Suzy's boss, Mark Gurdon – where did you do that?'

'I'm not sure. I think possibly he could have come into the station.'

'Okay, at what point did you go to 37 Shorrolds Road, the house that Suzy was supposed to be showing to a viewer that day, and check that out?'

Mick said nothing; he looked a little confused.

'Do you remember going there, to the house for sale?' I pressed the question again.

Mick frowned. 'Er… I didn't. I never went there.'

'You never went to the address?'

'I never went to that address.'

'Okay – do you know who did?'

'No, I don't…'

This was fascinating.

Mick and Steve had broken into Suzy's flat to look for something that might indicate what had befallen her, to enquire if she was ill, injured or even dead in her flat. Yet they'd not gone to the same trouble at the address where Suzy was supposed to have shown a client round a house?

This made no sense.

'Right, who else was involved that night then? Can you remember? Was it just the two of you?' I asked, wondering if our research had missed something. Mick Jones and Steve Hill would have done everything together, but perhaps there had been other officers involved in those very early stages?

'Initially it was just the two of us and the relief inspector, Thompson – I can't remember his first name...'

I knew Thompson's name. It was Ken Thompson. He was the uniformed duty inspector responsible for the oversight of all the officers on duty that evening in Fulham, though the CID would likely have disputed this, claiming they reported to the detective chief inspector, not anyone in uniform.

But Ken Thompson was the supervisor. As the duty inspector, his role was to stay behind the desk in the office and supervise. It wasn't his role to undertake enquiries.

I tried again. 'Okay. So, you think you met Mark Gurdon at Fulham police station?'

'I can't remember,' replied Mick.

'Do you think that somebody from the uniform relief team went to Shorrolds Road?'

'I can't commit myself to yes or no... I would presume, initially, somebody would have gone there. So who's to say that Mark Gurdon hadn't gone there himself, you know?'

'So we don't know who went to Shorrolds Road?'

Mick shook his head.

'Did anyone go there?'

'If I was her boss, and she'd gone missing, having gone to Shorrolds Road to do a viewing – I'd go there. I'd – I'd go in there myself.'

I sat in silence for a moment.

I knew that it had been suggested that Suzy's work colleagues, Mark Gurdon and Nigel Hindle, had gone to Shorrolds Road to look for her. I'd seen them re-enact it in the *Crimewatch* reconstruction broadcast in October 1986. The footage shows them banging on the door of the premises and not going inside the house; they'd just knocked on the door to see if Suzy had perhaps locked herself in.

Caroline had pointed out to me that 37 Shorrolds Road was a three-storey house with a south-facing roof terrace forty feet above the ground. The 'For Sale' listings and house particulars from July 1986 confirmed this. What if Suzy had fallen from the balcony and were lying somewhere?

Why had Mick Jones assumed that Gurdon had been inside but not checked the premises for himself?

Of course, in hindsight, Suzy wasn't found inside the house and she hadn't fallen off the balcony. There would be no mystery if the police had subsequently found Suzy dead when the place had been dusted for prints the following day. Yet these sorts of assumptions in the initial stages of an investigation, about who had done what and why, meant things could fall through the cracks. I knew this myself. It was where mistakes had been made in Joanne's case; how we'd messed it all up.

It bothered me.

'Have you thought about talking to the review team?' Mick asked, filling the silence as I continued to ponder the significance of what I'd just been told.

'I've already spoken to someone on the Murder Review Group, yes,' I replied, referring to my conversation with Graeme Gwyn.

'Oh right. Is it active then?'

Murder cases were referred to as either active or inactive. They were only classed as closed if there was a conviction or the suspect, upon whom charges would have been brought, was now dead.

'Not at the moment, no – it's inactive,' I responded.

Mick sat in silence, waiting for my next question. I hadn't meant him to feel as if I was interrogating him, but here we were, and I sounded as if I was being critical. I wasn't. But it was these sorts of tiny discrepancies which often pointed to something that had been missed and could make the crucial difference between getting to the answers and not.

'Were you involved in the case the following day, when it was considered an abduction?' I asked as a large group of Japanese tourists rushed in and filled the Wesley Café with the sound of clattering trays and plates.

By the following day, everyone was convinced Shorrolds Road was an integral part of the investigation; the place where they believed Suzy had last been positively sighted.

'Yes, I was involved throughout.'

'The case ran for about a year, is that right?'

'I was on it for about eight months. I wasn't on the last knockings because they reduced the squad somewhat. It was on the old card system as well. Those cards are still there, the decision logs would still be there…'

Mick and I talked about the incident room logs that were still in existence, held by the police. Incident rooms were resource intensive and difficult to run, so they weren't something every inquiry had. The creation of one in Suzy's case had become a necessity due to the hundreds of calls and letters that had flooded in from the public. All those thousands of pieces of information needed to be recorded and processed somewhere, just in case they were potential leads that helped to solve the investigation.

We talked briefly about the police press conference held the day after Suzy's disappearance at Fulham police station. Mick explained that he'd had nothing to do with it.

'I was a detective constable; I would never have been involved in the press conference. Superintendent Carter did that. He's dead now. Everyone was so passionate about it – it was a massive inquiry. The whole nation got behind it. Everybody on the team was very passionate about finding her and finding her alive.

'There was no such thing as a family liaison officer at the time,' Mick continued, 'so I was probably the first family liaison officer if you like, going to her parents' house. There was Mum and Dad, a sister – she was in New Zealand at the time. A brother was there, he was working away somewhere, on some fish farm. Mum and Dad, they were very intelligent people and they just couldn't get their heads around the fact that she'd just gone missing. They even brought in mediums like Doris Stokes and Uri Geller to help. I remember being in the house with those two one night and it was a bit surreal.'

Doris Stokes was a prominent British spiritualist and professional medium who gave public performances and appeared on television. Geller was a self-proclaimed psychic. Both had been household names at the time.

I'd read about Diana's attempts to solve the case using the supernatural. Within two weeks of Suzy's disappearance, she publicly confirmed that she'd contacted Doris Stokes after a friend suggested it might help. 'We need every bit of help we can get,' Diana had said.

But what I hadn't realised was that Diana had invited the police to observe their activities too.

'They were a very, very nice family,' Mick continued. 'Mum's dead now, dad's still alive...'

'Her dad died in June,' I added.

'Oh bless. Is the brother still around?'

'I haven't spoken to anyone in the family, not yet.'

'Have you spoken to the Sturgis staff – Mark Gurdon, her boss, especially?

'I've interviewed him once, yes. I'd like to talk to him again. Maybe I will...'

We talked about the case for another ten minutes and batted around some of the theories that had been put forward over the years as my coffee went cold.

After confirming that he'd be happy to help if I thought of anything else, we shook hands and Mick left me sitting alone at the table. I had the feeling he was sincere about that, despite me making him feel uncomfortable with some of my questions.

Sitting in Wesley's Café, now surrounded by Japanese tourists, I called Caroline's mobile.

'Hey, how did the meeting go?' Caroline asked excitedly.

'Not bad; he seems like a nice guy.'

'Did he say anything interesting?'

'He did. He says he didn't search Shorrolds Road for Suzy the night she went missing.'

'Okay...'

'He thinks Mark Gurdon went inside and searched for Suzy, but of course we know from all our research that he didn't

– Mark just knocked on the door. Suzy could have been dead inside that address and no one would have known.'

'But Suzy wasn't dead inside that address.'

'I know she wasn't.'

'Does it really matter whether the police searched 37 Shorrolds Road that night or not?' Caroline asked, sounding confused.

'So an estate agent has gone missing, and her desk diary states she has an appointment to show a Fulham house to a viewer. Yet the police totally ignore this and decide to break into Suzy's own flat in Putney. They don't bother to even look inside the Fulham house she was supposed to be showing a client around? That just seems strange to me. Why didn't the CID search 37 Shorrolds Road?' I said, finishing the last of my cold coffee. 'I want to understand their thought processes.'

'Right...' replied Caroline, sounding unconvinced.

'It will likely tell us something important. Trust me.'

'Alright.'

'Can you go back through our research and see what we have on the police actually going inside 37 Shorrolds Road? I want to know who went inside and when.'

'Okay, it might take me a little while though,' she said, hanging up.

I could tell by the sound of Caroline's voice she felt this might be a waste of time.

Yet I was sure it was important. Somehow.

24

My dining-room table was awash with newspaper cuttings, photos and binders. The cherry-wood tabletop was barely visible above the mountains of paperwork.

'By the following morning, the police were forensicating 37 Shorrolds Road as they would a crime scene,' Caroline confirmed. 'These two photos pop up in numerous places the week Suzy disappeared. Both shots were taken by professional photographers on Tuesday, 29 July.'

I looked at the two black-and-white images showing police officers standing guard outside 37 Shorrolds Road.

'I'm guessing by the direction of the brief shadows on the cars here' – I pointed at the photo on my left showing a police officer in his tunic and tall, custodian helmet – 'that *this* one was taken earlier in the day, before noon. So there was a crime scene at Shorrolds Road at some point on Tuesday morning?'

'There was.' Caroline nodded. 'And in this *other* photo we have a different police officer in a short-sleeved shirt standing guard outside 37 Shorrolds Road.' Caroline pointed at the second photo, which was on my right.

'Okay. So the shadows here would indicate to me this second photo has been taken later in the day, perhaps mid-afternoon. Both pictures are confirmation they forensicated Shorrolds Road on Tuesday, hence the police officers controlling entry to the scene through the front door...' I mused.

'Yes,' Caroline agreed.

'How did they get into that address on Tuesday morning?' I

asked, picking up one of the photos and looking closely at the open door.

She frowned at me. 'What do you mean?'

'How did the police get the front door open – did they break in?'

Caroline nodded. 'I suppose they must have done. Suzy had the key to do the viewing…'

'Which is why Mark Gurdon only knocked at the door of 37 Shorrolds Road on the Monday night looking for Suzy and didn't go in?'

Caroline nodded again.

'So who broke into the house then?' I asked.

'I can't find any record of it.'

'Do we know how many locks were on that front door?' I asked, wondering how much noise and damage it had taken to get in.

'How would we know that?'

'Have we got any other photos of it? Or maybe we have a description of the keys Suzy had with her to do the viewing – that would indicate the number of locks perhaps?'

'There were some photos and video taken of the door a week later, during the police's one-week anniversary reconstruction… hang on.' Caroline grabbed her binders full of different pieces of paper, photos and newspaper cuttings, all filed away in protective plastic sleeves.

She pulled out a black-and-white photo of the two police officers who'd played 'Mr Kipper' and Suzy. They were standing outside the closed front door of 37 Shorrolds Road. 'That was taken on Monday, 4 August 1986,' she said, passing the photograph to me.

'The lost key is described by the police several times in their 1986 appeals for the public's help. Let me just pull that information up…' Caroline grabbed her laptop.

I examined the photo she'd given me as she searched the database she'd compiled.

'The key for 37 Shorrolds Road is described as… "a single Yale key on a large, yellow plastic fob".' Caroline looked up.

'Identical to the one which the blonde police officer standing by that undamaged front door has in her hand then?' I pointed to the key and Sturgis key fob dangling from the Suzy lookalike's hand in the photo.

'Like that one, yes,' she agreed.

'*Like* that one? Or *exactly* that one?'

'I don't know what you mean?'

'That front door isn't damaged, six days after the police have forensicated the inside of the address. They didn't break in through the door.'

'What about the back?'

'That involves scaling high walls, clambering over fences and cutting through undergrowth. We never do it.'

'Maybe that's a spare key she has there?' she said, pointing at the key in the Suzy lookalike's hand in the photo.

'Why would the estate agent need more than one set?'

'That photo was taken at a police reconstruction seven days later though…'

'We know the police had that key to 37 Shorrolds Road on Tuesday morning when the place was forensicated. The police didn't break in; there's no damage to the door – so where did the police get that key from by Tuesday morning?'

'I see your point.'

'And we know Mark Gurdon *didn't* have a spare key. He *didn't* go inside to look for Suzy because he *says* he assumed Suzy had the key. Mick Jones from Fulham CID *doesn't* go to 37 Shorrolds Road that night because he assumed that Mark Gurdon had looked inside. Which we know he didn't. Nobody goes inside the house for sale.'

'But by Tuesday morning the police somehow have a key?' Caroline asked rhetorically.

'By Tuesday morning, within hours, the police are using a key to get in and out of 37 Shorrolds Road, so that fingerprinting can be done on that house, yes,' I agreed.

'Someone at the estate agent's found the key in the branch and gave it to the police?'

'That would be my guess…'

'But that would mean Suzy didn't take the key with her to do the viewing?'

I smiled. 'It would. Why would you go and do a house viewing without the key?'

'How could you do a house viewing without the key?'

I shook my head. 'You couldn't…'

'That's absolutely unbelievable if that's right,' Caroline concluded, her eyes wide in astonishment.

We needed to find the evidence to back up our theory, and that wasn't going to be easy, not more than thirty years on. But if we were right, it meant Suzy *hadn't* done the house viewing which the police always claimed had led to her disappearance.

25

'Dad was a bit over it all at the end. The Lamplugh case exhausted him, mentally and physically. The sleepless nights got to him, you know?' Andy Carter mused over his cup of coffee. 'There's a picture of Dad in the major incident room taken by a newspaper. He'd aged. He looks shattered.'

After what former CID officer Mick Jones had told me, Caroline and I had decided that we needed a greater understanding of the decision-making within the police investigation. Many of the early decisions would have been those of Det. Supt Nick Carter, the original senior investigating officer on Suzy's case. But as Mick Jones had said, Carter had sadly passed away, aged seventy, in the rural retirement idyll of the West Country.

Back in July 1986, Carter had been married with a young family. His youngest, Andy, who we'd driven deep into the countryside to meet, was now in his forties. Dressed in jeans with the dark hair and young looks of his dad, he reminded me of a cattle rancher. He explained what sort of man his father had been as we drank coffee at a round, wooden picnic table outside a busy farm shop.

Carter had worked upward of fourteen-hour days over the months that he'd frantically led the investigation, desperately hoping for a break that would locate Suzy. Yet, it was to be the last ever case of his thirty-year policing career. He would retire from the Met at the end of 1986, just five months after taking the role in the Lamplugh investigation, before his team had barely made any headway at all.

The problem was the senior investigating officer in the Lamplugh case hadn't put himself forward for the role, nor did it appear he'd been singled out by some special selection panel specifically for this investigation. Our research suggested that when Suzy went missing, Carter just happened to be the senior officer on standby.

I wanted to understand what made Nick Carter tick. It would help me grasp why he'd made some of the decisions he had during his stewardship of the Lamplugh investigation. Understanding those decisions might help me unpick anything else that might have gone wrong or been overlooked and shine a light on something that would help us find Suzy.

Andy explained how a school trip to London had motivated his father to join the police: 'At fifteen or sixteen, Dad went from Chippenham on a visit to the Big Smoke. He was quite naïve then. Him and his best friend got ripped off by somebody; they took all his money. He decided that was it, he was going to sort those bastards out! He ended up joining the Met and his best friend joined the military police.'

From a fresh-faced constable in the mid-1950s, Nick Carter worked his way up through the ranks, eventually heading murder teams as a senior investigating officer. By the time Suzy went missing, he was forty-eight years of age, a veteran of fighting gangland London and due to retire from the force in just five short months.

In anticipation of his retirement, his wife and their two children, Andy and Sally, had already relocated to the West Country, where their father, Nick, had grown up. Carter was left behind in London, living alone in a tiny West London bedsit, crossing the days off the calendar until he could join them to enjoy his countryside retirement.

Andy explained that the lead-up to his father's retirement and beyond had not been happy ones; they'd been dogged by personal tragedy. 'Back in the early eighties, my mum's parents both died in quick succession. My grandad had suffered with a terrible brain tumour and died at home in July 1983. Then, in the December of the same year, my grandmother went missing whilst trekking in the Himalayas. She'd had a difficult life, brought up in quite a tough environment, and she was very close to her husband. Looking back on it, I think maybe once she'd lost her soulmate, that was it...'

'What happened?' I asked, as Andy tailed off.

'She was with a group of people hiking in Nepal. One night the group said they were going one way, and she just said that she was going to go another way, on her own, for whatever reason... So off she went. We don't know whether it was a deliberate decision or not...' Andy shook his head. 'She could have slipped and fallen – you just don't know. They never found her. The older I get, I think it's possible she may have committed suicide, but there's no evidence for that. They never found her body. She just disappeared. Gone.

'My dad went out there with my mum's brother,' he continued, 'did a bit of investigating to see if there were any clues about what had happened, but nothing was ever found.'

But there was more. In addition to the tragic disappearances of both Suzy and his mother-in-law, Det. Supt Nick Carter's life had been affected by a third unsolved missing person case that he also worked on.

Back in 1979, Martin Allen, a fifteen-year-old schoolboy, had vanished as he travelled home from school. Police hadn't been informed of the schoolboy's disappearance for over twenty-four hours; family members had assumed he'd gone to a Guy Fawkes party on the evening of 5 November. Much like the Lamplugh case, the investigation, when it finally began, hit a brick wall very early on. The police never uncovered what happened nor brought anyone to justice. And just like Suzy and Carter's mother-in-law, the body of Martin Allen was also never found.

Being put in charge of the Suzy Lamplugh case, months before retirement, must have been somewhat of a poisoned chalice for a man with the ghost of Martin Allen on his conscience and that of his missing mother-in-law in the Himalayas.

'Did you or your sister never show any signs of wanting to join the police?' Caroline asked, wondering if perhaps other members of the Carter family had carried the police torch onward, as was often the case.

Andy began to look very upset, his eyes filling with tears. 'My sister's dead.'

'I'm so sorry,' Caroline apologised. 'When did that happen?'

I felt awful. How had we not picked this up prior to our meeting?

'In 1990. I can remember it clearly, like it was yesterday...' Andy's eyes filled with tears and I could see he was struggling to keep them from flowing down his cheeks. 'It was a bad day. We were at a friend's house. A mate down the road had a swimming pool, so we were round there having a swim. She was just a teenager. Always had asthma and had an asthma attack. We called 999 and the ambulance didn't... couldn't get there in time.'

The years leading up to Carter's retirement and beyond had been dogged by personal tragedy, death and a lack of opportunity to find the truth.

I changed the subject. 'When your dad retired, what did he do to keep busy down here?'

'Well he took a few years enjoying his retirement, just doing odd jobs,' Andy sighed, 'and then he decided he still had plenty of years left in him. He was only in his early fifties. So in 1990 he joined Allied British Foods in Bristol. It was the day after he'd joined that my sister went swimming, had the asthma attack and died...

'He carried on there with the same company afterwards though. They had brands like Burton Biscuits and Twining Teas. He worked on security, investigating any criminality, from rustling loaves of bread on a Sunday morning right up to financial fraud at a senior level.'

'Was he quite bored at home, do you think?'

'Yeah, I suppose he was. He set up a business with his old neighbour making signs at first – that didn't really float his boat much, so then he joined the food company.'

The silence hung in the warm air as Andy fought to keep the tears back.

I was left with the impression that Nick Carter had been a man who felt that there was unfinished business with the police, and that Suzy weighed heavily on his shoulders. It was something that he could never let go of.

The field behind Andy was dotted with half-moon, steel-roofed, pig arks that looked like mini air-raid shelters. While Andy tried to compose himself, I took in the earthy smells and sounds and watched the large white sows and their piglets as they rolled around in the mud, flicking flies with their ears. I felt like hugging him, and perhaps I should have done, but I wasn't sure how he'd react and if it was the right thing to do.

It was the second time we'd upset someone by asking questions in this case. There were so many bad memories attached to it.

'There was a detective inspector who worked under my dad on the Lamplugh case – DI Pete Johnstone. I could have a chat with Pete,' Andy said, finally regaining his voice and wiping away the tears. 'I wouldn't say I knew him well. Haven't spoken to him for a long time. They both used to volunteer on a fundraiser – an annual missing persons walk from Scotland to London. Between about 2002 and 2006, my dad and Pete were part of the support team. I joined them a couple of times. It was quite a good laugh. Drive a bit, support the walkers, have a few beers at the very end of the day… That's how I know Pete Johnstone. Would it be worth me having a chat with him?'

'I'd love to talk to him, yes, please,' I responded.

We shook hands and agreed to speak in a few weeks, after he'd made contact with Pete. Andy left us sitting outside the farm shop, climbed into his car and drove off into the warm afternoon. I liked Andy. I felt desperately sorry for his father and disappointed that I'd never met him in life.

While we all say we leave home at home and work at work, it's never the truth. It was impossible to separate them. Home and personal life always affected our decision-making at work, and vice versa.

How much of Nick Carter's personal life was in the Suzy Lamplugh investigation?

The decision to go to the media and to call a press conference, both within hours of Suzy's disappearance, and before they'd barely interviewed a single witness, all made a little more sense to me now. All of this decision-making had been Carter's; desperate for the trail not to go cold, as it had done in both the Martin Allen schoolboy case, and in his mother-in-law's.

26

It was unseasonably warm.

London should have started to become a little cooler as the city's parks were splashed with autumnal colours, but not thus far.

Sitting in my garden in the leafy shade of a golden ash tree, it was shaping up to be a very strange year in so many ways.

As I typed up a report on my laptop, my phone rang.

'Hello, is that David?' the voice on the other end asked.

'It is,' I responded.

'You asked me to call you?'

Our investigation had become so vast, and had so many individual moving parts, names and addresses, that we had to meticulously record everything we did in daily reports. It was simply the only way we could keep track of what we'd done, who we'd spoken to, what we'd found out and where we were going next.

Often the phone would ring like this, and someone would say, 'It's so and so – you asked me to call you…'

But I was placing so many calls to people, firing off emails, or visiting addresses and leaving contact details, that it was easy to lose track of who was who, and what we'd contacted them about.

It was common sense, of course, to keep detailed records to ensure you didn't make mistakes. Laziness was the biggest enemy here. You had to fight it.

This time, however, as soon as he said his name, I knew who the caller was. I didn't need to search the files and read our notes to remember why I needed to speak with him.

I'd spent the last few weeks researching Harry Riglin and his family. As the chief and only witness immediately after Suzy's disappearance, he was an integral part of the case.

Harry had been fifty-eight years old when Suzy went missing; he was one of the oldest witnesses in the police investigation. Born in 1928, he would be ninety years of age now, if I could find him.

He had lived at 35 Shorrolds Road, the house immediately next door to the one Suzy was supposed to be showing to 'Mr Kipper' and was widely reported that week as the last person to have seen Suzy alive. He was said to have seen her standing outside with 'Mr Kipper'.

So Harry wasn't just one of the police's oldest witnesses; he was also their most important.

In the twenty-four hours following the sighting, the police would work with Harry to produce an artist's impression of the man he'd seen; an artist's impression that would take on a life of its own and everyone would associate with 'Mr Kipper' – even to this day.

After speaking to Andy Carter about the pressure his father was under in the final months of his career, the ghosts that haunted him, his desire to get a quick result on Suzy's case, we'd gone back and looked at every interview Det. Supt Nick Carter had ever done. When we went back to the original press conference Carter had held on the Tuesday afternoon in the police canteen, where he'd talked about Harry Riglin's sighting, there was something very odd about the way he'd worded it: 'We have a witness who says that he saw a fair-haired lady and this man leaving the property at about ten past one. And that is the last time she has been seen.'

While Carter had used Suzy's name repeatedly throughout the press conference to describe her, she'd been reduced merely to 'a fair-haired lady' as he introduced Harry's sighting into the police's narrative. Why did Carter *not* refer to her as 'Suzy', when in his very next sentence – 'And that is the last time she has been seen' – he implies that is exactly who he is talking about?

I needed to know exactly what Harry Riglin had told the police. Though I'd already encountered a problem.

I wasn't supremely confident Harry was actually still alive.

Harry was from a very large family which had lived in the Hammersmith area for at least four generations. In comparison to some of the other enquiries we were doing, this made the task of finding someone who knew whether Harry was alive or not easy. Research was all well and good, but the only way to really move this case on was to actually speak to people.

I'd established a phone number for one of Harry's nephews and left a message for him to call me back.

But before I'd even typed my report, with all the names of those connected to Harry, my phone was ringing. It was his nephew on the other end.

If only all our enquiries were this easy!

But my feelings of triumph were quickly dashed.

'I am his nephew, yes – and he did live at that address,' he said, 'but I'm afraid my uncle Harry died in 2005.'

This was sad news.

Harry had worked previously in the insurance industry in the City of London but had taken early retirement to look after his mother who was in failing health.

His nephew described him as a kind, caring man who was very well thought of by the entire family; a man who was very conscientious, and 'really switched on', and someone he'd always looked up to and admired.

Lena, Harry's mother, was agoraphobic and suffered severely from travel sickness; she scarcely left the house. She had died in December 1984, but Harry had left his job to care for her in her nineties as her health failed. He had never lived away from his parents. Apparently Harry was also gay, but he kept this very private.

'I don't suppose your uncle Harry ever talked about what he'd seen that day to anyone – about what he'd told the police?' I asked.

'I was very close to my uncle,' he responded. He went on to explain how it all held particular personal interest for him, as he'd actually grown up living at 37 Shorrolds Road. It had been his own family home from 1958 to 1969, so he knew the house well, as did Harry, who'd been inside it hundreds of times.

'Uncle Harry owned a nice car; he parked it in the street outside,' he continued. 'Parking was always a nightmare in Shorrolds Road. So he used to keep an eye on the car...'

I listened and made notes.

'That day, Harry had heard a bang. He assumed it was a car door banging. He looked outside and saw a man and a woman on the pavement. He could describe the man quite well. But he couldn't describe the woman at all.'

'What?' I exclaimed. 'He never – he never – he...' I stuttered, trying to comprehend what he'd just said.

He never identified the woman as Suzy to the police?' I asked, regaining my composure. 'Is that what you're saying?'

'He never said he saw her, no; he just told them he saw a woman there with a man. That's all,' he responded.

This was beyond incredible.

If there was no positive identification that the woman was Suzy, how could the police claim it was her? How could they claim 'the man', whose artist impression they'd circulated, was 'Mr Kipper'?

But it was just what we'd suspected. Det. Supt Nick Carter had given the game away at that first press conference. There was talk of a blonde woman but zero confirmation it was Suzy. Everything the police had claimed had happened that day was a story; a narrative; their best guess.

We had already exposed serious uncertainty about the house key for 37 Shorrolds Road. We couldn't yet prove it, but we had grave doubts about Suzy having ever had the key. On top of this, despite all the police insinuation, Harry had *not* identified Suzy nor seen anyone hanging around suspiciously in wait for her, as the televised police reconstruction had alluded to.

I thanked Harry's nephew for his call and said I'd be in touch.

I needed to speak to Caroline. She wasn't going to believe this.

27

I wasn't sure if I could hear it – or feel it.

But it wanted me to wake up.

The room was a pale grey. The early morning light was trying its best to fight its way round the edges of the curtains.

My phone was vibrating again. It was in the bed with me, somewhere. I could feel it buzzing against the mattress or the bedclothes. Maybe I'd let the answerphone get it?

It stopped. Almost immediately it began buzzing again. This time I made an unsuccessful scramble around for it, bleary-eyed, in the half darkness of my bedroom.

Someone had something urgent to tell me.

I got up, pulled the duvet off the bed and shook it in the hunt for the elusive handset. It thudded onto the floor at my feet before going to answerphone again. Picking it up, I could see that there were three missed calls, all from Caroline. Before I'd even had a chance to hit the button to call her back, she was calling for a fourth time.

I accepted the call, putting the handset against my ear. 'Hey, what's—'

'They're digging up the garden!' Caroline shouted down the phone at me before I could finish the sentence.

'What?' My head was still hazy from the sleep I'd been torn from. I still couldn't grasp what she was talking about.

'They're digging up Cannan's mum's old garden to look for Suzy Lamplugh,' Caroline repeated again.

'Who is?'

'The police!'

'How? *Why?*'

'Turn the TV news on – call me back.' Caroline hung up.

I'm never very good when I first wake up, especially not when I've been ripped from a deep sleep like that. Today was the first and only day off I would have in a stretch of two weeks in my security work.

I pulled on a pair of tracksuit bottoms and made my way downstairs. Groggily, I turned on the television, and hunted for the news.

'… the current owner says he purchased the home in Sutton Coldfield, in 1992, from John Cannan's mother…' a reporter explained, as an aerial shot of a garden filled the screen.

The news footage cut to an officer in a full white bodysuit in the middle of a housing estate in the West Midlands. He was pushing a wheelbarrow of rubble down a narrow alleyway toward a yellow skip.

'It's not the first time police have been at this particular family property,' the reporter continued. 'It's believed that officers first visited the premises in 1989, as part of their investigation into John Cannan, and again seventeen years ago, declining to do anything on both occasions. Yesterday, all of that dramatically changed when police returned to dig parts of the premises up. Police are investigating the theory that Cannan drove Miss Lamplugh 125 miles from Fulham to Sutton Coldfield, before dumping her body in his mother's garage, using an inspection pit which he filled with concrete.'

I called Caroline back. 'I can't believe it,' I said as she picked up the phone.

'Have you heard from the police? Did the bloke from the Murder Review Group call back?' Caroline asked.

'I feel as if I'm still asleep, dreaming,' I joked.

The police had not looked at Suzy's case in more than eight years.

'Have you heard from the Murder Review Group bloke?' Caroline repeated her question.

'I would have told you if I had, wouldn't I? Or you'd have read it in the updated progress report that I only just finished!'

'I was just checking.' She didn't sound convinced.

'I've not spoken to him since June, since his retirement drinks do at the pub. He said he'd call me, but he hasn't. I suppose I could have chased him up, but we were making good progress – I just wanted to crack on before we went back to the police.'

'What are we going to do?' Caroline asked anxiously.

The semi-detached house in Shipton Road, Sutton Coldfield, where the police were digging had been owned by John Cannan's parents, Sheila and Cyril, since the early 1980s. But it was never truly John's home.

Cannan had married in 1978; he'd lived with his wife and child before embarking on a series of other relationships over the next three years. These other relationships would last almost until he was imprisoned in 1981 for robbery and rape.

Cannan would then spend the next five years behind bars. This was all before his parents had even owned the house in Shipton Road. The fractious relationship he had with his father, Cyril, would ensure that they could no longer readily share a house.

While Cyril would die before Cannan's release from prison, the fifteen months between his release in July 1986 and his reincarceration in October 1987 were spent being monitored by the probation service.

A flurry of media coverage had pressured police into temporarily considering the house as a deposition site back in 2002, before it had eventually been discounted.

'There's nothing we can do,' I responded. 'We've just got to let them get on with it.'

'Do you think Suzy's really there?' Caroline enquired.

'Do I think John Cannan gets released from prison, within days he kills Suzy for some unknown reason, then drives her remains more than 100 miles north to a house he barely knows, to hide it in the garden for his mother to potentially find?'

'It is a little far-fetched,' she agreed.

'A lot of the finger pointing is because Cannan looks like that artist's impression, the one of the man Harry Riglin described to the police. And now we have grave doubts that Suzy was ever even at that address in Shorrolds Road. So, if Suzy never went there, any description of a random man seen in the street has no relevance whatsoever.'

'Yeah, I know. But why now? Why go all the way to the West Midlands and dig Cannan's mum's old house up now? Is it connected to Paul Lamplugh's death? Maybe they know something we don't?'

'They've known about this house for over thirty years.' I was starting to feel angry. 'I told you this is what would happen. This is why I asked my contacts not to tell anyone which case we were working on. It ruffles feathers...'

'Are you going to ring the police?'

'And say what to them exactly?' My voice was probably louder than it should have been. I was angry, but not at Caroline; I didn't mean to sound angry at her. This all seemed so ridiculous. Frustrating.

Caroline pressed again. 'To do this now – it makes no sense. I thought maybe you might be able to find out why now?'

'They've had a meeting. Someone has asked if there's anything outstanding on the file, anything that could embarrass the organisation. They've realised that the previous teams decided against digging a garden in the West Midlands. And someone's suggested, "Maybe we should have a go at that?" And they've gone and done exactly that.'

'Just like that?'

'Just like that, yes. They're the police,' I snapped.

'Maybe you should go back to bed?'

'Not now – I can't. Not after this. I'll call you later, shall I?' I tried to calm myself down.

'Yeah, you can try,' she said, before hanging up.

She could hear the frustration and anger in my voice.

I shouldn't have been surprised. I knew exactly what the Met as an organisation was like. This was them flexing their muscles, exerting their authority over the investigation. Telling the world, and our tiny, little, insignificant investigation, exactly how it was going to be.

120

28

'Specialist forensic teams are in their second week of a search at a garden in Shipton Road, Sutton Coldfield, West Midlands. Police said they will remain at the site until the search is complete. The semi-detached house was once owned by Sheila Cannan, the mother of convicted killer, John Cannan. He was named by police as the prime suspect in Suzy Lamplugh's disappearance in 2002 but has always denied any involvement in the case…'

Caroline and I were in the car, travelling out of London for another meeting. There hadn't been much conversation between us since I'd picked her up at the station. She seemed vexed with me, almost as if she blamed me for the police conducting the searches in Sutton Coldfield.

The police search for Suzy's body had dominated news bulletins for the past week. It was a huge story. There was no escaping it, not even in the car.

'At the end of last week, John Cannan expressed hopes that the search of his mother's former home will conclude swiftly… His solicitor provided the following statement: "Mr Cannan hopes this will end speculation as to his involvement in the 1986 disappearance of estate agent Suzy Lamplugh. He has no idea why the search has come now, with the development coming 'out of the blue'." '

Caroline reached forward from the passenger seat and turned off the radio.

'I can't listen to it anymore,' she said, sighing.

'Let's just focus on what we're doing. Focus on today,' I said, trying to console her.

'We've wasted years on this project. We should have stuck to writing the crime-fiction books and just left this investigation to the police,' she lamented.

'Don't let it get you down. Let's see what today brings, shall we?'

Caroline didn't reply as I followed the satnav directions off the motorway and onto a stretch of single carriageway, passing open fields and rolling countryside.

At short notice, Mark Gurdon, Suzy's former boss, had agreed to another meeting with us. I wanted to move forward with our investigation, even if Caroline had been disheartened by the recent surge in police activity on the case. I was sure we were on to something important, something the police had missed, and we needed to get to the crux of it.

As I pulled into the car park at Mark's chosen meeting point, there was one thing I could say about Mark Gurdon with certainty: he had a knack for knowing a good pub.

On a cold Monday afternoon such as this, many pub car parks would be filled with builders' vans and motorway maintenance trucks. But not this one. High-value sports cars, Ferraris and Aston Martins gleamed – straight from a garage where the weekend's rain hadn't touched them. Rather than a clientele in filthy jeans and hard hats, drivers in posh silk scarves and cravats headed for a gourmet lunch.

What I couldn't say with certainty about Mark Gurdon was why we kept finding anomalies in his story about the day Suzy had gone missing.

Since we'd last spoken, I'd managed to track down David Craddock, the sales negotiator who'd been away on holiday when Suzy disappeared. He told me that the police had asked him virtually nothing when he'd returned to work; his sense was that the police felt there wasn't anything useful he could offer the investigation. But I'd found it particularly enlightening to talk to him, because, during our discussions about life in the office and Suzy's work ethic, something very significant was said.

Sturgis estate agency had a strict office staffing policy.

None of the people we'd spoken with until that point had mentioned an office staffing policy. The policy stipulated by head office, Craddock said, was that there had to be a 'fee earner' in the office at all times. In the case of the Fulham branch, this meant one of the three negotiators or Mark Gurdon. But with David on holiday at the time, and Mark at lunch the day Suzy went missing, this meant Suzy or Nigel would've had to remain in the office.

When coupled with the idea that Suzy hadn't taken the key with her to do the viewing at Shorrolds Road, and that she was never seen by Harry Riglin at that address, it seemed to give Nigel's argument with Suzy that day, and his 'subplot' relationship with Stephanie, a whole new meaning.

I was hoping Mark could help us shed further light on it.

Whilst scouring the lunchtime menu in a cosy corner by the fireplace, we began by discussing the dig the police were currently undertaking.

'Do you think it's possible that the "Mr Kipper" appointment was completely fictitious, made up just so Suzy could leave the office that day?' I asked, after we'd finished chatting about the recent events in Sutton Coldfield.

'There was nothing that people couldn't do,' Mark replied, 'I didn't sort of say, "You're out at twelve and you're back at one for lunch. Where have you been?" It wasn't like that at all. If she'd have wanted to have a two-hour lunch, or she wanted to go shopping, or she wanted to meet someone, I like to think she would have just asked me.'

'I know, you did say that last time,' I responded.

'And I'd have said, "Yeah, fine, no problem." She didn't need to lie to conceal her whereabouts.'

'You know she'd fallen out with Nigel that morning about the house sale? We discussed last time that there'd been a fallout that morning as a result of it...'

'That's right – there'd been two offers on. Yeah,' Mark agreed, nodding.

'David Craddock was on holiday. You were out to lunch that day. That would have meant that either Suzy or Nigel would have *had* to have been in the office. One of them would have *had* to have been in the office at all times?' I repeated the office staffing policy to Mark, as David had explained to me.

Mark attempted to bypass this office protocol with his answer. 'Well, or Stephanie the secretary or James the office junior. Somebody had to be there.'

'You wouldn't have had to have a negotiator in the office – a "fee earner"?' I asked again.

'No, not around lunchtime, not if everyone was working—' Mark stopped himself and began to think about his answer again.

'I don't know,' he continued. 'Normally, normally there would be, yes, because there was enough cover, but there wouldn't necessarily have to be, no. *If* people had appointments, Stephanie would be the one who would man the fort. I know you've spoken to her, haven't you?'

'I have,' I responded, nodding in agreement. What he'd just said was important: 'if people had appointments'.

'Steph, more often than not, was the one told to "take your lunch later" or "go and buy a sandwich later" because, as a secretary, you didn't often leave the office,' he continued. 'Suzy would always have taken precedence over Steph or James. It was 1986, we were selling properties every day, so it was just a lot of fluidity and movement. So she could have said anything really and—'

But of course, that day, Stephanie had left the office before Suzy, and it was possible Nigel had joined his girlfriend for the duration too.

'What I'm thinking, Mark,' I cut him off; I needed to nail this point with him.

There was an undeniable office staffing policy – David Craddock had been crystal clear what it was, and what it meant for Nigel or Suzy that afternoon she went missing. Why Mark didn't want to talk about it or agree that there was a policy at all was very much the issue here.

'David Craddock's on holiday; you're out for lunch; Stephanie's already at lunch…' I leaned forward onto the table as I spoke. 'If Nigel was about to go out too, perhaps with

Stephanie… it's almost the perfect storm for a false entry in the diary if Suzy needed to go somewhere as well, isn't it?'

Mark stayed silent.

'Suzy could only go out, as you've just said, *if* she had an appointment. If the "Mr Kipper" entry in her diary wasn't there, she'd have to be *in* the office. Maybe she had something she needed to do?'

'Possibly. Possibly…' Mark nodded and fidgeted with his menu, palpably uncomfortable.

I looked across at Caroline. Her eyes lit up. We were on to something. Both of us could see it.

The desk diary entry was the centrepiece of the police investigation; the centrepiece of their entire narrative about what had happened to Suzy that day; the foundation upon which everything they claimed had happened was based. Without it, their entire 'house showing' narrative collapsed.

On the afternoon Suzy had gone missing, in the leafy and affluent suburb of East Sheen, Diana Lamplugh recalled the phone ringing at about four o'clock.

It was Suzy's boss, Mark Gurdon, and according to Diana, he'd asked something like this: 'Do you have any idea where your daughter might be, Mrs Lamplugh? We wondered whether she could have called into home for lunch?'

Although Suzy's parents lived little more than a three-mile journey south-west from the Fulham branch of the estate agency, the heavy and unpredictable traffic along Richmond Road and the surrounding area meant that it would have been foolish for Suzy to even think about attempting to shoehorn in a lunchtime visit to her parents.

There had been no mention of a house viewing to Suzy's mother, not in those initial phone calls. I'd noticed this the last time we'd spoken to Mark Gurdon. His initial thoughts were that Suzy was 'out at lunch', not that she was out working and showing houses.

'That was your original thought though, wasn't it?' I pushed him for an answer. 'That she had somewhere to go, something to do, not a house viewing?'

There was a brief period of silence.

'I thought she'd gone off to—' Mark paused and looked up from his menu. 'I thought she'd gone off to have her lunch and then go shopping, in Putney or something, where she lived, yeah…'

I wanted to scream but somehow held it in. We were close to a full admission about the diary entry here.

'This is why it was odd, that she had to sort of say that,' Mark continued, referring to the entry in Suzy's diary. 'It's why we phoned her friends first of all, and then we phoned hospitals, and the last person we phoned was her mother.'

Mark knew the diary entry was false?

29

'Which brings me on to the key you held for 37 Shorrolds Road, Mark.' I moved forward, hoping that he'd finally get it all off his chest now we'd got this far.

Mark frowned at me and didn't answer.

'I'd like your brutal honesty here, Mark – I don't think Suzy ever had the key to Shorrolds Road. Have you ever had the feeling she didn't have the key?'

There was a long pause.

'Never even occurred to me,' Mark finally responded.

Was that the truth? I didn't know. I waited in silence and looked at him, trying to make up my mind.

'But Suzy must have had the keys to Shorrolds Road with her… Were they not found?' Mark asked, filling the silence I'd left.

'That's the next question we're going to come on to,' I said as our drinks arrived.

'You've got my brain ticking…' Mark picked up his glass of white wine and took a big gulp.

I sipped the lager shandy I'd ordered, allowing its arrival to provide a further period of silence in our meeting. People hated silence. They felt it needed to be filled with words; even good friends found it hard to sit quietly and just look at each other. I'd always found it very useful in interviews.

'We never checked, you know, to my knowledge… We never checked that she had the keys.' Mark shrugged, directing his gaze away from mine as he placed his drink down in front of him.

'You didn't check to see if she had the key to do the viewing?' I asked, incredulous.

'She had it in her diary, Shorrolds Road, so she would have had to have had the keys to do the house viewing?'

This didn't tally with his earlier response that he thought Suzy was going shopping in Putney. It was the finger-pointing tone of my voice that had made him retreat from his earlier answers. Even I could hear it.

I had to get him back onside. We were taking two steps forward and one step backward.

It was annoying.

'Someone had a key to go in and out of the front door the next day, Mark – the police must have had a key – someone at the estate agent's had to have given that key to the police?' I pushed again, this time a little more softly.

We'd examined the front door of 37 Shorrolds Road. The door on the house was still the same one that had been there in 1986, in the original photos. The Met have only ever had one method of breaking open locked front doors: brute force. In the 1990s, a specially designed battering ram was introduced, but before that, the police used sledgehammers to attack locked or jammed doors. Both styles of battering ram leave scars on wooden doors which can never be covered up – but there were no such telltale marks on the door at 37 Shorrolds Road. We'd contacted various people, including photographers who'd seen and recorded the state of the front door on 29 July, when the police were at the premises, and no one had seen any damage.

'Hmm.' Mark appeared deep in thought.

I had to remember that everyone appeared to have missed this, not just Mark, and I didn't want it to sound as if I was blaming him personally for the error. I wasn't. But he'd already indicated that he felt Suzy was off shopping in Putney and not doing the house viewing that day. It was a logical conclusion that she wouldn't have the key, wasn't it?

'You don't remember changing the locks? Anything like that?' I decided to try another route to where we needed to go – less direct, less accusatory.

Mark shook his head. 'Definitely not.'

'The police didn't ask you to change the locks on the house so they could get in?'

'No. Not that I remember at all. No.'

'The police didn't have the locks changed and then give you a new set of keys?

'Don't remember that happening, no,' He half smiled.

'No. This is what I mean. Can you see what I'm saying?'

'Yeah, I can.'

'I think it's a simple mistake. There was a lot of confusion on the day. But, somehow, the key that Suzy was supposed to have with her to do the viewing has been handed over to the police, and the police haven't realised that it was the original key.'

'The police must have had the key, yeah,' Mark concluded with a sigh and nodded.

I picked up my drink again and began to swig it slowly. I needed to stop asking Mark questions, wanting this all to settle in, to give him a moment.

But Caroline, who'd been quiet the entire meeting, suddenly smelled blood and decided to go in for the kill.

'How or where did the police get the keys from?' she asked, sounding rather angry at him.

There was a pause.

'In Suzy's car? I don't know.' Mark shrugged and held his hands up, looking more than a little defeated, and sounding harassed.

'There were no keys found in her car,' Caroline said abruptly. I could see she was beginning to fray at the edges. The searches at Sutton Coldfield had caused a lot of friction between us. I still wasn't sure why, but she was very stressed. She was angry.

It had taken us months to arrive at this point, meeting people and carefully interviewing them. We couldn't have Mark scared off and scolded like this now.

I touched her arm, wanting her to give Mark some space and stop her playing the full-on bad-cop role.

She backed off.

'I don't know where the keys were,' Mark finally said. 'If you're certain the keys weren't found in her car, that's the... that's the only place they would be... She must have just gone out—'

He stopped himself. But he didn't need to finish his sentence. It was plain for all to see.

Did Mark have suspicions that the Shorrolds Road entry in Suzy's diary could be false? Was he also indicating that she probably didn't have the key to do the viewing, as we'd suspected? On top of this, we now seemed to have a reason for the false entry in her diary.

We weren't there yet. But it was all now much more than just an idea – Suzy *hadn't* gone to Shorrolds Road.

As our food arrived at the table, I decided we'd not press Mark any further. Not today. I didn't want to upset him too much. Although we had a reason for the false diary entry, we still didn't understand what had motivated Suzy to do it. Understanding that motive was probably crucial to the entire mystery.

While I suspected Mark was still holding a lot back, he actually did want to help. I'd collect my evidence elsewhere and keep Mark as a friend, an ally to our investigation.

'Let's just enjoy our lunch,' I announced, hoping that Caroline would know that this was directed at her.

Did he know about Suzy not having the key? I wasn't sure, but beating him up about it, harassing him and making him feel bad about it wasn't going to change anything all these years later.

The police should have established this. But they hadn't.

And it wasn't Mark's fault they hadn't. After all, he wasn't the one whose job it had been to investigate Suzy's disappearance.

30

'I told you. I don't know anyone called Noel,' said the small, hard-faced woman on the doorstep.

In contrast to her miniature stature, she seemed overly combative and quite fearsome. Her short, greying hairdo, thick with hairspray and a hint of yellow tobacco stain, didn't move – like a plastic figurine.

'What do you mean you don't know him?' I asked, unsatisfied. 'Are you sure?'

'I'm sure,' she snapped back at me, curling her lip into a smirk.

The sun was starting to set in the winter sky, and the air was beginning to take on a chill. I'd been cooped up in the car for much of the afternoon, parked on the edge of a run-down housing estate, waiting for this woman to come home. Her neighbour had told me that she was probably only at the local shops, as she never went very far.

It always surprises me how much information people are willing to share with total strangers in the street, but I'm thankful for it. And sometimes it's the most useful information of all.

Sitting under an airport flight path, with just the harsh whine of jet engines for company, I'd watched the woman's house for hours. Just as the light began to fade, and a seed of doubt had set in about the accuracy of the neighbour's information, the small woman had eventually returned in exactly the vehicle her neighbour had described – a shiny, new, white Volkswagen Polo – and parked outside the house. She'd also

131

been in the company of a man who'd helped her carry in some shopping from the car. The neighbour hadn't mentioned a man.

Up in the West Midlands, the police had completed their recent searches in Sutton Coldfield. They'd dug up the garden, excavated the old garage and completely removed the concrete floor of the kitchen, leaving a huge crater in John Cannan's mother's former home. The family who now owned the house were livid; the kitchen was unusable.

The police had found nothing. Not a single shred of evidence.

Two weeks of digging holes at a cost of several hundred thousand pounds, and the only things they had to show for it were a disgruntled, angry householder, and a pile of bills for the forensic teams.

After our second meeting with Suzy's boss, Mark Gurdon, Caroline and I believed that we were beginning to see gaping holes in the police narrative.

There had been a conscious decision to base the early part of the police investigation on the assumption that the 'Mr Kipper' diary entry in Suzy's desk diary was correct. This was despite the police's chief witness, Harry Riglin, not actually supporting this assumption at all. His evidence suggested the contrary. He had seen 'a woman' but hadn't identified her as Suzy. Regardless of this, the police had pressed ahead as if he had, producing the artist impression of the man they now called 'Mr Kipper' and telling reporters at that first press conference that Harry was the last person to see Suzy alive.

It was a complete fabrication.

Our interviews with Mark had exposed grave doubts about the integrity of the 'Mr Kipper' diary entry. I had struggled to see why this hadn't been established in 1986 by the police. But in those early days, Det. Supt Nick Carter – haunted by his failure in the Allen case, by his mother-in-law's disappearance, and short on time – had ignored any doubts that he might have had about the veracity of Suzy's diary entry. He'd decided that Harry Riglin's inability to make a positive identification of Suzy was possibly due to other reasons and something that could be managed. There would be other witnesses that would come forward, surely? The police just needed to find these other witnesses.

The drive to find these people culminated with a televised reconstruction on the seven-day anniversary of Suzy's disappearance. Again, the police's story – their narrative about what they believed happened to Suzy when she walked out of the Sturgis office that day – was presented as fact. But what the police were actually doing was simply asking members of the public to come forward and confirm their assumed narrative was the correct one.

The public stayed silent. No one called in and confirmed this. In the days that followed the televised reconstruction, there were a series of panicked appeals from the police in the press saying exactly this.

But that all changed at some point around 20 August 1986, almost a full two weeks after the reconstruction and three weeks after Suzy's disappearance. That day, the police triumphantly claimed they'd found two witnesses who were positive they'd seen Suzy in Shorrolds Road, in exactly the circumstances that her work desk diary would suggest.

There was Nicholas Doyle, who claimed to have seen a woman and a man near to 37 Shorrolds Road. But he couldn't confirm the time, only that it was sometime between noon and 4 p.m. And Doyle didn't agree with the artist impression created by Harry Riglin; this wasn't the man he'd seen, he said. The woman was with a different man altogether. It was hardly dynamite.

The other new lead came from a man called Noel Devere, said to be an unemployed bar and cellarman at the time, and his account seemed to stand out in a rather odd way. It was literally everything the police claimed had happened to Suzy in their suggested story, repeated verbatim.

Noel would claim that he'd been walking along Shorrolds Road at 12.50 p.m., on the afternoon of Monday, 28 July, when he'd seen a woman. She was standing beneath a Sturgis 'For

Sale' sign in the gateway of 37 Shorrolds Road. He'd remembered the house, he said, because it was one he particularly liked. He described the woman as clutching a set of keys in her right hand on a large yellow tag and looking out toward the street. Although he hadn't taken much notice of the woman or her appearance at the time, following weeks of non-stop media coverage about the case, he had now come to believe this woman might be Suzy.

But even Diana Lamplugh, by December 1986, would come to dispute the eye-witness testimony, saying: 'Of course there have been tons of people who were sure they had seen her. But I think that was just because they wanted to.'

Where had the police found these witnesses, and why, given the excessive detail in their statements, had it taken these people so long to come forward with their information? I was keen to speak with both of them to understand more, particularly in view of our new information, which suggested Suzy's desk diary entry was false.

But hunting for Nicholas Doyle and Noel Devere was like hunting for ghosts. They proved to be the most elusive characters we'd tried to track down so far. Noel, in particular, was like looking into a black hole. He had virtually no data footprint at all. I eventually settled on the idea that Noel Devere wasn't his real name. It couldn't be. It was an alias.

Whilst using an alias isn't illegal, because you can call yourself any name you desire, it did make finding him problematic. It also introduced a whiff of suspicion about why both of these men were so difficult to find. Why wasn't Devere even using his real name?

After much searching, I eventually found a single trace of someone who had called themselves Noel Devere, previously living with the helmet-haired woman. And so here I was.

'So you don't know Noel Devere?' I asked again.

'No, I told you,' she said sternly.

I pulled out a printout of the electoral register from my coat and pointed to her name on the record. 'That is you there, living at that address?' I asked.

She leaned forward and looked at where my finger was pointing before snatching the piece of paper out of my hand and examining it more closely.

'That's me, yes,' she responded with a nod, every strand of hair remaining as tightly in place as her puckered face.

'Well, as you can see here' – I pointed to a section lower down the page she was now holding – 'it shows you were living with Noel Devere.'

'But I don't know *anyone* called Noel!'

'Look, this man is not in any trouble,' I tried to reason with her. Perhaps I looked intimidating in the fading light, standing at her door asking strange questions. 'I'm not a police officer, I'm not a debt collector, or anything to do with the benefit agency. Nothing like that. I'm a writer. I just need to speak with him. He's a witness in a case I'm investigating. An important case. Perhaps he used a different first name. Do you know anyone called Devere?'

'I don't,' she responded curtly.

In all my decades as a police officer, and in all the subsequent years I've been tracing people for various assignments, I've never found cohabitees listed on the electoral register that didn't know each other. Not once.

I wanted to call her a liar, but I didn't. It served no purpose.

Local councils are responsible for compiling the electoral register in their area. They send out a single form to 'The occupier' of each household, and the occupier, normally the council-tax payer, would reply on behalf of everyone living there. As this woman was the occupier, she would have been responsible for filling out the form and returning it on behalf of everyone living at her home. As the responsible householder she must have declared the name Noel Devere when she filled out the form.

I tried a different tack. 'You don't know anyone called Devere or Noel and you've never lived with anyone who goes by that name?'

'No.' She shook her head again. Her hair stayed mesmerisingly in place, as if superglued.

'Who's the man I saw go into your house a moment ago carrying the shopping from your car?'

The woman frowned at me, narrowed her eyes into a dour stare and exhaled. She now realised that I'd been watching her.

'I don't know any Noel Devere, and there is *no* man in here,' she huffed back.

It seemed increasingly unlikely I was going to get anywhere with her. I'd probably be here until the sun rose the next morning, with the first airport departures of the day flying overhead.

'Noel Devere, I'd like to talk to you,' I shouted over the top of her head, into her empty hallway, and waited.

There was no response and no movement. The man inside stayed away from the front door and out of sight. What sort of person leaves someone in their sixties, on their own, at the front door, to fend off a stranger like this? I wondered.

'There's no one there!' she shouted at me, shoving the printout into my chest, stepping backward, not a hair out of place, and slamming the door in my face.

'Clearly the police won't be relying on that witness to prove their case,' I said to myself, screwing up the printout and stuffing it into my coat pocket as I walked back down the road to my car.

Noel Devere was a ghost and ghosts were strange things.

Where on earth had the police found him so long after Suzy's disappearance and why was his account of events such a perfect fit for their own made-up story?

31

'How the hell did you get this telephone number?'

Martin Sturgis's voice, bellowing down the phone at me, weighed heavily on my mind as I made my way down Buckingham Palace Road to meet him. The Sturgis family had owned the chain of estate agencies where Suzy worked. As I fought my way through the sea of commuters, I replayed our earlier telephone conversation in my head.

'Look, we spent a lot of time asking ourselves if there was something that our estate agency should or could have done to prevent it. I don't think there was anything that we could have done differently!' he'd shouted at me. I was a little nervous to be meeting him.

It had taken me quite some time to locate Martin. Given the passage of time, tracing witnesses in Suzy's case was one of the most challenging things I'd ever undertaken. I could tell Martin wasn't particularly happy about it.

Martin Sturgis's great-grandfather had worked as a builder on arrival in the UK from Ireland. His family had then been involved in building, renting and eventually selling many large residential developments in South West London. Following the Second World War, Martin's father had returned from the RAF and transformed one of the family's old sales offices into an estate agency. By the eighties, with Martin as a senior partner, the Sturgis family had a dozen or so sales outlets, plus lettings, professional services and a commercial division, and would go on to open yet more branches across Greater London before being sold to Prudential in 1988.

As Caroline and I wandered through the crowds toward our face-to-face meeting, I wondered if Martin Sturgis would be as volatile in person as he'd seemed on the phone.

We wanted to discuss the door key to 37 Shorrolds Road and check the office staffing policy. It was best to check matters of policy with the man at the top – the man responsible for actually setting it.

Our meeting place was the Grosvenor Hotel, a four-star railway hotel often assumed to be part of Victoria station itself. The magnificent, yellow-brick building exuded the glamour of 1860s holiday travel to the south coast for the well-to-do.

Behind the heavily veined marble columns, we found Martin Sturgis in the Tea Lounge. We all shook hands and exchanged greetings, the impeccably dressed Martin exuding class and manners. The ranting man I'd experienced on the phone seemed like someone else entirely. He was calm and pleasant, not at all what I had been expecting.

The waiter brought us refreshments in minuscule china cups. I wondered if the Victorians on their way to Brighton had ever asked for a mug.

Martin began by explaining what he could remember of the day Suzy went missing. He described being at Langan's Brasserie in the West End. At between 4 p.m. and 5 p.m., he'd received a call on his brick-like mobile handset from Mark Gurdon.

'Do you remember what Mark said?' I probed.

'Yes. "There's been a problem. Susanna" – as we used to call her, rather than Suzy – "hasn't come back to the office and she's been declared missing." Mark's a very level-headed guy. He told me, "There's nothing much you can do about it because everybody's trying to find her. I'm just letting you know." '

There was a quiet confidence about Martin as he spoke. He was sincere – the sort of man that you learned to trust easily. He'd been ten years older than Suzy when she'd gone missing. It was hard to believe that the beautifully spoken and well-dressed, silver-haired man sitting across the table from me was now nearly seventy; he could easily have passed for twenty years younger.

'Mark handled it quite well,' Martin continued. 'In fairness to him, he said, "I'm the Fulham manager, I'm responsible, there's nothing very much you can do about it. I will keep you informed. If I need your help, I'll ask you." That was pretty much how it worked. I couldn't change anything. What had happened had happened. But to what extent does it impact upon him? Should he have been there?'

I asked where Mark had been at the time.

Martin frowned – he didn't seem sure how to answer at first.

'He might have been with Keith Perry, who was responsible for all the branches. I don't really know. No one told me because I might get annoyed,' he said finally.

It was an odd answer. He either knew Mark was out at lunch or he didn't.

I'd never heard the name Keith Perry before. Mark had described being out with 'other managers' and we hadn't thought it important to check who he'd been with. Yet Martin described Keith as someone more senior than Mark. I made a mental note to come back to it.

'We didn't discourage managers if they wanted to have lunch and a chat. Was it Mark's responsibility to make sure he knew what Suzy was doing? I can't say. If someone goes out to do something without letting you know, then how do you stop them? I think he probably told me that he'd spoken to her mother too.'

My ears pricked up at his comment: 'If someone goes out to do something without letting you know'…

'Did you know Diana at that point?' I asked. I knew that Martin's family had lived fairly close to Diana and Paul Lamplugh during the 1960s.

'No. We used to live in East Sheen, as they did too, but we had no knowledge of them, or their family, as far as I'm aware,' he replied.

As yet, we'd failed to unearth how Suzy had originally become associated with Sturgis estate agency. There was a belief that seemed to emanate from within the Lamplugh family that she'd just wandered into the Fulham branch and talked her way into a job on the spot, but nobody we'd spoken to remembered actually giving her the role.

'Do you remember how she got the job?'

'No idea. She wouldn't have got it from me. She would have got it from Mark Gurdon or Keith Perry, the guy who oversaw the sales offices at the time. We regularly advertised jobs, but it could have been by word of mouth. I don't really know how she got the job.'

Keith's name again. This time mentioned as someone who might have recruited Suzy.

Martin's words seemed to elevate Keith Perry as someone of importance in Suzy's story. I needed to understand who he was, but I'd wait and see what else was said first.

We knew the Sturgis family had sold the business a couple of years after Suzy's disappearance. Caroline asked Martin if there had been any legal pressure from her parents – perhaps complaining that the estate agency had been at fault, or if there had been any insurance claims?

'Good question,' Martin responded. 'I think at one stage there was some talk, but it disappeared fairly quickly. Any suggestion that the family had made, that we might in some way be responsible, was very quickly pushed aside, I think by the police. Fairly quickly Diana was advised that that wouldn't go anywhere. At the end of the day, we weren't responsible. Susanna worked for us, but no one could prove that she was taken in the course of business by a client. If Susanna had her Plan B that day, she hasn't told anybody about it. And that's her responsibility, nobody else's. And I think that therein lies the problem. What could Mark have done about it, even if he'd known?'

I thought about our meeting with Mark and his suspicion that Suzy was going shopping in Putney.

'Did anyone ever put forward a different theory to you about what might have happened to Suzy? Where she might have gone? Rather than the "Mr Kipper" abduction idea?'

Martin paused before replying. 'Everybody was, and is, still totally mystified to this day. I mean, did she even go there?'

'Did she even go there?' I repeated his rhetorical question.

'I don't know, I really don't know.' Martin answered it anyway, shaking his head. 'Did she make the appointment up? Was she just going off for a fling with somebody? To an interview with a competitor? Off on a bender? Or was she on some sort of excursion to meet a boy?'

I stayed quiet and let him continue.

'I don't know. No one knows. You'd have thought, if it was unusual, her going off on her own in work time, people in the office would have spotted something. Working in close proximity to each other, they do notice these things that are abnormal. Did she give any indication that she was going off somewhere? No one seems to know.'

'It's possible...' I began to answer, thinking again about Mark's answer in the pub, but Martin was still talking.

'We had plenty of post-mortems at the time.' Martin was still in full flow. 'In the estate agency business, people are supposed to write down where they're going, but are they *really* going there? People assume that you're just doing a normal viewing. You take the keys and off you go. It's an empty property.'

'The key, yes, you should take the key with you,' I mumbled as he continued talking.

'So there wasn't a great big witch hunt afterwards, of what the hell did she think she was doing, because she wasn't there to ask of course,' Martin said wistfully.

'More tea, sir?' A waiter with a Spanish accent appeared at my side. I'd already drained my ridiculously small cup.

'Yes, please.' I nodded at our cups, but Martin smiled and politely declined.

'Can I get you some cake?' I asked Martin, pointing at a cake tier on another table. This interview was proving much more fruitful than I'd imagined. And far from Martin being the ogre I'd thought him to be on the phone, he was very pleasant and remarkably astute. If he was declining more tea, he plainly thought we were nearly done. Cake was my way of trying to bribe him into staying as long as possible.

He shook his head and screwed up his face. Maybe avoiding cake was how he'd kept his youthful looks? I made a mental note of that too – to avoid cake, if I could.

'How much did you have to do with day-to-day running of the offices? Would you have known if Suzy had a habit of sloping off work, to do things she shouldn't have been doing?' Caroline asked as the waiter returned with a stainless-steel teapot and began pouring.

'All that sort of stuff was down to individual managers at each branch, who looked after their own affairs.'

I sipped my tea as he spoke.

'Obviously we ran central accounts and mostly did administration centrally from a financial point of view, but the day-to-day running of the office and control of the staff was down to the manager, not other individuals.'

I thought again about the argument between Suzy and Nigel the day she had gone missing.

Martin carried on. 'Maybe she'd skived off once or twice before and done something? From what Mark's told me, he was totally unaware of what she was up to. But he might have put two and two together on a previous occasion and probably doesn't want to mention it now because, well, why land her in it when she's not here? And she's suffered from whatever she's done… But was it his responsibility? Well, he's dealing with grown-up people. He's not dealing with children. You're dealing with people who work in an office environment.'

Martin confirmed everything that we'd suspected. Mark's belief in the integrity of the diary entry appeared to have waned over the years, despite what he'd told us in his first interview. Today, neither he nor the managing partner of the firm seemed to stand behind the diary entry as a thing of absolute truth. Yet, back in 1986, the police had presented Suzy's desk diary to the public as indisputable fact.

'Was there an office staffing policy? Generally, to your knowledge, would there always have had to have been a sales negotiator in the office at any one time?' I asked.

'Yes! The office was never left empty,' Martin said sternly and rather loudly, as if I'd just called him up on the phone for the first time again. 'It was very unusual for a secretary to be left in the office on their own.'

'Or an office junior?' asked Caroline.

'Or an office junior, yes.'

'This is starting to make more sense to me now,' I replied.

Martin looked confused.

'You had three negotiators and Mark in the Fulham office,' I continued. 'There was an office junior, one permanent secretary and a temporary secretary. There were four fee earners: Mark, David, Nigel and Suzy. David Craddock was on holiday. Mark was out to lunch. Which left Suzy and Nigel in the office alone. Did Suzy deliberately put a false entry in her diary because she wanted to nip out and she couldn't do that without having some legitimate reason for leaving the office?'

'It's a possibility, yes,' Martin agreed.

'Because if Nigel had ducked out for lunch first, Suzy would have been confined to the office.' I was half talking to myself as some of the puzzle started to drop into place in my head. The argument that Nigel and Suzy had had that morning was important. There was no way Suzy was going to let him go out to lunch with his girlfriend, Stephanie the secretary.

'Yes.' Martin was agreeing with my chain of thought.

'And that would mean that the entry in her diary about "Mr Kipper" was completely false,' I mused.

'Possibly. You'd have thought that if she was that intelligent, she'd have used a less recognisable name?'

'But as you've already said, there was no big witch hunt afterwards of "what the hell did she think she was doing?" because she wasn't there to ask, so it's never really been talked about.'

Martin nodded. 'To what extent did anybody know that she was doing something she shouldn't have been doing? With someone that she shouldn't have been doing it with? That's what you're trying to find out?'

It was true. All I needed was some proof, something that I could hang my hat on.

'I think that if anyone knew what she was up to that day, they're not going to tell you or anybody else,' Martin continued. 'In a fairly open working environment, where people are coming and going, it's not at all unusual that someone would just write something down and dip out. Particularly if the manager wasn't there and you've only got another equally junior negotiator in the office – it's not his problem. It only becomes a problem when she doesn't come back.'

Which is exactly what happened. They could all see it. It was a pity the police hadn't.

I wondered if Martin was for hire as a trainee investigator. His thought processes seemed much more consistent with that of a criminal investigator than the managing director of an estate agency chain.

I moved on to the next area that was still gnawing at me. 'I'm looking into whether Suzy ever had the keys to Shorrolds Road.'

'Well, you would assume, if she's showing the empty property, that she'd have had the keys with her. But, if the keys weren't found, and they weren't at the property, and apparently there was no evidence that she went inside the property... then maybe she didn't bother to take the keys with her?'

'Would that have been unusual? For a negotiator to go to a property showing without the keys?'

'Without the keys? Unusual? *Yes, of course*! Doesn't make much sense. So yes, if she didn't have the keys, the whole "Mr Kipper" thing could have been a complete charade. That's the difficulty that everybody has thirty-odd years later. How do you try and work out what happened when there isn't anything to show for it? No CCTV. No nothing.'

'Has anybody ever mentioned this to you, the idea that Suzy didn't have the key to the property?' I asked.

'No,' he fired back.

I was shocked. Perhaps there were two sets of keys? I tried a different line of questioning: 'If you were holding keys for a property for sale, how many sets would you have?'

'There would be one. It would be very unusual indeed to have had two, because two sets are difficult to keep track of and sometimes keys go missing. So that's always an issue. Generally speaking, one set of keys. Normally one set would always suffice.'

'And if you did have two sets of keys, would they have been held separately or together?'

'They'd have been held together, on the same bunch. On the same key board.'

I'd asked this question in recent weeks to several former Sturgis employees. But I wanted confirmation from Martin. His answer was the same. Duplicate keys were extremely rare, and they were *never* split up. Everyone was paranoid that spare keys would go walkabout. They were always kept together on the same bunch, on the same hook, on the same key board. They were *never* detached from each other.

'The property that Suzy was supposed to be showing "Mr Kipper" around. Did you ever remember anything about the locks being changed?'

'No. The office certainly would have told me if someone had lost the key to someone's house.'

Naturally, it would have been quite a nightmare if a set of a customer's keys had gone missing and they'd had to change all the locks. Martin explained that all correspondence for this sort of thing would have passed over his desk, and the invoices over the desk of his brother, who ran accounting.

Other Sturgis employees had also agreed with this scenario. 'Mark Gurdon also said you didn't change the locks,' I replied.

'Yeah, I didn't think so. The whole thing was very mysterious. We assume she's gone to show this property and taken the keys, but if they weren't missing...'

'It appears they weren't missing. You didn't change the locks. It's very unlikely you had duplicate keys. If you did have two, they'd have been on the same bunch. They were never split up. Everyone agrees Suzy would have taken the whole lot. The door wasn't damaged. You didn't break in. The police didn't break in. You didn't pay for the locks to be changed...'

Martin nodded. 'We must have had the key?'

'Yes,' I agreed.

Suzy didn't have the key to 37 Shorrolds Road with her, I was now certain of it. What we'd found out also put a whole new slant on the integrity of her diary entry.

Martin was sitting in silence, looking a little shell-shocked. I wondered now if he'd accept a piece of that cake.

I wanted to ask him about Keith Perry.

32

The festive period was upon us, together with the betting on a white Christmas. Although the weather had been very cold for over a week, the odds were drifting, unlike the snow. The bookies were now offering 8/1 for the white stuff to appear in London.

I was taking a quick break from more research in my office at home. My ex-wife had made me some Christmas cake. Vanilla marzipan, icing, brandy, raisins, sultanas, currants, cherries, cranberries. It was all there. But five days before Christmas and I'd already nearly eaten it all.

Sitting with my tea and cake, my thoughts were never far from Suzy these days. Had she ever experienced a white Christmas in her short life?

She had to be dead, surely? She couldn't have just gone to ground, reinvented herself and started afresh, as some conspiracy theories suggested.

As we slowly unpicked the details of the day she'd gone missing and peeled back parts of her personality to reveal things she'd kept hidden from most, I wondered, tentatively, if I were slowly beginning to understand her.

I thought about how far we'd come since we started: 2019 was fast approaching and as we edged toward the precipice of a third year investigating Suzy's case, I was pleased with what we'd already established. We'd spent thousands of hours and thousands of pounds on our investigation, and we were finally making progress.

I hoped the New Year would bring more answers about what had really happened to Suzy.

The conclusion we'd drawn, especially after speaking to Martin Sturgis and establishing that Suzy hadn't even taken the key with her, was that "Mr Kipper" was as elusive as Father Christmas. Neither seemed to exist – except in our imaginations.

The police had somehow come into possession of the very house key that they'd been telling everyone in their public appeals was missing. It was both comical and incredibly tragic all at the same time, that the police could be asking for the public's help to track down something they'd had in their possession all along.

When it came to the name 'Kipper', we knew that during the original investigation, the police had gone through all the Sturgis files and the London phonebook and not a single 'Kipper' had been found. It seemed to be a wild goose chase.

The evidence we'd uncovered about the key, and the feedback we were now getting from Suzy's colleagues, indicated the 'Mr Kipper' appointment had been entirely fictitious. If this was the case, then we should be able to prove *why* Suzy had chosen the name 'Mr Kipper' in the first place.

This was our next task.

In the early eighties, Suzy had lived with her sister, Tamsin, in Walham Grove, just a stone's throw away from Shorrolds Road. During this period, Suzy became acquainted with many of the Fulham locals, some of whom became her friends. The area and road were both familiar to her professionally and personally.

I'd become particularly interested in a pair of brothers whom Suzy knew who went by the name of 'Herring'.

Herring are fish that move in large schools, often around the coastlines of the northern hemisphere. They have been consumed as staples for thousands of years. A kipper is a whole herring, split in a butterfly fashion from tail to head, gutted, salted or pickled, and cold-smoked over smouldering wood chips.

John Herring was known to the original police investigation team. His name was in one of Suzy's diaries. John, as well as his brother Peter – coincidentally a Sturgis estate agency client – were quickly eliminated from the police investigation as being of no interest.

A Herring split in two? I couldn't help wondering if the police had overlooked something else, something significant. So I'd spent several days locating and trying to contact the Herring brothers.

As I wondered about another slice of Christmas cake and a further cup of tea, my phone began to ring. It was a number I didn't recognise and turned out to be John Herring, replying to one of the messages I'd left.

He turned out to be a thoroughly affable chap.

'To be honest, I only met her a couple of times. She was a friend of a friend. I met her at a drinks party six months or a year before she disappeared,' John explained. 'At the time I was living at an address in Wardo Avenue…'

As soon he said Wardo Avenue, my mind started doing somersaults. It meant something, but I couldn't remember what. I brushed the cake crumbs off my keyboard and pushed my plate aside.

'I was nicknamed Kipper at primary school, but no one really uses it these days,' John continued as I searched through my notes and spreadsheets for Wardo Avenue, 'and no one ever called me "Mr Kipper" – just Kipper.'

'And where did you move after you'd lived in Wardo Avenue?' I asked as I toggled between spreadsheets and the thousands of photos I had, desperately trying to find the information I needed.

There was quite a long pause before John answered.

'Well, er… I moved out of the house in Wardo Avenue about six months before she went missing and then… and then into a house in Shorrolds Road.'

'Okay,' I said, the hairs on the back of my neck standing on end.

'I don't believe Suzy knew that I'd moved out of Wardo Ave to Shorrolds Road,' he added.

'But you were living in Shorrolds Road, Fulham, when Suzy went missing?' I asked.

'I was, but I don't think Suzy knew that.'

As he finished his sentence, I brought up a photo of Suzy's work desk diary. It lay open at the date of her disappearance, the page with the infamous 'Mr Kipper' entry on it. The top of the page held the address '142 Wardo' and what looked like the words 'bike contract' written after it.

'Wow,' I said accidentally.

'What?' John asked.

'Does "142 Wardo bike contract" mean anything to you?'

'No. I lived at number twenty. I was sharing a house with three other people. That's where I'd met Suzy. She came to our place in Wardo Avenue on at least one occasion.'

So there were two roads on the same page of Suzy's diary that related to the exact same day she went missing and both held some personal association with John Herring who used to be known as 'Kipper'?

'What number Shorrolds Road did you live at, John?'

'I can't remember – it was about fifty yards up from the main road on the left.'

I knew that number thirty-seven was about a hundred yards up. The two addresses were within feet of each other.

'Look, I'm really not sure Suzy necessarily knew that I was living there,' John repeated again, sounding slightly concerned. Perhaps he was worried I thought he could be the infamous 'Mr Kipper'. Our research had also shown that Suzy had attended a party at 54 Shorrolds Road at around the same time John would have moved into the street.

There was a logical connection between Wardo Avenue and Shorrolds Road and that connection was John Herring, who had on occasion been called 'Kipper'. That connection could all be made by looking at what Suzy had recorded in her work desk diary for the date she had gone missing.

I also knew from our research that 37 Shorrolds Road had only come onto the market with Sturgis in the days before Suzy had gone missing, and the house details were displayed in the window right next to Suzy's desk; she could see it from where she was sitting.

So, sitting at her desk, looking at the board in the window where 37 Shorrolds Road was newly displayed, then looking at her desk diary with the word 'Wardo' at the top of the page, Suzy had written down the words 'Mr Kipper' and 'Shorrolds Road' underneath.

Suzy's *own* mental associations were likely responsible for the creation of 'Mr Kipper', the bogeyman that has haunted her case from that day to this.

Given everything we'd found out so far, I was satisfied that this was the case.

I thanked John for his information and asked if he could get his brother, Peter, who had been a Sturgis client, to give me a call, before wishing him a Merry Christmas. John Herring's revelations might be the best Christmas present we'd get this year.

33

'I'm just interested in trying to find Suzy's body,' I said, sounding far too much like some overenthusiastic, amateur sleuth – even to my own ears.

'Yeah, well,' Pete Johnstone said dismissively under his breath.

Pete Johnstone, the former detective inspector on the Suzy Lamplugh case, hadn't been an especially difficult man to locate, but over the past twelve months he had persistently ignored both my letters and Caroline's to his home. He'd also ignored requests from people such as Andy Carter, the son of the original senior investigating officer, asking him to get in touch with us.

I was a little surprised by his silence to the different approaches that we'd made. Both of us had spent decades in the same police force and had colleagues in common, one of whom, a close friend of mine, had described Pete as a 'good bloke' and 'approachable'.

Nevertheless, he had ignored us.

As we slowly began to make headway in the investigation, and there was finally some light shed on the dark, forgotten parts of the inquiry, providing tangible answers, people like Pete Johnstone, who were refusing to engage, had started to become barriers that needed to be overcome. We needed to speak with those who'd ignored our requests for contact, even if that meant involuntarily on their doorstep.

Unlike some of the witnesses, Pete didn't live too far away from me, but the late January snows had made travelling tricky.

Today, as the big freeze began to thaw, we'd decided it was time to go and knock on his door, hoping that, despite my current track record with interviews in this case so far, he wouldn't shut it in our faces.

At the time of Suzy's disappearance back in July 1986, Pete Johnstone had been a fresh-faced, 36-year-old transferee who'd just come off the back of three to four years spent policing the streets of Brixton in uniform. At Fulham, Suzy's case was to be one of his first investigations as a newly promoted detective inspector.

It was easy to blame Det. Supt Nick Carter, the senior investigating officer, for any mistakes that might have been made along the way. But DI Pete Johnstone had been second in command as the investigating officer, or IO, working directly under him. Arguably, it was Pete who would have made more of the hour-to-hour and day-to-day decisions on the ground in the first few days of the investigation. If we were to understand what had really taken place, it was important that we speak to him.

The planners of the medieval village that Pete Johnstone now lived in had never envisioned the need for car parking, and consequently it appeared to be banned by the modern-day local council. In hammering rain, we'd had to park quite a way from the grade-II-listed, fifteenth-century cottage and by the time we arrived at Pete's front door, we were soaked through to the bone.

As I knocked, we could see the glow of a laptop screen burning brightly in the gloom through one of the front windows. It gave me some hope that our journey wasn't a wasted one.

Moments later, we were finally standing face to face with the man who had ignored us for a year.

'You'd better come in for a minute,' he said, looking us both up and down.

We were sodden and cold, and I wondered if he'd merely taken pity on us rather than actually wanting to help with our quest. He beckoned us in – down some steps and into a kitchen with low ceilings and exposed oak beams.

Pete placed a flat-bottomed kettle on the blue Aga. 'Did you want a cup of tea?'

'That'd be great. Thank you. Nice Aga,' Caroline replied.

'It's actually getting refurbished tomorrow, funnily enough,' Pete said cordially.

Pete and Caroline discussed the merits of Agas for a few minutes while I stood there and dripped water onto his floor. I'd never met Caroline's parents, but apparently they had an Aga too, and Caroline was a clear enthusiast.

The smell and feel of the old timber-framed house reminded me of days spent on the Kent coast, at my own mother's place, before she'd died. This familiarity put me at ease too, and despite Pete having ignored us all this time, it didn't take me long to settle down at the large, central table in the kitchen, my damp coat slung on the back of my chair, steaming in the warmth of the kitchen.

'To be honest with you, I don't really want to be involved with this…' Pete placed a bone-china teacup in front of me, pushed a bowl of sugar next to it and sat down on the opposite side of his kitchen table.

For a man of sixty-eight, who'd worked shift patterns in various London boroughs, Pete looked well. He hadn't put on much weight in the thirty or so years Suzy had been missing. Although greying, he'd retained his hair, and despite drooping eyelids behind the wire-framed glasses he now wore, he looked very similar to the photos I'd seen of him from 1986.

Sitting around Pete's kitchen table, Caroline to his left and me directly across from him, I noticed an awkwardness in him. Strangely, he'd positioned himself side on to the kitchen table, facing away from Caroline – practically sitting with his back to her. It almost seemed rude. I wondered if she'd been too enthusiastic with her discussion about Agas, or whether he knew in advance that she loved playing the bad-cop role in our team?

I could see Caroline was confused by his behaviour and a little bit put out.

I heaped three large teaspoons of sugar into my cup and began to stir, trying to ignore Pete's awkwardness.

'I can't tell you how many calls I've had over the years on this case,' Pete began as he sipped his own tea. 'Journalists, foreign journalists, television companies, people all over the place... And to be honest with you, it's just a long, long time ago. I always feel very sorry for the family that it wasn't resolved. I always admired Mrs Lamplugh, because she turned something so negative into something so positive. There's not many people who can do that actually. She was a nice lady. It was such a high-profile case.'

'It was probably the biggest missing person case conducted on home soil, wasn't it?' I asked, hoping to prompt his memory.

'You know the way it goes, don't you? It's silly season, Parliament's not there,' he responded, looking into his tea. He was referring to the time of year Suzy had gone missing, but it was an unusual way to describe it.

The term refers to the part of the year when Parliament and the law courts are not sitting – the six to eight weeks in late July, August and early September when the lack of hard news transforms the normally serious press diet into a hunt for more inane and inconsequential stories. This terminology seemed to be completely at odds with Pete's old-school policing demeanour. And surely Suzy's story was a *serious* one? Not exactly what you'd associate with the light-hearted silly season?

'You've got to take yourself back to the eighties,' Pete continued. 'She was a young, white, good-looking girl with her own flat, car and a job. It just tickled everyone's fancy, didn't it? Nothing else to write about, so they pick on something like that, and it went mental.'

I paused while I thought about his terminology – 'tickled everyone's fancy'.

'Who made it like that – was it the family or Diana?' I wondered about the decision to organise the press conference so early, before the police knew anything at all. I had blamed Det. Supt Nick Carter for going to the media so quickly, haunted by the ghosts of people who'd gone missing in his past. But maybe it wasn't totally his fault?

'I wouldn't say that actually. I liked Mrs Lamplugh. I thought she was a different sort of woman, but I really liked her. She was *what you saw is what you got.* And she'd lost a daughter, for God's sake.' Pete spoke passionately but remained with his back to Caroline.

'It was another pressure on you when you're doing an inquiry. You have to put all these things in little boxes to deal with them. And deal with them correctly. Because if you don't, you know what the media's like – once someone makes a mistake, they're all over it like a rash, aren't they? Oh, the police didn't do this. Police aren't allowed to make a mistake, are they?'

I knew this from hard experience. Learning to investigate crime and learning how to be a good detective took many years. And if you were going to learn your trade, the best place to make mistakes was with crimes at the lower end of the harm spectrum. If you messed up on your very first investigation into someone's bag being stolen and the offender got off, it was a lot less serious than if you messed up in a murder investigation or the largest missing person case on home soil.

But I also knew that Pete's career progression had been very different to that of a traditional career detective – those who'd had that chance to make their mistakes early. Pete had made a sideways move and transferred laterally across from uniform.

While Pete's career progression wasn't unheard of, especially not on promotion, historically it wasn't considered the preferred, or more esteemed, career pathway. For many police services back in the 1980s (particularly for those forces that weren't able to fill all of their detective supervisor roles, because not enough detectives passed the promotion exams that particular year), officers were just expected to pick up the necessary detective skills for the role as they went along.

'And we all do, we all make mistakes, don't we?' Pete continued. I wondered if he was referring to something in Suzy's investigation. 'Well, we're all human, aren't we? If you're a divisional man, you have a murder inquiry to do, you can work forty-eight hours non-stop, quite often. And I did on that occasion.'

Pete moved on to talk about the sheer amount of work being heaped upon him by the Area Major Investigation Pool (AMIP) at the time of Suzy's disappearance.

There were sixty-seven different divisions in the Metropolitan Police district. Fulham was just one of those divisions. Divisions were divided among eight numbered geographical areas, with each area having a headquarters. AMIP was designed to assist area headquarters with the investigation of major crimes, such as non-domestic murders or those that crossed the boundaries of divisions in their area. Officers whose names were on the AMIP list were often called upon to assist other divisional CID officers across the area.

The problem was that AMIP teams could be involved in any number of investigations at the same time, and while investigations were supposed to be prioritised according to a strict criteria dependent on the severity of the crime, it was well known that this didn't happen. Things normally got dealt with on a first-come-first-served basis.

'We had another job going at the time actually, when the Lamplugh job broke. We had a big cement factory in Fulham…'

Could this have impacted upon Suzy's case in those crucial first hours and days? The complete lack of investigative leads in the first week of Suzy's case suddenly made more sense to me.

'And there was a big con going on at the cement works,' Pete continued. 'It was costing the company millions every year. And basically these guys, these drivers, were picking up eight pallets to take to their company, but picking up another eight and selling them privately. So the company put in a private investigator from Scotland who became a driver and understood what was going on. And the day after Suzy went missing, at five o'clock the next morning, we arrested thirty-eight people in one swoop all round the Home Counties. Regional came and helped us because we had to arrest them all at the same time, at about five in the morning.'

At the very moment that Det. Supt Nick Carter was doing that first press conference with Diana and Paul Lamplugh in front of the British media, it seemed that the entire Lamplugh investigation team was involved in another huge operation – a completely separate project, and one which meant police resources and man hours were stretched.

'So when we started the Lamplugh job, we had to run that cement job right the way through it. Because we couldn't stop it – we had everything in place. You know what it's like?'

I did know what it was like. Only too well. What he was telling me was that there was no real investigative focus on Suzy's case until all the arrests from the cement works case and the associated paperwork were all processed and out of the way. And on an operation of the magnitude he was describing at the cement works, this would have taken days, perhaps even the entire first week Suzy had gone missing.

This wasn't Pete's fault. It was something that you learned to do in the CID – juggle lots of investigations at the same time. Yet here were both Suzy's case and the cement works case on the same DI's table on the very same day. Both huge cases sitting with a detective inspector perhaps not as experienced at juggling, because he'd transferred laterally into the role and his previous three or four years had been spent in uniform?

It likely explained why the story presented to the media on the seven-day anniversary of Suzy's disappearance was identical to the one Det. Supt Nick Carter had presented at the press conference a week earlier. There had been no new witnesses, no real progress and nothing new to investigate in seven days. The police had done little or no work on Suzy's case that week because of the huge cement works raid. It also explained the delay in interviewing some of the key witnesses, such as Suzy's lodger, Nick Bryant.

Perhaps that had been part of the police strategy, to appear to be busy as far as the press were concerned.

Police search teams had been organised to look in parks, in and along the River Thames and on railway embankments for Suzy's body – but all the while, the actual investigation team had been busy doing something completely different.

Our conversation moved on to Pete's superior, Nick Carter, and his son, Andy Carter, who we'd already interviewed. I wanted to understand how Pete saw his senior investigating officer.

'Nick retired between Christmas 1986 and the start of New Year 1987 in early January. He'd bought a place in the West Country by then, where his son Andrew and his wife now live with the family.'

I nodded in agreement as he continued to speak, drinking my tea.

'I think he was just keen to get there. He was living in a flat with hardly any furniture. So he needed to go there. He didn't *want* to leave, to be honest with you, because he wanted to finish the job, because he was a very, very good detective, was Nick.'

Pete continued. 'And that's when we were moved to a small office at Hammersmith. And then I had to go back to Fulham, because they started giving me rapes and things like that to deal with, because they didn't have anybody else. And so I sort of did the two. And Mike Barley sort of caretaked, really, with a couple of girls, I think. Can't remember their names… And that's how the thing with John Cannan came up.'

I saw Caroline wince as Pete referred to 'a couple of girls'. Perhaps he wasn't in the mood to go to the trouble of recalling their names for us, or perhaps he didn't think they merited a mention? In any case, Caroline appeared ready to launch into bad-cop mode.

But before she could do so, a loud, artificial voice suddenly announced from behind me:

'I don't have any jokes about that!'

We all jumped.

34

I looked round to see where the voice had come from.

As if reading the situation as it unfolded, a smart speaker device perched on the window ledge behind me had joined in our conversation uninvited.

I began to laugh. The timing couldn't have been better. It threw Caroline off her stride.

'Oh, that's just Alexa,' Pete said, smiling, before continuing with his recollections of the investigation.

'Nick Carter, myself and Mike Barley were probably the main contenders on that investigation to be honest with you,' Pete said. 'Mike was the office manager – he ended up at the Yard, didn't he?'

I didn't know a great deal about former DS Mike Barley's career yet, besides him being the office manager of the incident room during the Lamplugh investigation. I'd been told by others in the Met that he had come from uniform via a similar lateral transfer process to Pete Johnstone, and that at some point between 1984 and 1985 he'd worked as a police sergeant on public order duties in the Midlands and the North during the coal miners' strike.

Pete explained how DS Barley had ended up in the office manager's role on Suzy's case: 'I took Mike Barley, chose him, because he was my detective sergeant and one of my DSes at Fulham. He'd never actually done it before, but he really went into it very well.'

This information that the office manager on the case had never run an incident room before was news to us.

In 1981, Sir Lawrence Byford had conducted a review into the police mishandling of the Yorkshire Ripper case which had enabled the Ripper, Peter Sutcliffe, to go on killing despite being in the police database for the investigation. Sutcliffe had been interviewed by police a total of nine times during the Yorkshire Ripper investigation but still missed as a credible suspect. The Byford report stated:

> The career development, training and selection of senior detectives need to be improved so that they have the management skills to meet the demands of an inquiry. There should be adequate training for staff of major incident rooms. The operational efficiency of a major incident room will greatly depend on the extent to which the staff allocated to it are specially trained.

The office manager's role in an incident room is a specialist role. And Suzy's case was extremely complicated – it wasn't something you could dip in and out of, not even as a very experienced detective and criminal investigator. Nevertheless, Pete was describing to us exactly that. Neither he nor former DS Mike Barley had been accustomed to an investigation of this size and complexity, yet they were both trying to run it alongside the huge cement-works case.

Despite the recommendations in the Byford Report five years previously, Pete was confirming that his newly crowned office manager of the incident room had never worked in that capacity before? And that the senior investigating officer, Det. Supt Nick Carter, had retired around six months into the investigation – leaving Pete, the investigating officer, in charge. But even Pete wasn't spending all his time on the case, because he was dealing with rape dockets in another building?

Everything Pete was telling us sounded like a recipe for absolute disaster. It perhaps wasn't surprising that amongst the chaos of the first week, with the cement-works case and plethora of untrained, inexperienced staff, that mistakes around the house key, unconfirmed victim sightings and the false diary entry had been made?

As I wondered how Carter could have let all this happen under his watchful eye, Pete began explaining why he didn't want to speak about Suzy's case to me. It was to do with his memory, he said.

'I did an interview on ITN – did you see that?'

I confirmed that I'd seen it. In the interview footage, Pete had used the strange phrase 'and that's the classic first description we get of the person who became to be known by everyone as "Mr Kipper" '. It felt as if he were talking about the makings of an icon.

Pete continued. 'And that was filmed in about 2002. And even then, while we were talking about it, I got one thing wrong. Because I remembered. And they said, "Oh we'll have to reshoot that, because it's not right." '

'It does happen,' I replied, wondering if he'd got it wrong because the police narrative was so shaky that even they couldn't remember the stories they'd told the press.

'It does happen – well it does happen. With the best will in the world, you can't keep this information, particularly when you've moved on,' he replied.

'We notice it with witnesses, don't we?' I asked, wondering about the ghost witness, Noel Devere, and his statement popping up suddenly into the investigation all those weeks later. 'This happens with our witnesses? Even days after the event, they can be wrong?' I still found it odd how this 'ghost witness' had been uncovered so long after Suzy's disappearance yet seemed to support the police narrative so fully and effectively.

'Exactly. I think witnesses sometimes can be the most unreliable people in the world, which is why you need to get *a lot of witness statements* to see if you can get some resemblance [sic] of truth out of them. You know?'

It was almost as if Pete were reading my mind.

I asked him about Harry Riglin, the next-door neighbour, who was supposed to have seen Suzy at the house for sale in Shorrolds Road. His swift response cut me off before I could even finish my question.

'Which is where the, er, identikit came from, yeah. But if you recall, Harry only ever gave a very good description of the *man*.'

Had Pete just confirmed for us exactly what Harry Riglin's nephew had told us? Harry never identified Suzy on the day she went missing.

Pete was becoming increasingly defensive in his answers, but as he had been kind enough to let us into his home on such a cold and damp day to finally speak to us, I decided that now was not the time and place to put him on the spot about it. There were others I wanted to talk to first. I could come back to him if I needed to. We thanked Pete for his hospitality, pulled on our still-damp coats and made our way back to the car.

35

The rain hadn't let up. It was still being thrown from the sky by the bucketful as we ran back to the car, soaking us through to the skin again. Our clothes were so wet that the car's heater instantly lost its normally easy battle with the condensation on the inside of the windows. And as our warm bodies turned the moisture on our clothes into water vapour, the situation rapidly became worse, making driving off impossible. We were sitting motionless on the outskirts of Pete's village with the engine running and the heater on.

'What do you make of all that then?' Caroline asked, water slowly dripping from her hair onto the leather of the seat and running down the back.

'I get the feeling he knows they've made mistakes. I think that's why he was telling us about the cement-works case. I couldn't see any other relevance to that otherwise, if I'm honest.'

'You think the cement case is important?'

'In terms of how it's impacted on the Lamplugh investigation?' I responded, struggling to peel off my wet coat and throwing the sodden thing over my shoulder into the back, water splashing all over the roof lining.

'Yeah…'

'Of course – how could it not?' I carried on as I tried to brush the water in my hair off with my hands. 'He's just said the team were focused on another huge investigation at exactly the moment all of their attention should have been on Suzy. That's madness. Why did they go ahead with those arrests? Why not just put the cement case on hold for a couple of weeks? There's no time-critical element to that, but with Suzy there was. Those first hours and days are crucial in a murder or suspicious missing person case.'

'It must have taken a long time to organise something as big as the cement-work arrests?'

'Totally. Weeks. But it wasn't a priority. The victim wasn't even a person; it was a big company. It wasn't a priority, or it wouldn't have been for me. Carter let it happen. His choice.'

Caroline nodded but didn't reply.

'That is exactly how we messed up Joanne's case. You can't just leave it, you can't just get on with business as usual and simply wait for something to turn up. You've got to get out there and ask questions.'

I shook my head, water still dripping from my hair to the tip of my nose.

'There was no real investigative focus on Suzy's case in those first few crucial days at least – maybe not even in that first week?' I continued. 'They did the initial press conference at Fulham police station. Did some appeals. They organised uniform officers to go out with dogs and search open spaces, towpaths, perhaps even organised some divers to swim up the bank of the Thames.'

'It looked busy.'

'Exactly. You know this, and you've never worked in the police. But none of that stuff needed the CID.'

A small hole had started to appear in the condensation on the front windscreen. I reached down and turned up the heater to full blast, hoping that we could finally get on our way.

'It was all things that could be organised by less than a handful of people sitting behind a desk at Fulham,' I continued as I watched the hole in the condensation get larger. 'There was no real investigation going on, not really. There can't have been, not with thirty-eight arrests being made at the same time for something completely unrelated. We know there was no one asking real questions.'

Caroline nodded. 'Yeah.'

'Certainly no one asking, "How on earth could Suzy have done a house viewing if she didn't have the key and you still have it?" No questions like that, as there should have been. All the nuance has been lost. But you don't need me to tell you this,' I said as we moved off and slowly made our way through the winding side roads of Pete's village and back toward the motorway.

'No, I see your point. He seemed to be falling over himself to tell us that Harry Riglin only gave a good description of the man at Shorrolds, but only after you mentioned you'd spoken to Riglin's nephew.'

'He didn't actually admit that Suzy was never seen there by Riglin though, did he? He fell short of actually saying it.'

'Yeah. I thought you'd have jumped on him and clarified it. Why didn't you?'

'I don't think we need to nail him to the wall, not right at this moment. I want to see what else we find first. Leave the door open with these people. He talked to us.'

'He talked to *you*; he had his back to me.'

'Yeah, what was all that about?'

'I dunno,' she said, shrugging.

'He talked to you about his Aga,' I quipped.

'Maybe he thought I wasn't important; I was just the hired female help. I did say I was your assistant.'

'True. Why did you say that? You aren't my assistant.'

'I'm not sure. Maybe I was trying to make you sound more important – that you were so important, you had an assistant.'

I burst out laughing.

'We need to get this good-cop bad-cop thing sorted out,' I said, turning to her, seeing she was smiling.

'I broke the ice with him by talking about Agas.'

'You did. But don't call yourself my assistant again. We are equals in this, and I wouldn't want to be investigating this case with anyone else.'

'What are we doing next then?' she asked, ignoring the compliment I'd just given her.

'The lost chequebook and diary at the pub, the one Adam Leegood said to us didn't happen or didn't happen on the Friday night he was with her. I still don't know what he meant…'

'I don't either,' Caroline agreed.

'We need to know more about that. That's what we're doing next.'

'Yes, boss,' she replied playfully.

36

'Have you any idea how difficult it is for us to find this information for you?' the fifties-something woman in a white mohair cardigan asked me through the glass screen that normally protected her from irate people making enquiries about their court cases and fines.

'I can imagine, and I'm really sorry to ask, but it's important.'

'None of this information is on the computer – we can't just log in and get it for you. It's all held in the old ledgers downstairs, in the basement. We have to go down there, dust 'em off...' She wasn't listening to me. She was annoyed, I could see that. 'We have to find the right book, and do it all manually. This information is thirty-three years old.'

'I know. I'm sorry.' I repeated my apology, hoping it would appease her. 'I was here a few weeks ago asking for it.'

It was my second visit in as many weeks to the magistrates' court at Lavender Hill, an early-sixties monstrosity that housed both the courthouse and the local police station. It was unusual for both buildings to be co-located these days, but in Victorian times the South-Western Police Court and police station had stood side by side here.

Nowadays courts needed to be independent from the police for the public to trust the justice system. But the thick glass screen between us suggested that people still didn't quite trust the justice system enough.

'What exactly do you need this information for anyway?' she asked, frowning through the glass.

'I'm investigating a missing persons case…' I didn't have to tell her, but as I was asking her to dig through decades of grime in the basement in her pristine white cardigan, I felt that she deserved an explanation. 'It's a very old case, possibly a murder, but we can't say for sure, and I need the information in your basement to identify potential witnesses.'

'Well, you'll have to wait. We're short of staff. And as I said, it's a mess and very dirty down there. We might not even come up with what you need. I can't say for certain that we even still have it.'

I smiled. 'Thank you.'

'You're welcome. Come back later this afternoon; I'll let you know what we find.'

I nodded.

'I can recommend Café Parisienne, while you wait. It's across the road. Kazim's breakfasts are good.'

'I'll check it out. I really appreciate your help.'

She smiled back at me, before spinning on her heel and walking away from the glass partition.

Back in 1986, shortly after Suzy's disappearance, her cheque-book and personal pocket diary had been recovered by the police from the Prince of Wales pub at 138 Upper Richmond Road. It was the closest pub to Suzy's home – around 200 metres from her front door.

I still didn't completely understand exactly how and when Suzy's items had been lost or stolen nor how they'd ended up at the pub. I also felt that Adam Leegood's responses, on the two occasions he'd been asked about the incident, had been very strange – both when I'd asked him about it and previously on the documentary we'd watched. It gave me no confidence that the police actually truly understood how and when Suzy's belongings had ended up in the pub or come into their possession. Their understanding of it all seemed to be like many other parts of the case – assumption and supposition.

But with Suzy's items being found at a pub, it did provide us with a distinct advantage in our own investigation. All premises selling alcohol for consumption on or off the premises have to be licensed. Licensing laws of one form or another have existed since the middle of the eighteenth century. Licensing registers and records are public records which are kept for decades – and, in some cases, centuries.

The Prince of Wales public house fell into the catchment area of Lavender Hill magistrates' court. The system of licensing is slightly different now, but in 1986, they were responsible for issuing the licence to enable alcohol to be legally sold from the premises. And with licences being issued to named individuals and not breweries, I was hoping the court could help me find out who was licenced to run the pub at the time of Suzy's disappearance. Provided the records still existed, that was.

I crossed the road and walked into the Café Parisienne, its walls adorned with black-and-white photos of Hollywood stars and singers from days gone by. I made myself at home at a table and perused the menu, envisaging a long wait. All I needed from the court was the name of the pub's licensee at the time of Suzy's disappearance. Perhaps he or she would remember the circumstances back in summer 1986 which led to Suzy's belongings being retrieved by the police from their establishment.

37

26 February 2019
32 years, 6 months, 29 days missing

'I'm looking for Michael Hutchings?' I asked the woman as she answered the door.

'Well, you've found him, but he's in the shower at the moment,' she responded.

We were at the front door of a cottage on the edge of a sleepy English village after a very long drive, with a grey-haired woman who looked to be in her sixties in a plaid skirt and blue jumper.

After a long wait in the café, Lavender Hill magistrates' court had told me that they had granted a drinks licence for alcohol to be sold at the Prince of Wales pub to a 'Michael Hutchings'.

But there was no other information available from the court – no ages or dates of birth. This made finding this man hard work. We'd travelled coast to coast in search of him.

'I'm sorry to bother you. I'm not sure if I've got the right Michael Hutchings, that's all. Did your Michael used to work at the Prince of Wales pub in Putney?'

'I haven't been married to him forever, but... I believe he did, yes.'

Today was another good day, another small but hard-earned victory in tracking down someone that otherwise would have been lost to history. I wanted to jump up and down in celebration, but I had to hide my elation to all but Caroline who was standing by my side. I winked at her. She smiled.

'I wonder if we could have a chat with him about it?' I asked.

The woman invited us into a living room that backed onto a kitchen. At the rear was a large, well-tended garden. The lounge furniture seemed to be positioned at offbeat angles, and a strong new-carpet smell permeated the room. I wondered if this was why Michael was in the shower this early in the day, because he'd just moved his furniture back into a freshly carpeted living room?

'I'll go and get him,' the woman said, leaving us alone.

'We found him,' Caroline whispered through gritted teeth whilst clenching her fist.

'We don't know he knows anything yet. It might be a big waste of time,' I reminded her.

As we sat down on the oddly positioned chairs and surveyed the room in silence, a man in his seventies with a bright red face and wet hair, fresh from the shower, appeared at the living-room door. He was tucking his shirt into a pair of tracksuit bottoms; the shirt became wet as it touched his skin. He hadn't dried as well as he normally would have done.

'Hello. Are you Michael?' I got up from the sofa and shook the man's hand.

'I am, yes,' he responded, looking confused.

'I'm sorry this is completely out of the blue. And I'm sorry to get you out of the shower. I'm a writer. I understand you used to run the Prince of Wales pub in Putney?'

'That's correct.'

'It's taken me an awful long time to track you down. I've got a few questions to ask you and they're going to seem very strange, and—'

'Not if they're about Suzy Lamplugh, they're not!' he said loudly.

In the background, Caroline let out a faint gasp. We had the right man.

'Yes they are. How did you—'

'The strangest thing is that the police never came back to me,' he replied, cutting me off – stopping me in my tracks.

We had walked, unannounced, into this man's house and he knew the very thing I was here to ask him about after nearly thirty-three years. Every person we had spoken to in this case had come out with something odd, something strange, something unexpected and it was happening again.

I struggled with the peculiarities surrounding Suzy's case. I'd conducted hundreds of criminal investigations over the years, but never had I experienced this many witnesses constantly saying things I wasn't expecting to hear.

It had taken weeks and hundreds of miles to find Michael, and the moment we did, he'd broadsided us with an apparent complaint about a police investigation from more than thirty years ago; it was surreal. My elation at finding him was now replaced by feelings of regret. We were more than thirty years too late. Why had the police not come back to him and why was he complaining about it?

'Did you talk to the police originally?' I asked.

'I can't remember it all now...' He frowned. 'The purse, or bag, or whatever it was that was found... I can't remember now. It was handed in by a member of staff...' Michael tailed off.

He knew that I wanted to ask him about lost property. It was what I'd tried to talk to Adam Leegood about – the items Adam had half claimed were stolen on a documentary we'd watched. Though, manifestly, they *hadn't* been stolen, not if someone had handed them in to the pub management.

Our research had shown the police recovered a pocket diary, a postcard and chequebook from the Prince of Wales pub in Putney, all belonging to Suzy, though there seemed to be some confusion as to exactly *when* these items had been collected from the pub.

Our research indicated that police themselves didn't even seem sure exactly *when* they'd come into possession of the items. Nor could we establish how the police came to know the items were at the pub in the first place. Everyone we'd spoken to denied knowing anything about them being lost – except for Adam Leegood, who, oddly, had become upset when I'd asked about them.

We were able to prove that the police *had* collected the items, because they'd talked extensively to the press about working through the contents of Suzy's personal pocket diary. They'd described hunting among its pages for a 'Mr Kipper'.

But curiously, they seemed unconcerned about how the items had ended up at the pub, or how and why they'd been informed the items were there, and that was what I wanted to talk to Michael about. Who had rung the police to tell them that Suzy's lost items were at the pub?

'I think a member of staff handed it in to my then wife,' Michael continued, though he was struggling to remember the exact details of the particular items in question. I was impressed he could remember this much. 'We couldn't find anything in there, whatever it was, an address or anything.'

'And you rang the police and they collected it off you?' I asked.

'Did they collect it off me, or was it my then wife at the time?' Michael paused, trying to recall the chain of events. 'No, I don't remember actually physically handing it over to somebody, no.'

'Did you call the police to say you had it though?' Caroline asked, sounding a little impatient.

There was a long pause.

I looked across at Caroline, trying to indicate that she needed to give Michael more time.

'All I know is the police were called…' Michael finally said with a sigh 'And it was handed over to them.'

'We know the police were called,' I agreed, 'but why were they called – because you knew who Suzy Lamplugh was and she'd gone missing?' I tried again.

'Afterwards, yes.'

'But you didn't know that at the time, when the items were found?'

'No.' He shook his head. 'I think we'd asked, or somebody had asked around the pub, does anybody know this person? So that we could then have contacted them. I can't for the life of me… There couldn't have been an address in it. There couldn't have been, or else we would have known it either was or wasn't local.'

'You don't remember her?'

'No. Not at all.'

'You don't remember her as a regular in the pub?'

'Nope,' he said.

'Do you know where she lived?'

'Nope. Not a clue.'

It seemed that Michael had some concept of some lost property, but that he'd had little to do with finding it, or with the police becoming involved with the pub.

Michael explained that it was much later, on seeing some publicity about Suzy's disappearance and her case, that he eventually made the connection between the lost property at the pub and Suzy Lamplugh. He couldn't remember how he'd found this out.

He explained that he'd been married at the time to a woman called Zoe and they ran the pub together, but following a death in Zoe's family in 1988, their marriage had deteriorated, eventually ending in divorce. He had no idea where she lived now.

'How many members of staff did you have back then?' I asked.

'If I had a member of staff go off sick, I could ring a dozen people. So I had a lot of staff working not too many hours. So there were probably a dozen to fifteen, mostly female. I had a cellarman that worked with me, an Irish guy, Brendon something.'

'There's quite a lot of people in the pub then?'

'It got busy. I took it over from people who'd been removed by the company. I took it over when it was doing about £1,500 a week. When I left it was doing about £8,000 a week.'

'The police seem to think the items might have been found by an interim employee – does that mean anything to you?' I asked, trying to jog his memory.

'I was a training manager. I moved on to become an area trainer. I had about three couples that trained with me at the Prince of Wales. They normally stayed with us for about twelve weeks, because that was the length of the course. Once they finished the twelve-week training course, they then went round and did relief in various pubs around the country. They'd do a little pub somewhere, and a big one, and an awkward one – so they'd get a feel for all of the types of pubs that were around there.'

'Okay,' I encouraged him.

'When I was on holiday, I always insisted that the people I'd trained at my pub do my relief work. Those were the ones that ran my pub when I wasn't there. Because they knew how I ran it. They knew the customers, the staff, so once they get to a certain point where they know the system, and you can see that they get on alright with the staff, they don't have any major clashes or anything – then I was quite happy to leave them there, as long as they didn't change anything.'

Michael explained that in late 1985, he'd been sent on a course by his brewery, Imperial Inns & Taverns, in order to become a trainer. He'd taken his first live-in couple at the pub on their twelve-week course in January 1986. The brewery would normally only consider couples as relief workers for their pubs, and you came as a pair, as a team, just like he and Zoe were, so it was couples he'd train up. These couples would live with him, above his pub, whilst they trained.

'I had one couple that came from the North, one couple from London, and another couple from Cornwall.'

We were starting to make progress.

Some of what I'd read elsewhere now started to make sense. In 1987, just as the police were about to close the investigation into Suzy's case, they had taken a statement from a witness based up north, about finding Suzy's chequebook and diary outside the Prince of Wales pub in Putney. It was from a man called Clive Vole, a relief worker at the pub.

'Does the name Clive mean anything to you?' I asked.

'Yes, he's part of the couple from the north. They ran the Prince of Wales while I wasn't there, yes.'

'But you weren't on holiday at the time when this happened, when this stuff was found?'

'Nope. I was there when it was found,' he replied.

I asked Michael if he had copies of any documents or passports that would assist in showing when he had taken holiday in 1986. It was curious that the police had dealt with Clive Vole, the relief cover, if the actual licensee was present, as Michael claimed he was?

Michael had a rummage around but could find nothing that helped. We looked through his old photo albums at his holiday snaps from the eighties, but none of them had dates on them.

I asked Michael if he was still in contact with the couple from the North whom he'd trained up.

'No. Crikey, they actually split up. Probably within the next six months or so after that, they went their separate ways,' Michael replied. 'We knew Clive and Karen quite well. If they were in between relief duties and we were on holiday in that area, we would visit them and stay in the house they had up there.'

'Any idea why they split up?' I asked.

'No, not a clue. I think I spoke to Clive after I'd heard they'd broken up. I can't remember how I found out – somebody had told me, and there was something about his partner deciding she really didn't want to be running pubs. And I think that caused a rift, after the fact that they'd just been through training and what have you. So…'

Michael clarified that he had never been asked to give a written statement to the police about the items being found. However, as the full-time licensee of the pub who was present when the items had been lost, he felt he should have done.

It seemed to me that the police had gone back to the Prince of Wales in 1987 looking for Clive, to take a statement from him. They'd briefly spoken to the pub, alerting them that the lost property was connected to Suzy. However, as a stopgap employee, Clive was no longer there.

'At the time the items were found, I thought it's just somebody who'd lost their purse, handbag or whatever. It was handed in. That was it,' Michael explained.

But that changed when the police had begun searching for Clive Vole and Michael had found out the items were connected to a missing person case. Michael had been left with the impression that the police were going to come back to him, after they'd tracked down and spoken to Clive Vole – and he felt aggrieved they hadn't.

I pressed him on what he remembered of the police's attitude when he had spoken to them.

'As I recall they made some sort of comment about, "Oh somebody else being silly and left it after having had too much to drink." And off they went. That was how I felt they viewed it,' he responded.

'You mentioned that there was a rule back then that you had to be a couple to run a pub?'

'It wasn't a rule as such, but the brewery made it difficult for you as a single person, and it was very difficult for a single person to actually run a pub anyway. Because you're one person down to begin with.'

'So once Clive split from his partner, what would have happened to him running pubs?'

'If Clive was on his own and still wanted to run pubs, it would have made it hard for him. You would be landed with the little pub that's trouble.'

'Do you know if that's what happened? Did he then run pubs on his own?'

'I don't. I never heard from either of them again after that.'

We stayed and had some tea. Caroline talked to Michael about the antique cuckoo clock on his wall as we thumbed through more of his photographs, looking for anything that might be useful. I found a few photographs of the Prince of Wales pub in 1986, which Michael very kindly gave us to copy.

On our drive back to London, Caroline and I decided that we had three new people to find. Clive Vole and his former partner, Karen Furness, who'd both been employed as interim relief workers and also had dealings with Suzy's lost belongings. And Michael Hutching's ex-wife, Zoe. We had to get to the bottom of this lost or stolen chequebook saga.

It was something the police had dismissed, but the more we asked questions about it, the more intriguing it became.

38

The long drive north had taken us most of the day. I'd picked Caroline up on the journey from London in our bid to locate another of the witnesses in the case.

The address we'd found for Clive Vole, the relief barman whom the police believed had found Suzy's lost belongings, was located on the edge of a small mining town in the north of England, hundreds of miles from London.

We'd been unable to establish much about Clive's current lifestyle, only that he didn't appear to be in the pub trade any longer and that despite originally hailing from a different northern town, he now lived with a woman who'd grown up in the area in which he'd settled. We were unsure as to how long it would take us to actually find him at home, especially if he still worked or travelled. And with such a long journey, we had to build in the opportunity to go back to the address on a few different occasions at different times of the day, so we'd had to book accommodation nearby.

The mining town was located on the side of an ancient hillside within a breathtaking landscape. After dropping our bags at the cheap and cheerful stone cottage on one side of the town, we drove to the end-of-terrace house we'd identified on the other – to see if we could locate Clive.

The house was one of the better homes in the area: well kept, with rendered walls painted in a bright colour, and a small front garden separated from the road by a box hedge. The lean-to porch at the front marked the house out from the rest of the terrace. And, with a selection of ornaments and freshly cut flowers on display in the front window, the house had a distinctly feminine feel to it.

'Hello.' A short, stout man in his sixties, with bloodshot, bulging eyes opened the door. He had a bushy, unkempt moustache and a wild mane of white hair.

A small dog at his side barked at me but made no attempt to move past his leg and into the garden where I stood. His accent sounded like a good fit for the man we were looking for. Maybe this was him?

'Hello, I'm looking for Clive…' I said.

The man with the wild hair frowned at me but said nothing, eying me suspiciously.

'Are you Clive?' I asked again hopefully, trying to read what his frown meant.

'Yeah,' he responded, still peering at me with a frown on his face.

We were in luck. I introduced myself over the noise of the dog as a truck rumbled down the road behind me.

Clive was wearing a stained green T-shirt, blue jeans and a brown cardigan. His scruffy appearance seemed at odds with the neat and tidy house he'd emerged from.

'I wonder if I can have a chat with you about Suzy Lamplugh?' I ventured.

'What, sorry?' Clive responded as the incensed dog continued to bark at me as if I'd disturbed his afternoon snooze too.

'I was wondering if I could have a chat with you about Suzy Lamplugh? I'm writing a book and I understand you found a chequebook of hers in 1986? You worked down in London, at a pub?'

'Yeah.' Clive sighed as the dog finally lost interest in me and walked off, back into the house, probably to continue its sleep.

'There was a chequebook found of Suzy's? At the pub?'

The traffic calmed and there was near total silence for what seemed like a long time before Clive responded with a simple, 'Yeah.'

'Do you remember that?' I asked.

Again there was total silence, with Clive just looking straight at me but saying nothing. I looked across at Caroline. She gave a very slight shrug.

The dog appeared momentarily by Clive's side again, wondering what was going on here, though this time it didn't bark.

'I wondered if I could have a chat with you about it, that was all?' I pressed him again for an answer.

'I'm just not getting it. Sorry, having problems...' He laughed after another very long silence, now pointing at his ears. Hearing aids protruded from both sides.

'Would it be easier inside?' I asked, raising my voice and wondering if the passing traffic noise and the dog barking had caused him problems, though I was already having my doubts. The traffic was light and infrequent, and the dog was now silent. The very long pauses in Clive's replies didn't seem to fit with background noise being the issue.

Closing the inner door to the house, Clive beckoned me out of the front garden and into the porch.

'Can't hear very well, sorry,' said Clive pointing to his ears again, by way of explanation for our change of location and his long pauses. I wondered whether he truly couldn't hear me, or if he had deliberately brought me in out of the sight line of any nosey neighbours. There wasn't room for three of us in the small porch, but the door was open, and Caroline remained standing outside the front, watching us through the open door.

'No, that's alright. I'll speak up. Perhaps I was speaking too softly.'

He smiled but again said nothing.

'In 1986, you were working at a pub in Putney?' I started again, raising my voice this time round.

'Yeah,' he replied, nodding.

'And I think you were employed for a short period there, is that right?'

'Yeah.'

'A chequebook belonging to Suzy Lamplugh was found. Do you know who Suzy Lamplugh is?'

There was a long pause.

'No,' was his eventual response.

He'd already confirmed that he knew what I was talking about, so I tried again: 'It's a girl who went missing in 1986. And there was a chequebook of hers found. And I think you found it either inside the pub or outside the pub, or something like that?'

There was another very long pause before he answered, 'Yeah, I think, yeah, I…' he stammered, seemingly reluctant to confirm anything. Or maybe it was just so long ago, he was struggling to recall.

'I just want to have a quick chat with you about it. Can you remember anything about it?'

'I can't really. I'm going down to pick my friend up in a minute,' he said, before asking, 'But what do you want about it, in particular?'

I struggled to read whether he was nervous of us, couldn't remember anything or was just very unclear about what we wanted. Clive's odd way of speaking, as we would come to discover, often made him difficult to understand.

'Well, it's just the circumstances of finding it. And you did a couple of statements for the police – I'd just like to talk about that really.'

'Well, the thing was, it was years ago now. And I mean, when you're running a pub, finding something like that is just run of the mill. You find wallets, chequebooks, all things like that. Shopping bags, briefcases…'

I nodded in agreement, imagining how many people must leave stuff in pubs, especially tired or inebriated customers late at night.

'So it wasn't anything, particularly in that day,' Clive continued.

I started to wonder if we could make it back home that night – whether we could collect our bags and cancel the accommodation.

'All I remember really is that sss, er—' Clive began speaking again as I considered calling it a day but then stopped himself mid-sentence.

I looked over at Caroline. She shook her head. It was a waste of time.

But suddenly, Clive appeared to remember something.

'Well, it was a bit odd,' he said. 'Found the chequebook the night before. Then, when I found the chequebook, I put it on the shelf in the – in the cellar. And then I phoned up the bank the next morning, because there was no telephone number in the chequebook or in the diary.'

I hadn't mentioned Suzy's diary to him. He'd introduced it into the conversation. He definitely remembered.

'And they said to get in touch with her, and that she'd get in touch with me,' he carried on. 'I got a phone call back about dinner time, before we opened, saying that, "Got her chequebook and diary. And she'd be round to pick 'em up later."'

There was suddenly a mountain of information.

'Then I got a phone call about two o'clock from a woman, saying, "If she comes, tell her you can't find 'em and give us a ring,"' Clive finished with a chuckle.

'Right...' I tried to take stock of what he was now saying, but he wasn't the easiest of men to understand.

In the dying light of the police investigation into Suzy's disappearance, just before the case was closed in 1987, our research suggested that Clive had been interviewed by the police. From speaking to Michael Hutchings, and from what I could glean elsewhere, it seemed that this had been an administrative type of interview and statement; it wasn't an investigative line of enquiry.

There was a standardised procedure for running major incident rooms. That procedure dictated that the MIR had to know the provenance of all the information within it. In other words, there had to be an audit trail of how anything had ended up in the investigation. And in the case of exhibits, such as Suzy's chequebook and diary, that had to take the form of a written statement.

So it was likely the only reason Clive Vole was ever formally interviewed was to tidy up the loose ends in the MIR before the case was closed, hence why the police had never bothered to check any of the information with Michael Hutchings, the pub's permanent landlord.

'Bit odd,' Clive said, laughing.

It *was* totally odd what he was saying. Some woman had phoned the pub and asked him if Suzy had been to pick up her stuff on the day of Suzy's disappearance? Almost off the wall. But I knew that Clive's original statement had confused the police too, and I could see why, as he babbled his account at me.

'And do you know who that phone call was from?' I asked, still trying to process what he was saying.

'No!' he exclaimed. 'The police said it wasn't her mother, but... The phone call said, "Try to keep her there while I get round there..." And she said "Susan"; she didn't say "Miss Lampoo" [sic] or whatever. It sounded like some member of the family wanted to talk to her before, whatever...'

As I processed what he was saying, it seemed that he was suggesting that he'd found Suzy's belongings on Sunday night then called the bank on Monday morning, the day Suzy had gone missing. There had then been some sort of appointment made between Suzy and the pub for her to come and collect her belongings that day, and then there was an odd phone call to the pub from someone right after Suzy had disappeared.

As far as I knew, little of this had been said before. Clive stood laughing at me as I wondered what this all meant and how I should approach it.

'How did this person know that she was coming to the pub?' I pondered, trying to get to the bottom of it. It was a surprise to hear this incredible account, almost as if it was deliberately crazy.

'All I can assume is the bank must have phoned the work or somewhere to get in touch with her, coz then there weren't any mobiles of course, so you couldn't just ring somebody... So they, the bank, must have phoned the workplace or home or somewhere to tell her that it had got her chequebook and diary.'

'Right,' I said. None of it made any sense; *he* didn't make sense. 'It had got her chequebook and diary' – what the hell did that mean? 'It', the bank, didn't have these items – Clive had them. It was impossible to decipher from the way he spoke, but I played along with him, not wishing to break his stride.

I asked him about Suzy's plans to retrieve her lost belongings from the pub. 'She made an appointment to come later on?' I pressed, trying to understand.

'Yeah,' he responded after a slight pause.

'What sort of time was that?'

'Well, no, I mean—' Clive replied, before stopping mid-sentence.

I again looked over at Caroline; she looked as confused as I was.

'Dang. I'll tell you what happened, and then you can decide for yourself, but after then, about five, six o'clock, nobody turned up for the chequebook, we're shutting before evening session. And then I got a phone call, presumably it said from... Chelsea police station, saying that they'd be sending somebody round. "Had she been for the chequebook?" I said no. And then by ten o'clock, I'd got, what? Three police officers there?'

'Right,' was all I could think of saying. Was this guy mad and having us on?

'And which day was this on? That all this happened?' I asked.

'The same day. All in the same day, this.'

'She went missing on the Monday. So all of this happened on the same day?'

'I can't remember exactly what day of the week it was, coz it was just, like I say, like a normal day to me. It wasn't... when you work in t'pub, day in, day out, most days are the same. Only difference is the Sunday where you get, sort of, bit more time. But... Yeah, it was just odd, the way that everybody sort of... it happened, because there were... too many people interested too quick... I mean... Looking back on it, if I said to police there's me 23-year-old daughter's missing, they'd say give us a ring in a couple of days if she doesn't turn up. Not be round at ten o'clock the next, same day. I mean that was a bit weird!' Clive laughed.

'You're from this village, is that right?' I changed tack and asked him a question that I knew the answer to. From an unpromising start where he'd refuted knowing who Suzy Lamplugh was, the flow of information from him had now ramped up to a million miles an hour. I wanted to slow this torrent down a little and gain back some control over the conversation, but I also wanted to test his ability to tell the truth.

'I'm from the north, originally. We was recruited from up here. And we was sort of sent down there for pub training.'

He'd answered me truthfully.

'Who's "we"?' I enquired. I'd already guessed the answer from what Michael Hutchings, the permanent landlord, had previously told us. Again the question was a test of his veracity – plus it was sometimes helpful for people to underestimate your knowledge of the subject you were questioning them about initially.

He explained that he was referring to his former partner. 'I don't know where she is now. Couldn't tell you,' he replied, chuckling again.

'You're not with her anymore?' Again, I knew the answer to this question but wanted to hear his response. I hoped he might shed some light on when or why they'd split.

'But I dealt with it, coz the manager of the pub at the time was on holiday – that's why we were standing in. And I was in by myself while… this was going on,' he responded.

He'd avoided my question about his ex but provided an intelligible and straightforward response about the interim pub work – and an example of how he normally spoke in conversation.

'Right. Oh, so your partner didn't talk to—'

'She didn't have anything to do with it,' Clive said quickly, not allowing me to finish my sentence. It was almost as if he didn't like me directing the conversation.

He continued. 'But that's about all I can tell you. Because it, at the time, it was… sort of… was like I say, was just like a normal day to me – it wasn't anything special. So I didn't really take a great deal of notice.'

He seemed to remember much more than Michael – a lot more. There was quite incredible detail in some of what he was saying, if it was true. I started to wonder why the memory was so vivid.

'It's sort of lost in time. But I must admit it was a bit strange at the time. I thought it was strange…' Clive said, as if reading my mind.

'You found the chequebook one day, and—'

'Oh yeah, not the same day exactly,' he answered before I'd finished my question again. 'The night before, I found the chequebook. I was going to the takeaway. And I found the chequebook on the way out. Because there were two, like, tables outside, like picnic tables. And probably put bag on table and fell off and the chequebook and diary s'must of fallen on the floor. And I just went out and they were on floor, so I picked them up. Went to takeaway, came back…'

'And then what did you do? You rang…?' I decided to try again now he was speaking a bit more normally, more slowly.

'Bank. Yeah.'

'You said the police turned up that day, on the Monday?'

'It were all – all this happened on one day. It wasn't sort of, like, over two days or three days… Everything happened in one day.'

'Okay. Can I take a telephone number for you? Is that possible?' I decided to retreat and rethink how I was going to deal with this. I needed to analyse all of this information; I couldn't do it standing here talking to him. And besides, he'd said something about going to pick up his friend right at the start of our conversation, so I wanted to let him do that. Perhaps he'd be easier to interview on another occasion.

'Yeah. Just a minute, I'll have to…' Clive disappeared into the house leaving me standing in the porch and Caroline still waiting outside.

On his return we exchanged telephone numbers.

I tried to wrap up the meeting. 'Okay, well it was great to meet you.'

'Well, what I've found strange, like I say, was that everybody was so interested so quickly.' Clive wasn't finished. Although we were about to leave, he seemed to want to continue talking to us on the doorstep. 'I mean the phone call that I got in the afternoon, from her mother, or whatever. "Try and keep her there... while I get round." That was odd. I mean... Why would you say that to somebody?'

'You don't know how they got your telephone number?' I asked, referring to the mystery person who'd called the pub.

'I've no idea on that, because like I say, when I phoned the bank, the bank must have phoned her home, or business, or workplace... to give her... tell her. That's the only place I can think that they got the number from... Coz like I said, she just say, "Keep us Susan there while I get round."' Clive began to ramble again. 'That sounds like somebody's in... She's going to do a runner or something. Doesn't sound like she—' Clive stopped himself mid-sentence.

'Well it sounds like she was in a bit of trouble, do you not think?' I played along.

'Well, yeah, but... That was, what, three o'clock. And she only phoned me, what, two hours before that?'

I looked across at Caroline. Had Clive just said he'd spoken to Suzy at 1 p.m. the day she went missing, at about the time she would have been leaving the Sturgis office? I wasn't sure if I'd heard him correctly.

'It seems... It seemed a bit strange to me,' he continued.

'You spoke to her on the phone then?' I stopped him talking, wanting to clarify the point. Had he actually spoken to Suzy?

'Sorry?' Clive looked confused.

'You said she phoned you. You spoke to her on the phone?'

'Yeah, says it... Like I say, it's just odd that' – he began to chuckle a little as his sentences deteriorated into unconventional snippets again, not making any real sense – 'that everybody were interested so quickly.'

'Can you remember what she said to you on the phone?' I pushed him for clarification.

He paused before responding ,'What – what she said to me?'

'Yeah.'

'She said about, sort of, "Try to keep her there, while I get round,"' he replied.

It was a non-answer.

'No. Sorry, you were talking about speaking to Suzy on the phone. You didn't speak to Suzy on the phone?' I pushed him for an answer again.

'Sorry?

'Did you speak to Suzy on the phone?' I asked him again, more emphatically this time.

'Oh yeah. Yeah I did,' he responded. As he did so, he closed his eyes and covered his mouth with the mobile phone he had in his hand.

My heart thudded hard in my chest. This was hugely significant.

'And what did she say to you?' I wanted to be clear on what he was saying, that he had spoken to Suzy the day she had gone missing.

'Basically,' Clive continued, 'have you got me chequebook and diary? I said yes. "You have got the diary, haven't you?" Yes. "Ah, right. I'll be round for it later,"' he finished flatly.

'Fair enough. She does sound like she's got herself in a right load of trouble,' I replied, trying not to show my excitement at what he'd just told me.

If this was true, this would likely have been one of Suzy's last phone calls, perhaps even the last phone call before she'd left the office. We needed time to properly unpick and decipher all this. I couldn't do that standing on the doorstep with him in front of me.

'I mean, I can't give you much more help than that really.' He chuckled at me.

I shook his hand and told him I'd be in touch.

As we retreated, Caroline ducked behind me on the garden path and headed toward the gate. She hadn't tried to shake his hand.

'Ta ta now, bye,' he called after us. I turned and waved at him. He smiled, waved back and slowly closed the door.

39

'Do you think he's telling us the truth?' Caroline asked over her drink. I could see the bubbles jumping out of the glass atop the golden liquid. It was unusual for her to drink alcohol when we were working, but I could see this investigation, and particularly today, was taking its toll on her.

Earlier in the day we'd passed a redeveloped brownfield site that now housed a retail and leisure park. I'd retraced our steps so we could grab something to eat before we returned to our accommodation for the night; we'd not eaten all day.

The large, newly finished Italian place we were sitting in was next to a multiplex cinema complex. The place was deserted, despite it being a Friday. The area was like a ghost town; my car was one of just a handful in the whole car park. We had the restaurant completely to ourselves.

'He sounds slightly strange at times, and there's something very odd about him, but we can't dismiss it – it might be the truth. We'll have to see what we can find to corroborate it.' I sipped my own drink as a group of waiters and waitresses hovered, watching us from the corner of the restaurant. They were making me feel uncomfortable, as if we were under surveillance.

'What Clive told us about finding Suzy's chequebook and diary outside the pub on the Sunday night – that does have a ring of truth to it? There's that peculiar hole in the timeline we found for Suzy on the Sunday night, where no one seems to really know where she was for sure.'

'That does ring true, I agree – it fits perfectly with what we've already found,' I conceded.

'She should have been with Adam Leegood, but she wasn't, and we don't really know why, and—'

'And Adam Leegood *was* very strange with us when we suggested Suzy lost this stuff on the Friday,' I finished her sentence, agreeing that it all fitted like a well-made jigsaw in some respects.

'That isn't what I was going to say,' she chided.

'Oh, sorry.'

'And… that stuff about finding it under the picnic tables outside – the 1986 photos that Michael Hutchings gave us, they show two picnic benches outside the pub. I checked them while we drove here. The photos fit with the account he's giving. He couldn't possibly know that we had this information?'

'No,' I agreed. 'And his account of events is very detailed, possibly the most detailed of any of the witnesses so far.'

'Exactly. It's very different to anyone we've interviewed up until now. And, we already have some corroboration for what he's saying.'

'We do,' I mused as I sipped my drink again.

'So could Suzy have been going to the pub on that Monday afternoon to pick up her lost property?'

'It's possible, but he only said she was coming over to see him *later* – he doesn't say a time.'

'What does *later* mean?' she asked.

'You listened to him the same as I did. I don't know what it means. He's not easy to pin down with a solid answer. But maybe that is what she said. Maybe she did just say she was going to be over *later*?'

'What if *later* meant she was on her way? He said he spoke to her at about 1 p.m.?'

'Caroline, it's early days. It's a very significant statement. But we've got to work on it. Establish what the facts are.'

'He said the police knew all this…' Caroline sounded upset. 'How can they not have thought that it was all very odd?'

I shrugged. I had no explanation.

What worried me more was the level of detail that he could recall about the simple finding of a chequebook nearly thirty-three years previously. It's not even as if he had time to think about it. Two random strangers knock at your front door on a Friday evening when you're lying on the sofa with the dog. They ask you about an event which should be pretty much meaningless to you, and you suddenly remember details like it happened yesterday. How could he remember such vivid detail after all this time?

'What are we going to do?' asked Caroline.

'We've got to look at what he's said, piece by piece, and establish what we can prove or disprove.'

'How are we going to do that?' she asked, picking up her drink and taking a gulp.

'First, let's see if we can find out a bit more about him. I've got an address for his ex. Let's go and speak to her. She might tell us he's prone to making things up.'

'Where does she live?'

'Somewhere in the back of beyond. It's several hundred miles from here. She's married now and lives with her husband.'

Caroline sighed. 'And when are you planning to do that?'

'First thing in the morning. No time like the present?'

Caroline nodded as our food arrived.

Each of the waiting staff appeared to be carrying something. With no other customers to serve, they'd all joined in – a line of them placing items on our table. A plate each, knives, forks, salt, pepper, parmesan.

I tucked into my pasta. I was starving. Caroline was sitting looking at hers.

'You alright?' I asked as I finished my mouthful of food, putting down my knife and fork.

'What if he's telling us the truth? What if Clive *was* the last person Suzy spoke to before leaving the office? Does that mean she *was* on the way to see him? Does it mean she *did* go and see him?'

'One step at a time,' I counselled.

'It gives me the creeps thinking about it.'

I'd dealt with plenty of criminal investigations before; some of them had been murders and killings. Compartmentalising and processing unpleasant thoughts was something that you learn to do to protect your mental health. Caroline hadn't ever had to do this.

'Don't focus on what might have happened, on some imaginary event. We don't know what's happened. Don't let your imagination run riot. Focus on the information we now have; focus on what he's told us and where we go next. Prove or disprove. It's that simple. That's the job in front of us now.'

'He said some weird things,' she replied as she took another sip of beer.

'But every single person we've met in this investigation has said things we really didn't expect,' I reminded her. 'Anyway, are you going to eat your food before the chef comes over and tells us off?' I indicated with my eyes to the gaggle of waiters and waitresses who had now been joined by the chef from the kitchen, watching us.

Outside, the weather was dry and mild. It was a Friday night, and as the first day of the month, this would be just after payday for many people. But here we were at 8.30 p.m., the only customers in this cavernous restaurant. It was as if we'd broken a lockdown after a zombie apocalypse.

'What the hell is wrong with this place?' Caroline said with a smile.

But I could tell that the smile was wrong; false; an act. She was using barely half the facial muscles that she normally would. There were no wrinkles around her mouth or at the corners of her eyes like normal. I'd known her long enough to see these things.

'God knows where everyone else is tonight. They *are* very attentive.' I chuckled, not letting on to her that I could see how spooked she was by all of this.

40

Karen Furness had been in her mid-twenties and employed as a relief worker in the kitchen of the Prince of Wales pub when Suzy had gone missing. At that point in time she'd been together with Clive Vole for nearly a decade.

Their relationship had long since ended. According to Michael Hutchings they'd split up within months of Suzy's disappearance. Karen now lived in the countryside with her husband. After driving for what seemed like an eternity, we'd eventually located the Victorian home that they shared.

I parked my car next to a garage. Rooks circled in the overcast sky and the gravel crunched under our feet.

As I walked round to the front of the house to hunt for a main entrance, Caroline shouted at me to come back. She'd already pressed a doorbell at a side door, and a woman wearing jeans and an old fleece sweater had appeared. The woman was in her late fifties or early sixties and held a cat in her arms.

I made my way back round to the door at which Caroline was standing, but as the woman saw me approaching, she inched backward slightly.

'Hello. Are you Karen?' asked Caroline.

'I am, yes,' the woman replied.

'Hello. I'm David; I'm a writer,' I began, making the introductions. 'Sorry, I wasn't sure if this was your main door or if there was a front door around the other side we should have tried?'

I paused to gauge her reaction.

She didn't reply. Her face was expressionless, and she gave nothing away.

'I'm a writer,' I repeated, trying again to break the ice. 'I wondered if I could talk to you about the Prince of Wales pub in Putney?'

There was another pause and more silence.

'I'm sorry to catch you unawares…' I tried to put her at ease. 'I'm investigating something that may or may not have happened there, and there was some property found, of somebody that went missing, a long, long time ago.'

I made sure not to mention any names. I needed to know if Karen was aware of who we were talking about here.

'Mm-hmm,' she replied, nodding.

This was a start. She seemed to recognise what I had come here to speak to her about.

'Do you know anything about it?' I asked.

'Yes,' she replied clearly.

This was good. There was another reply in the affirmative.

'Yes. Could I come in and talk to you about it?

There was a pause.

'I'd rather not,' replied the woman in a half whisper, hunching her shoulders and gripping the cat a little tighter.

'I'm sorry?' I asked in surprise.

'I'd rather not,' she replied, louder now, a steely tone in her voice.

'You'd rather not? No?'

She shook her head at me.

'Okay…' I replied. 'This is my card.' I passed my business card to her, still trying to engage her as I did so. Perhaps she would still talk to us on her doorstep. 'I take it you know about the property that was found there?'

'Yes,' she responded, confirming once again that she knew what I was talking about.

'Yeah. What do you know about it and the circumstances of it being found?'

'I'm sorry, I don't want to discuss it,' she replied, wrinkling her nose as if there were a bad smell underneath it as she took my card.

'You don't want to talk about it?' I pushed again.

'No,' she said flatly.

'Okay… Umm…' I stumbled over my words, baffled at this stonewalling and wondering how I might overcome it. She understood what we wanted to talk to her about, yet she wouldn't answer questions about it.

'Okay. Goodbye,' she said, taking a step back from the doorway and grabbing the door handle.

'Thanks…' I said, still wondering how I might convince her to talk to us.

But it was no good.

It was too late.

'Thank you,' she responded as she shut the door in our faces.

Caroline and I stared at one another, shocked, the rooks still circling overhead, their caws breaking the silence.

Karen hadn't even enquired what our questions were about, how we'd located her, or why we'd come to this part of the country to speak with her about Suzy's lost property. It bothered me that she wasn't even curious, especially given what Clive had told us just the day before, about his phone contact with Suzy during the lunchtime she'd gone missing.

Clive's insistence that Karen 'didn't have anything to do with it' was replaying in my head as we walked back to the car. What did he mean by that? Did she know something about Suzy's lost property?

Caroline and I got back into the car. I turned on the ignition and a flock of wood pigeons which had taken refuge in a nearby tree scattered into the sky. There was sudden pandemonium in the air as rooks then chased the pigeons off.

'How bizarre…' I said.

I moved the car slowly onto the road that led back the way we'd come.

'Are we just going to leave it like that?' Caroline asked as we drove away.

'We can't make her talk. If she won't answer questions, there's nothing we can do about that,' I said as we began to pick up speed.

'Go back,' Caroline barked.

'Drive back to her house?' I asked.

'We can't just walk away. She knows something.'

'She does, but she's not going to tell us what that is.'

'We've driven for bloody hours and hours today, and we've spent years getting to this point – we can't just walk away. Let me try again. Maybe she doesn't feel comfortable talking to you; maybe I should go and talk to her on my own?' Caroline suggested.

It was a fair question. Was Karen scared of me? Had she been the victim of something in the past? Some form of domestic abuse or violence at someone's hands?

'Okay, we can give it a go,' I said, turning the car around in the gateway of a field and heading back toward the property.

I pulled up on the main road this time, away from the property, and stopped the car.

'Do *not* go into the house with her under any circumstances,' I warned, wagging my finger at Caroline. 'I want to be able to see you. We know next to nothing about this woman.'

'Okay, boss,' Caroline said, opening the car door.

'If I park here, I can see the main door in the rear-view mirror. Don't move from that spot while you talk to her, so I can see you at all times.'

'Okay, I'll be fine… I'm a big girl,' Caroline said, rolling her eyes and closing the door.

I watched as she trudged back up the road, to the door of the house. We didn't know why this woman wasn't answering questions or how she might behave when Caroline called at the door again.

My palms began to get clammy. Cold sweat gathered under my collar. I didn't like being this far away, but it was possible my presence might have been the issue. Being at the door might ruin Caroline's opportunity.

Sitting in the car, I watched Caroline in my mirrors as she rang the doorbell again. No answer. She waited for a while and tried again. No answer.

Caroline walked over and checked the garage. We'd spotted cars there when we'd arrived the first time. Perhaps the woman had popped out to the shops in the meantime.

But I guessed the vehicles must still be present because Caroline returned to the door and rang the bell again. She waited for several more minutes with no response. She then walked around the side, glancing from a distance through the windows. From where I was located, I could see the lights still on inside the house. Caroline could see signs of life too, and she was refusing to give up.

Just as Caroline returned to the door of the house again, Karen yanked it open, a grim expression on her face. She looked angry. She began waving something at Caroline in her right hand. Something grey, perhaps metallic. My heart raced.

I scrambled to get out of the car. Swinging open the car door, I began running toward them, fearing it was a knife. Karen extended her arm, and jabbed whatever was in her hand toward Caroline.

As I raced across the road, Caroline took the item from Karen's hand and placed it to her ear.

I stopped running.

It was a telephone.

Karen hadn't been brandishing a weapon at all – she'd passed a grey handset to Caroline. I watched as Caroline entered into a deep discussion with the person on the other end of the line, whilst the woman waited at the door of the house.

Had the woman called the police? I watched them from my new vantage point in the road.

After a few minutes of back and forth between them, Caroline handed the phone back to the woman, who promptly went back inside the house and slammed the door behind her.

Caroline walked back to the car.

'Jesus, what happened?' I asked as she came back into the roadway. 'I thought she had a weapon as she came out of the door then.'

'It was fine. She was pre-prepared. She said she didn't want to talk to me and handed me the phone. She'd already got her husband on the other end. He was really angry and shouted a lot, accusing me of harassing his wife whilst he was away on business. I told him it was just me on my own, and all I wanted to do was just ask her a couple of questions. He said that if I didn't leave they were going to call the police.'

'Weird,' I concluded.

'Yeah. I don't know what she's told her husband. As I was talking to him on the phone, she kept saying stuff to me like, "I'll have the phone back now. Can I have the phone back?' all the time I was still talking to him. It was almost as if she didn't want me explaining anything to him. I got the impression she hadn't really told him what we were actually there about.'

'Okay,' I sighed. I didn't know what any of it meant.

'What do we do now?' asked Caroline.

'We drive back home…' I said, starting the car and moving off. 'Well done. You tried your best.'

We needed to plan what to do next. We could use the driving time to bat some ideas about between us.

41

'Be careful!' I screamed as Caroline stood on the brakes of the car, bringing us to a halt just millimetres from the vehicle in front of us.

'Sorry,' she said nervously. 'It goes quite fast, doesn't it?'

'Yes, and it's got very good brakes, but it weighs two and a half tons, so it's best not to travel at its maximum speed capacity.' My heart was thumping in my chest.

We'd barely been on the motorway for ten minutes. Caroline was driving my new car. I'd financed myself to the hilt to purchase it for my security business after my last one had literally fallen to pieces with the miles we'd put on it looking for witnesses in Suzy's case.

I was simply too tired to tackle the drive down into the depths of the countryside this morning; I'd unexpectedly been at work most of the night again. The drive was about an hour. I'd try to get some sleep on the way there and be ready to interview another potential witness when I woke up.

'This is probably a waste of time,' Caroline said dismissively as she concentrated on the road ahead.

'You're only saying that because you don't want to drive my car. If I was driving, you'd be saying the opposite.'

Caroline didn't reply, though she'd slowed the car down considerably.

'None of the people we speak to in this investigation say what we're expecting them to say, so who knows what this man is going to say until we talk to him?' I added, hoping to give her some enthusiasm for the drive as I closed my eyes.

'He's not going to know anything, is he? He left the pub a year before any of this stuff happened.'

'He did, but he might have an insight into the staffing of the place. Perhaps even some names.'

'I need you to read something before you go to sleep – that's really why I'm here today, not to be your chauffeur,' Caroline said as I drifted off.

'When I wake up. Just drive,' I mumbled before I was cloaked in the darkness of a dream.

I didn't hear her response, if there was one.

Norman Bubbers was now eighty-one years old – but back in December 1984, aged forty-six, he'd been granted a licence by South-Western magistrates' court, (now renamed Lavender Hill), to sell alcohol from the Prince of Wales public house in Putney. He'd been engaged to marry the woman helping him run the place.

Norman had been the licensee of the pub right before Michael Hutchings. It had taken me a while to actually track him down because the court had misspelled his name. But, eventually, I'd worked out that Lavender Hill magistrates' court, who'd kindly rummaged around in their dusty cellar for me for a second day, had made a mistake. Norman was alive and well, and living an hour or so from my home.

We were trying to trace people who had worked at the Prince of Wales pub at around the time Suzy had gone missing and needed to speak to anyone that might be able to provide us with some information on the workings of the pub. But with Karen refusing to assist us, that hunt was a convoluted one; a full week's worth of research just to find someone that might have more for us than a Christian name and a description of someone's accent.

I was dragged from my slumber by a terrible grinding sound as my alloy wheels scraped against a rough stony surface.

'Bugger, sorry,' I heard Caroline say as I opened my eyes. 'This thing *is* awkward to park.'

'Are we here?' I asked, trying to get my bearings. I decided not to moan about any damage – she had driven here under duress after all.

'His flat is just up there, yeah.' Caroline pointed toward a set of concrete stairs ahead of us; they led up to a tired, old-looking building that appeared as if it had seen better days.

'I appreciate you driving, thank you; I'm shattered.'

'I can do this interview if you want?' she enquired, turning off the car's engine.

'It's fine. What was it you wanted me to read before I fell asleep?'

'This…' Caroline reached across to the back seat behind me and produced a newspaper article headlined: 'Estate Agent's Girl Kidnap Fear'. It was dated Tuesday, 29 July 1986 and taken from *The London Standard*.

I read it.

One of Miss Lamplugh's neighbours said, 'Her mother phoned me yesterday afternoon to ask if I had seen Susan… Susan is a young girl with a very good social life…'

'That neighbour calls her Susan?'

'Yep.' Caroline nodded, looking rather pleased with herself.

It was one of the oddities we'd come across while talking to Clive Vole. He'd claimed that there had been a telephone call to the Prince of Wales, around two hours *after* he'd spoken to Suzy on the day she'd gone missing. He'd described a woman on the end of the phone who'd said to him: 'Try to keep her there, while I get round there…' And he'd told us the woman had used the name 'Susan' in reference to Suzy.

I remembered reading this newspaper article during our searches at the British Library. I remembered it because it was one of the very first pieces published about Suzy's disappearance. But I hadn't remembered that one of Suzy's neighbours had used the name 'Susan', and its significance was only now clear after having interviewed Clive Vole.

'Is this corroboration that someone might have called the Prince of Wales pub looking for her, as Clive claims?'

'In one way, I suppose, yes. But for the neighbour to have done that, Suzy would have to have told her she was going there?'

'Maybe she did?' Caroline shrugged. 'Maybe Suzy did go to Putney to do some shopping or for lunch, just as Mark Gurdon thought she was doing, and then she bumped into this neighbour, and she told her she was heading to collect her lost property from the pub?'

'And the neighbour has called the Prince of Wales after Diana has asked if she knows where Suzy is?' I asked rhetorically.

Caroline nodded.

'The times don't fit; Diana didn't allegedly become involved until later in the afternoon, well after three o'clock, so this means any subsequent phone call from the neighbour to the pub would have been later than that.'

'Clive might not have the times right,' Caroline concluded.

'True. But then that would mean that Suzy was going to the pub in the period she went missing, and the neighbour knew this?'

'It would. And that might explain how the police came to know the lost property was at the pub?'

She had a point.

We had spent some time trying to establish how and why the police came to know the lost items were at the Prince of Wales. We'd found no one who seemed to know Suzy was going there. It was possible that someone at Suzy's bank had made the connection following lost and found enquiries from the pub and from Suzy regarding her mislaid chequebook. But equally, a neighbour calling the police and telling them that she'd bumped into Suzy, who in turn had told her she was going to the pub that afternoon, would offer an explanation for this.

'Do we know who this neighbour is?' I asked.

'No idea – their name's not mentioned in the article.'

'Have we got the journalist's name – the journalist who wrote that piece?'

'We have, but...'

'He's dead?' I asked before she'd finished, guessing what she was likely to say.

'Sadly.' She nodded. 'He died a couple of years back.'

'Let me go and speak to this former landlord. I'll be back. Good work, really good work,' I said, getting out of the car and leaving Caroline inside.

42

'I'm just checking I'm doing the right thing when I go fishing,' the spritely old man said, gazing at his laptop screen as I sat down opposite him.

'You go fishing, do you?' I responded as I pulled out my notepad and pen, but Norman appeared to be more interested in his online research.

I sat quietly for several moments as Norman stared at the laptop, the glow of its screen lighting him in an eerie blue colour and casting skeletal-like shadows on his face. As I waited, I wondered how many other octogenarians were as computer literate as this one. A young lady had let me into the flat and pointed me in Norman's direction before disappearing into the kitchen, leaving us alone to chat. It was one of the reasons I did some of these less formal interviews alone – one person knocking at your door and asking questions was less intrusive, less intimidating.

'What is it you want to know?' Norman asked finally, placing the laptop on the floor and giving me his full attention.

Norman Bubbers had been the licensee of the Prince of Wales from Friday, 7 December 1984 to August 1985, right before Michael Hutchings had taken over.

It was a long shot, but I'd originally traced him in the hope some of the pub staff from his tenure had carried on working with Michael Hutchings, and that perhaps Norman could remember their names.

I explained to Norman how I'd got his details and that I was trying to track down other employees of the Prince of Wales – could he remember any of their full names or contact details?

'No. I would have known Christian names, nothing else.'

'Do you hold any old records or papers that might help me?'

'No.'

'Do you have anything written down anywhere – old letters, cards?'

'No, no, no.' Norman shook his head.

Norman explained that he'd lived above the pub while he worked there, and how it had been newly refurbished at the time. He had moved in at the end of 1984, following completion of the building works and redecoration.

The Prince of Wales pub was located on a corner plot, just south of the Fulham Railway Bridge spanning the Thames. Back in the early 1900s, a billiards room had been incorporated, with a huge, glazed Victorian skylight directly above, so that players could see the table clearly. But as Britain's pub trade evolved in the 1970s and 1980s, customers became less and less interested in watching live billiards and snooker. That became the preserve of Sundays at home in front of the television, while pubs became places that were expected to serve food.

In 1983, just six miles from the Prince of Wales, Harvester broke the mould of the British pub, opening its first premises in Morden. It revolutionised what was expected of 'the Great British boozer'. The Prince of Wales' owners at that time, Imperial Inns & Taverns, wasted no time in following suit. They began to apply for planning permission to put kitchens in their own pubs to serve food, and the Prince of Wales was among the first in the chain to get a makeover.

In the eighteen months before Suzy had gone missing, her local pub had gone through a dramatic transformation. Norman explained to me that when he took the pub on, it had been newly refurbished and redecorated, now with a kitchen on the ground floor.

An open yard and pot house next to the billiard room had been converted into the kitchen, and the billiard room changed into a dining room. At the same time, a new entrance was created, the ladies toilets were moved and the floor height of the billiard room was raised. This created a 'stage' section several feet high, upon which local office workers could dine on lasagna or shepherd's pie, at tables located away from the kitchen. Outside on the pub forecourt, next to a bin store and two phone boxes, customers could choose instead to sit at picnic tables. These were separated from Upper Richmond Road by just a low picket fence.

If Clive *was* telling us the truth, then rather than opting for a soggy sandwich and in order to collect her belongings, could the pub have been where Suzy was actually going that lunchtime? What if the police had just completely overlooked it as a line of enquiry, after placing too much emphasis on the 'Mr Kipper' appointment?

My visit to see Norman had been a valuable one. It was important to understand this pub inside out, from its foundations to the tip of its chimney. I thanked Norman for his time. I'd be visiting Wandsworth Council to check what he'd told me and to see what information they held about the Prince of Wales pub.

43

'That room used to be the office, before we moved it upstairs,' Claudette said, pointing into a small room that held bottles of red wine and spirits on a steel shelving unit.

Claudette, a twenty-something French Lyonnais native with a backcombed hairdo and a stud in her nose, was our guide. She'd been working at the Prince of Wales for the past ten months but was due to leave in the next two weeks for a larger pub in the same chain in Central London.

We were nearly finished with our tour. Claudette had shown us round the entire building, finishing here in the cellar – a messy, cold and uninviting place. The weather outside was foul. But where the rest of the pub cocooned you from its assault, here in the cellar, you were partially exposed. As I listened to the heavy footsteps of pedestrians pounding over the barrel hatch on the street above, rivulets from the torrential rain dripped down between the gap in the drop doors. Here in the basement, all the glamour and grandeur from the imposing Victorian gin palace above was gone.

The pub was leased through a complex chain of arrangements from a freeholder in Westminster. The company that currently ran the pub had very kindly granted us the opportunity of a tour. I explained I was writing a book in which the pub would feature, and they'd agreed to show Caroline and I around the premises.

I was happy that neither the pub company nor Claudette, our guide today, had enquired as to whether the book was fact or fiction. It suited me not to have to explain too much to them at this stage; I didn't know where this might lead.

Prior to our visit, I'd spent an entire day at Wandsworth Council town hall, looking through everything that they had on public record about the premises. I'd learned that the history of the pub dated further back than we'd realised. There had actually been a public house called the Prince of Wales on Upper Richmond Road for nearly 150 years. In the early 1870s it had occupied a spot nearer to Wandsworth, at number seventy-six. But as Putney grew and became more affluent following the Waterloo to Richmond railway upgrade from two lines to four in 1885, and with the arrival of the London Underground at East Putney in 1889 – the flourishing shops, businesses and significant urban development all afforded better opportunities closer to Putney. So, as Queen Victoria breathed her last words just after the turn of the century, a new building was erected at 138 Upper Richmond Road, on the site where we now stood.

'It's a lot smaller down here than I thought actually,' I concluded as Claudette showed us round. The basement's dimensions didn't seem to match the voluminous proportions of the four-storey premises above us.

'Well, actually it's because there's a wall right there...' She pointed at the bricks on the northern side of the basement room. The wall was mostly concealed by cardboard boxes stacked high. 'So as of that wall – behind that – that's the space under the dining room.'

At its original premises, the Prince of Wales had hosted billiard tournaments and prize-givings for Thames River swimming races. When the new premises were built, they were constructed with a billiard room and separate saloon bar in order to continue hosting such events. The billiards room, with its special, light-giving, roof-lantern windows, was now used as the dining room, which sat on the floor above and beyond the wall we were now looking at.

'Is there nothing underneath the dining room then?' I asked, looking at what appeared to be a large inspection hatch in the wall lined with the delivery of crisps. The cellar area seemed to stop too soon.

'It's just empty…' Claudette screwed her face up.

'There's a hole there though. Why's that hole there?' Caroline pointed at the inspection hatch.

'I don't know what that's for. My pest-kill guys, they have to go in there sometimes.'

'There's mice and things?' Caroline asked.

'Yeah…' Claudette grimaced. 'And there's lots of pipes from the kitchen that's in the corner – they need to access it.'

'So the pest-control guys actually climb in there?'

'Uh-huh.'

I'd learned a bit about the evolution of the pub from Norman Bubbers and from Wandsworth Council. I'd read through the building's various planning notices and permissions over the years; how it had developed from separate saloon bars for men and women and a sports billiards room to a large open-plan pub with a kitchen and flashy dining room. The Prince of Wales would eventually morph into one of the country's first gastro pubs.

Our guided tour galvanised my view of the place. They were huge premises, with plenty of places that the transient staff left unexplored, and the basement area in particular was virtually untouched from the day it had been built.

If I was honest, in the hundreds of pubs of which I've been a customer, I'd never really thought much about the mechanics or the logistics involved in ensuring how beer arrived into my pint glass. I knew that beer was delivered in kegs and they were dropped into cellars through holes in the road by the sides of the pubs, and that there was a gas system that somehow pumped the liquid upstairs and into my glass.

As I stood in the basement, with the rain running in from the street and Claudette the manager by my side, there was little sign the basement had been touched by the building works during the 1980s and early noughties. The new kitchen, which had been added just as Norman Bubbers had moved in at the end of 1984, occupied what used to be an enclosed yard, away from the basement area.

The pub was virtually as it had been in 1986.

What if Suzy *had* gone there and never left?

44

'Hello, Clive,' I said with a smile as he opened the door.

'Hello there.' Clive Vole chose not to return the smile. He didn't look especially pleased to see us, though I couldn't say if he seemed surprised either.

'I wanted to ask you another couple of questions. Is that alright?' I asked over the dog, which was again barking at me from behind him.

'Yeah,' he responded with a slight sigh. Clive looked as if he'd lost some weight since we'd last seen him eight weeks ago. He appeared healthier, leaner. Perhaps he was just standing more upright. He seemed somehow more combative in his tone too.

'I've spoken to Karen and she says she knows about this stuff,' I added, looking to see if there was a reaction from him.

We'd been unsuccessful in identifying any new witnesses at the Prince of Wales – Zoe Hutchings, the ex-wife of Michael, the full-time landlord, was proving especially difficult to locate.

But we were finding more intel and there was enough corroboration for Clive's story about Suzy coming to the pub on the day she went missing for me to consider it our main line of enquiry. And having visited the pub, it had revealed itself as a place that remained largely unchanged since 1986. The cavernous premises contained spaces which appeared to have been untouched for some decades.

It was a very strange situation. I honestly didn't know for sure if Suzy had disappeared at the pub or not. It was of course possible she had. But, because of a lack of other witnesses, I needed some additional corroboration that Clive was telling us the truth about speaking to Suzy and her agreement to visit the pub.

In the instant after Clive's admission to us that he'd spoken to Suzy, his body language had changed. He'd placed his hand, containing his mobile phone, directly up to cover his mouth. In my eyes, it hadn't seemed deliberate. To me it appeared to be a sudden involuntary reaction. Perhaps that pointed toward this admission being a mistake on his part, and one that he wasn't happy about?

We needed a way of checking the veracity of Clive's entire account of events. His account of finding Suzy's chequebook and diary on the Sunday night, the day before she went missing, and then the subsequent phone call with Suzy and others on the day she'd disappeared was so far from what the police claimed had happened that it would be easy for them to dismiss it as fantasy.

One way we could do this was look for the consistency in Clive's account of the events in a second interview. But, just asking him to repeat what he'd said before wasn't very scientific, and probably wouldn't hold up to close scrutiny. So I'd devised an interview plan that would test the account he'd given us eight weeks previously, while at the same time increasing what is known as cognitive load during a second interview.

Cognition refers to the mental processes of the brain: thinking, knowing, remembering, judging, problem-solving. Higher-level cognitive functions include language, imagination, perception and planning.

Being interviewed on your doorstep by someone about an event from many decades ago, without warning, would be quite mentally taxing – there would be a lot of cognitive processes involved. Clive seemed to have no problem remembering the events, unlike some of the witnesses we'd interviewed.

Our meeting with Karen, while largely unsuccessful from an information-and-intelligence-gaining point of view, provided us with a way of increasing the cognitive load during a second interview with Clive. I would use our meeting with her as a way of trying to influence Clive's account, looking for changes in what he had said previously in comparison with today by making him think that his ex had spoken in detail to us about the events.

If he was lying about them, he might deny that they'd ever happened. If he was telling the truth, not too much would be changed – he might even provide further detail. It was also fair to Clive to give him a second shot. If he'd made a mistake in some of the things he'd said previously to us, now was his opportunity to set the record straight.

'I'll just put the dog in,' Clive said, turning back to the house, either ignoring what I'd just said or not hearing me.

He grabbed the barking dog and shut it inside the house. As he did so, a dark-coloured cat ran past him and into the garden, giving Caroline an evil feline stare. 'Errrgh, cat's out!' he exclaimed.

Clive beckoned me into the porch area where we'd had our last conversation. This was all going according to my plan. I wanted to recreate, as much as I could, an identical environment to what we'd had when I'd last interviewed him.

We'd arrived on a Friday evening, as we had before, with no prior warning, and at about the same sort of time. Caroline remained outside in the garden while I talked to Clive in the lean-to porch. It was all identical, only this time Clive wasn't saying he had to go and pick anyone up.

'I know you said you called the police on Monday?'

Clive hadn't actually said this. He'd said that the police had called him, but I wanted to see if he picked up on me changing the direction of the contact, again increasing the load on his mind.

'I... er... I'm not sure about the day now. You're workin' in t'pub, you're working seven days a week. One day's same as the next day...' Clive stumbled slightly but ignored my precise question.

'Just a couple of hours different on a Sunday, that was it. But what I remember, what happened is that...' Clive then launched into a script-like account of the events he'd told me eight weeks before. 'On the night time when I went for a take-away, I found chequebook and diary. Next day, I phoned the bank about ten in the morning to say I'd found a chequebook and diary. Then she phoned me to say she'd be in later for it. Then I got another phone call off a woman saying that, "Tell her you can't find it and give us a ring, so I can get down there... Keep her... Keep her talking," whatever. And then, that was about it really... And, erm... Police turned up later.'

'The thing that I'm confused about is you say the police turned up later. How did the police get the chequebook and diary? How did that come into their possession?' I'd decided to change the order of the questioning too, asking him things in a different order to how he presented them.

'They came and collected it,' he responded.

Although it was the police collection of Suzy's lost items that I'd asked about, this was right at the end of the timeline. Clive had started talking about the events chronologically from the start, the opposite end.

'Did you give the chequebook to the police? Or did Karen give it to them?' I asked, using the name of Clive's ex deliberately for a second time, hoping that it would stab at his subconscious.

'I gave them the chequebook and diary,' he responded, seemingly oblivious to what I was doing.

'So you – you physically gave that to the police? Karen didn't have any part of giving it to them?'

'No.'

'Right. Okay. How come she knows about this stuff then?'

'Sorry?' Clive looked confused.

'Karen, your ex – was she present when this happened?'

After a long pause, Clive said, 'My ex? How could...? Sorry?'

'Karen,' I pushed him again. The strategy appeared to be working.

He frowned. 'Yeah.'

Clive hadn't used Karen's name when we'd spoken to him eight weeks previously; he'd only referred to her as his 'ex', adding that he had no idea where she was.

'I've spoken to Karen,' I explained. 'How does she know about all of this? Was she present when it was happening? How does she know about it all?' I asked, smiling at him.

Clive stayed silent.

'Was she there on the Monday?' I asked again.

'No,' he said flatly, staring back at me in an odd way.

Before I could ask another question, Clive began another monologue. 'Er... well, I presume, when I phoned the bank and asked the bank to tell her, that the bank phoned her house or her workplace or something like that. That's as much as I know.'

I wasn't sure why he was repeating all this. Perhaps he'd misheard what I'd asked, or perhaps he was just using this to fill the space because my constant use of Karen's name was causing a riot in his subconscious mind.

I wasn't sure.

'So the chequebook and the diary...' I returned to the point I wanted to understand. 'The police took it from you. When did they take it from you?'

'Er, oh... Er... It was either the same day, or the day after. I cannot remember one hundred per cent. I think it was the same day. I'm sure there were, they turned up about ten o'clock. Sommat like that... you know in the evening time.'

'And did you call the police? What was the reason you called them?'

'They turned up there – didn't call the police or anything,' Clive replied.

'You didn't call the police?'

'I've nothing to do with the police,' Clive replied, laughing.

'You didn't physically call the—'

'I had nothing to do with the police. 'Bout six o'clock on that same day, I'd put the – the—' He stopped and changed tack before continuing. 'Somebody phoned up, they said they were from Chelsea police station. Had she been for the chequebook and diary? And I said no. And that was it.'

'Then they came in to get it off you?' I asked.

'Then they came to pick up the chequebook and diary. Yeah.' He nodded.

Despite the problems I was creating for him, Clive was sticking to the answers he had given us last time.

'Right. And did they take a statement off you then or not?'

'I gave them a statement, I think the following day. Somebody came to get... take a statement and everything.' Clive's sentences were beginning to get vague and woolly again.

'Right. Okay. And so they took a written statement off you then, or – or did they take a written statement off you later?'

'Uhh, pretty much straight away, I think,' Clive replied.

'My understanding was they came and took a written statement a lot later. Like a year later, or something like that?'

'Nooo, they... They were quite quick off the mark actually. I was surprised how quick they were... Coz it, er, I mean, I don't know how old actually she was when she went missing, but she certainly wasn't young. I mean, young girls that are seven or eight, maybe police involved straight away, but not twenties, whatever she was.'

'The thing is, a lot of the information I've got, it sort of indicates that Suzy might have come to the pub.' I left open *when* I was actually talking about Suzy coming to the Prince of Wales, to see how this might affect how Clive answered.

'Nah,' he whispered.

'Do you think that's possible?' I probed.

'Noooo... unfor— Noo...' Clive stuttered a little.

I stayed silent.

'As far as I know, she must have been in the pub the night before,' he said. 'So, the night when I found the cheque book and diary.' He clarified his point, reinforcing what he meant, ensuring that it couldn't be misunderstood.

Had he noticed I was playing games with him?

'Why do you think that?' I asked, wondering if he had seen her there on the Sunday evening before she disappeared.

'I mean the chequebook and diary were just outside the door. As you stepped out of the door, there were like a little area with a couple of benches on it. And the chequebook and diary was on the floor just in front, side of the benches. So

216

whether she's actually gone out, put her handbag on the bench and it fell off or whatever or…'

'Do you remember seeing her that night?' I asked.

He'd mentioned the items falling out of Suzy's handbag during our previous conversation. Who says that Suzy was carrying a bag and that the items were in there? Why does he think she was in the pub and then went outside? Could she just have been passing but paused briefly to use one of the phone boxes on the pub's forecourt to call Adam at around 10.15 p.m.?

'Sorry?'

'Did you see her that night? On the Sunday night?'

There was a pause before Clive stuttered again. 'Sss… Did I see her?'

'Yeah.'

'I wouldn't know if, er, I saw her. I mean, the pub, the Prince of Wales got a heck of a lot of people, passing trade as well as regulars. The regulars usually stood at the bar. Everybody else, it was a face. You'd served 'em. Went.'

'And she definitely didn't come in on the Monday, when she went missing, to collect her stuff?' I pressed, wondering how he'd react.

'Sorry?'

'She definitely didn't come in to collect her stuff on the Monday?' I repeated.

'I say… Monday, Tuesday, Wednesday, Thursday… It could have been any day of the week.' Clive laughed.

He hadn't answered the question I was asking.

'Well, you know she lost her stuff on the Sunday, because that's when you found it?'

'Er… could be, yeah.' Clive laughed again. 'To meeee, it makes no difference, like I said!' He smiled, seemingly pleased with his answer.

'So it was that Sunday night you found the stuff. On the Monday, Suzy goes missing. That Monday you've spoken to her on the phone. She says, "Have you got my diary?" I'm asking you – did she come over and collect it? Did she come over to collect the stuff from the pub that day?'

217

'No,' Clive stated flatly.

'Are you positive?' I asked, giving him a second chance, a get-out clause.

'Pohhh-zitive.' Clive laughed again at the end of his answer. Was he mocking me? Had he caught on to what my game plan was here?

Before I could ask another question, he blasted back, 'Coz her chequebook and diary was still on top of the power box on the stairs!' He smiled, as if this proved his point.

'Okay. It's not possible that Karen met with her or anything like that?' I asked, specifically introducing his ex-partner's name again.

There was a pause, and Clive's smile disappeared from his face. 'How do you know about Karen?'

I explained how we'd found her and that we'd been to speak with her.

'Have you been in touch with her?' he shot back. There seemed to be a flash of panic on his face.

'Yes, as I said to you earlier on, I've spoken to her…'

'Been in touch with my ex?' Clive's face reddened and his words became harder and louder. He was beginning to get angry.

This was interesting.

'Yes, I've spoken to Karen.' I reinforced the point by repeating her name.

'You can interview *her* then,' he said sharply, flicking his arm in the air, as if physically trying to shrug off his annoyance.

'I'm asking you, is it possible that Karen spoke to Suzy?'

'I've got nothing else to say. Bye!' he said with bitterness in his voice now.

'I don't understand why the change in tone? What's the problem?' It seemed unusual that he'd be so angry about me speaking to his ex.

'What's the problem?' he blustered back.

'Yeah, what's the problem?' I was surprised he hadn't asked me to leave or slammed the door on us. While he was visibly angry, he also seemed reluctant to end the encounter. I wondered if he wanted to know what she'd told me?

'I don't like my ex. Simple as that! If you've been in touch with other people, then that's great. I've told you what I want to tell you! That's it. Bye!' he said angrily.

'You don't want to say anything else?'

Clive was starting to reach boiling point – I could see it in his face, in his wild bulging eyes and menacing stare – but he stayed silent.

Was this anger over me talking to his ex about some simple lost belongings, really?

I tried again. 'Is that possible? That Suzy came to the pub and Karen met with her. Is that possible?' I asked him again.

'You can ask me as many times as you want…'

'Well…' I began.

'YOU'VE JUST—' Clive exploded. I'd made him lose his temper.

He tried to compose himself. 'You've just upset me by saying that,' he said, this time more quietly, as he tried to pull himself back from the edge.

'Why have I upset you?' I asked, not letting him off the hook.

'I DON'T KNOW WHY YOU WAS IN TOUCH WITH HER! I TOLD YOU' – he began shouting again at the top of his voice; this time he couldn't control himself, getting angrier by the second – 'SHE HAD NOTHING TO DO WITH IT!'

'I don't understand why I've upset you,' I verbally prodded him.

'I told you she had nothing to do with it.' Clive lowered his voice.

'I know you did.'

'And then you've been in touch with her.'

'I've been and spoken with her. Yes.'

'Yeah. Bye! That's it. End of story,' he replied, pointing toward the garden gate.

'She knows all about it,' I repeated.

'SHE KNOWS NOTHING ABOUT IT!' Clive began shouting again and moved to grab the door. There was a danger

219

now that he might slam that door, trapping me in the porch and resorting to violence; he seemed to be angry enough.

I'd pushed him as far as I could.

I made a hasty exit from the porch area and into the front garden, just in case he decided to do something rash. While causing a stir within him over his ex had been part of my strategy from the start, I was somewhat surprised at quite how much it had upset him.

I glanced over at Caroline. She'd sensibly retreated a few steps back from this apoplectic, bulging-eyed man, bellowing down from his front step at the top of his voice. I could tell she was scared. Her body language indicated to me that she was ready to run.

But she didn't. She stood there. More than that, over the next several minutes she helped me talk Clive down from his temper, calming him and enabling us to ask him some more questions.

Once Clive's outburst had passed, I tried again. 'So how come Karen knows about all this stuff – can you just answer that?' I asked, hoping he would keep his calm. 'I don't know why this upsets you, but can you just answer me, how does she know about it?'

'Because I've told her about it. Everything...' Clive sighed and paused. 'The night I went out for the Chinese, it were a takeaway, a Chinese. I come back. Put the chequebook and diary on the bar. And then went to the takeaway. So if she had a look at 'um as well. See if there's any name and address in it. We didn't talk and say, "I've had a phone call off so and so, telling her to keep, keep her here while they could get down to the pub," etcetera.'

'Right...'

'We seem to be going round in circles here.' Clive laughed, his temper now gone.

He was right, we were. But Clive's story had remained remarkably consistent, even with the cognitive loading I'd designed, and despite his loss of temper, there was a high level of consistency. There was even some extra detail added – it was now a Chinese takeaway, and not just a takeaway. And the explanation about why his ex knew about the lost property was plausible.

But what was most interesting was his last sentence: 'We didn't talk and say, "I've had a phone call off so and so, telling her to keep, keep her here while they could get down to the pub," etcetera…'

I decided that enough was enough. We'd tested what we needed to test; it was time to retreat and consider what to do next.

45

'If I was going to hide a body in this pub, that's where I'd put it…' Ben pointed up toward a small opening in the wall on the other side of the cellar, the hatch that Caroline and I had seen on our last visit here.

Fortunately Ben hadn't baulked at my question. The pub's leaseholders, Food & Fuel, were being supremely helpful with all of our enquiries here; I really couldn't have asked for more. They'd allowed us to come back for a second look around.

With Clive Vole so adamant about his version of events, and apparently telling me the truth about a woman calling the pub looking for 'Susan', we had to seriously consider the possibility that Suzy had come to the Prince of Wales pub the afternoon she'd gone missing, even if Clive hadn't seen her.

I'd spoken once again to Michael Hutchings, the pub's full-time landlord in 1986, and asked if he'd experienced any problems with pests in the cellar, with rats and mice, as Claudette had mentioned.

While Michael didn't remember experiencing these, he said he had had a problem with flies. He said it was a constant ongoing issue, and something that every pub suffered from. Michael described them as mostly being bar flies and midges that were attracted to the empty ginger-ale, orange, and pineapple-juice bottles. But as we discussed them, and what they looked like, he also mentioned that there had been some rare problems with blowflies in the cellar.

Blowflies, more commonly known as bluebottles, feed on a variety of materials as adults. But their larvae are scavengers and live on the carcasses of dead animals, feeding on decaying flesh. Within minutes of a human dying, blowflies can arrive on the scene. The sudden appearance of dozens of blowflies in a building, such as Michael had described, was a signal that there was likely to be a dead rodent, bird or other animal in a wall, ceiling, attic or crawl space.

I couldn't say for certain that Suzy was here at the pub, but there now seemed a very plausible, strong line of enquiry, with mounting evidence, that she might have come here the afternoon she'd gone missing.

Might something awful have happened in the pub when she arrived? Was it possible that somehow, by accident or design, she had met her end here, never leaving the building again? Who was responsible for her death, or for covering it up? I didn't know.

So we were back, standing in the damp cellar of the Prince of Wales pub in Putney.

Just as the last time, it was a cold and very wet day outside.

Ben was the new manager; Claudette, the ultra-cool French girl, had moved on, and Ben was back at the Prince of Wales for another stint, having worked there previously. He'd probably assumed that I was talking about a fictional yarn when I'd asked him upstairs, a few moments ago, where he'd hide a body in his pub if he had to. But here he was pointing at the entrance to what looked like a secret tunnel.

'Can I go and look in there?'

'Sure, if you can get to it...' Ben looked at the piles of plates, cups, pots, pans, suitcases, boxes and other property piled all around the entrance to the hatch in the wall, obscuring any path to it. 'We've been having a bit of a clear-out.'

I gingerly stepped over the mass of property and toward the hole in the wall, slowly surveying for space on the floor for my next step as I moved, where I could.

At first glance, the hatch in the wall appeared nothing more than an opening about a metre up from the cellar floor. A fairly large concrete slab served as a step up to look inside. The hole, about two or three feet square, provided access to the underside of the suspended wooden floor of the dining room on the ground floor above; it looked like an inspection hatch.

The Victorians and Edwardians were prolific builders and largely used what were known as suspended timber floors, alongside rudimentary solid floors in hard-wearing areas such as kitchens and hallways.

I crawled the short distance on my hands and knees to an opening in the sleeper wall, used to feed water pipes and electrical wire through. The opening was smaller than the hole in the cellar wall but still big enough to crawl into. As I peered into the hole, I was predictably met with total darkness and an eerie silence, though my movement had caused years of dust to fill the blackness in front of me and I could taste its gritty staleness in my mouth.

I began to wheeze and cough as I kneeled there, scrabbling around in my pockets for my phone to use as a torch. When I turned it on and pointed it into the darkness, the space was much bigger than I had expected. This secret unused area under the dining-room floor was as vast as the rest of the pub's working cellar, only not as high. I struggled to make sense of the shapes and figures quickly looming out of the darkness and then suddenly slipping back into it as I moved the phone's beam around the cavernous space.

My visit to Wandsworth Council had revealed there had been some small changes at the pub over the years. The fencing and signage were now different, the bin store and phone boxes had eventually been removed from the forecourt, and there had been some cosmetic redecoration and rewiring completed in 2007. But there had been little actual building work carried out on the place since 1984, when the extensive remodelling of the ground floor was completed and Norman Bubbers took over.

So as I waited for the dust to settle and my wheezing to stop, I knew as I surveyed the darkness with the torch that I was looking into a space, untouched, underneath the dining-room floor, almost exactly as it had been in 1986.

'You can get right round the sewers from in there,' Ben piped up from the cellar behind me.

'Really?' I coughed.

'Yeah, it's off to your left.'

'So you wouldn't notice any foul smells coming from in here either?' I asked as my torch fixed on what appeared to be a pile of rubbish.

'You'd think it was the sewers, I guess,' Ben mused from behind me.

The ground underneath the billiard room was mostly flat, giving about three feet of headroom to the floorboards above. There was some red fabric underneath an old wooden board directly in front of me, but off to the left and on the far side of where I could see, there was a strange mound of rubbish. Some of it was rubble, probably from building work in 1984, but there was also what appeared to be detritus from the cellar.

On top of the mound, I could see a large plastic paint tub filled with brown bottles and at least one beer can.

Why was there cellar rubbish in this void, in this total darkness, and why was it all piled in one particular spot?

'Ben, do you mind if I take some photographs in here for my records?' I called out from under the floor.

'No problem,' he shouted back.

46

Sitting in the King's Café in the British Library, the people at the next table were discussing Geoffrey Chaucer, and what a joy his work was to read in eleventh-century Middle English. It felt like we were inside a beehive, the humming of voices around us interspersed with the sound of heels on stone as someone walked past.

Not much to look at from the outside, the beauty of the library at Kings Cross is all internal and the café has one of the most dramatic backdrops on the globe – a six-storey, smoked-glass-and-bronze tower full of books. The centrepiece of the library, it holds over 75,000 leather-bound books, volumes, pamphlets, manuscripts and maps collected by King George III between 1760 and 1820. Works in the collection date from the mid-fourteenth century, Chaucer's poems among them, along with countless other of the rarest books in the world. It's one of the best-kept secrets in London.

Sitting opposite me, Caroline cradled a cup of hot chocolate in her hands. She'd been researching the Met's sudden decision at Christmas 1999 to commission a review into Suzy's case. The review became the trigger for the consequent rein-vestigation of the case that took place from 2000 to 2002. This reinvestigation had culminated in the police naming John Cannan as the prime suspect in Suzy's murder.

It was somewhat baffling to us why the police had named Cannan at all, let alone decide to publicly pronounce that he was their 'prime suspect'. After spending several years investigating the case, we'd not come across a single shred of evidence that pointed in his direction. To me, there seemed to be nothing more than a very thin circumstantial case against him, supported by a mountain of innuendo in the media. I'd concluded that if we were to stand any chance of understanding it, we would need to get to the bottom of what had reignited the police activity at the end of 1999.

We were now so far *left field* of the police's own narrative on what had happened to Suzy, so far removed from their insistence that Cannan was *the chief suspect* in the case, that the police's obsession with him wasn't something we could simply ignore.

Just how on earth was he connected to the case if we hadn't found a shred of evidence?

'How did you get on?' I asked.

Caroline had been at the library all day, sifting through newspapers, books and media footage stored there.

'Well, I can say with absolute certainty that the precursor to the reinvestigation was the information given to Diana Lamplugh from the anonymous source in November 1999. That's what kicks everything off again, just before the turn of the millennium.'

'Okay,' I replied, sipping a cup of tea as she spoke. I'd been working with a security client all day while Caroline had been busy at the library.

'The police have never really talked publicly about the specifics of that information, or where it came from, but Diana does, to some extent. On 4 December 1999, she's all over the media saying that she's come into possession of some new, important information on Suzy's case. She claimed that the information had come from the prison education system.'

'Okay, go on…' I said, eyeing the lemon drizzle cake in front of me, happy that Caroline was doing the talking.

'Now, what she also says on the fourth is actually the key to deciphering who that secret, anonymous source is,' Caroline said intriguingly. 'One of the things Diana says is that she hasn't heard anything from the police regarding the new information, despite having passed it to them a fortnight ago.'

'Okay…' I encouraged, putting down my tea and tucking into the rather excellent lemon drizzle cake that the British Library served.

'Graham McGredy-Hunt – you remember we interviewed him about his book, *Searching for Suzy*, published in 2011?'

'The guy who kept the ferrets in his house in Gloucestershire.'

Caroline and I had travelled to interview McGredy-Hunt at his home. He lived in a tumbledown, eighteenth-century thatched cottage located halfway between Gloucester and Worcester. It was perched on a busy A-road about twelve miles from the site of the former Norton Barracks. The house was falling apart at the seams and needed a great deal of money spent on it, but he had long since retired and appeared to spend more time looking after his menagerie of animals than he did on his DIY.

'Him, yeah. We know that he contacted the Suzy Lamplugh Trust about the information he had in November 1999. Remember he said that he'd badgered the trust for over a week with constant phone calls until eventually he got to speak to Diana on 15 November?'

'I do remember,' I agreed.

'Well, he said that during that phone call, he shared his theory with Diana about who he thought had killed Suzy and where he thought Suzy's body was concealed. Straight after that, he forwarded on a written synopsis in the post to her.'

'That's quite close to when Diana is saying she got the anonymous information from the prison education system…'

'Well,' replied Caroline, 'he *is* the anonymous secret source and he's got the letters to prove it.'

Caroline explained that McGredy-Hunt held a letter from Diana dated 18 November 1999, thanking him for sending on his thesis to her, and in that letter, Diana explained that she'd passed *this* thesis to the police.

Today, Caroline had discovered that the police themselves had confirmed they'd received some written information from Diana Lamplugh on 20 November 1999, two days after Diana had written to McGredy-Hunt. And Caroline had now seen the official letters from the police to McGredy-Hunt, remind-ing him that he had agreed in their meeting not to go to the press.

'Excellent work. So we can categorically prove that the anonymous source who kickstarted the police reinvestigation in 2000 was Graham McGredy-Hunt?' I responded.

'We can,' Caroline replied, though the smile and trium-phant look was now disappearing from her face, 'but I know you're not going to tell me that this is good news, are you?'

She could read the expression on my face.

'You've done a good job. Please don't misunderstand me, you have. But it's not good news, no; it's not good news at all,' I said flatly.

Back in the first week of December 1999, the media had been all over this exciting news story, which told of an anon-ymous source from the prison education system who had corresponded with Diana Lamplugh by letter and phone. The source had suggested a general site of burial, although one which had been presented in the press on numerous previous occasions.

The problem was we knew exactly what McGredy-Hunt's secret information was and how it had been taken out of context. Diana Lamplugh had completely misled much of the press by weaponizing the info she'd received – using it to reopen the case and implicate John Cannan.

47

'It's rather difficult for us to move forward with this I'd say?'
Caroline asked.

I stayed silent.

Having interviewed McGredy-Hunt at length, Caroline
and I both knew the complete content of the information he'd
passed to Diana, the same information that she'd subsequently
passed to the police. And we knew this information was next
to worthless from an intelligence or evidential perspective.
But Diana had allowed the press to believe something entirely different, that McGredy-Hunt's thesis was somehow a step
forward in her quest to find Suzy, and that it somehow dovetailed into old rumours that the police had already considered.

The police had not taken a statement from McGredy-Hunt.
Just like Diana, they'd wanted to treat him as an anonymous
source of intelligence. And given the content of his thesis, it
could be argued that a formal written statement wasn't necessary. But the lack of one would mean that, other than the two
police officers who'd spoken to him, and besides a very small
group of others, few would ever understand what he'd actually said to Diana; few would actually know the content of
his thesis. This, of course, meant that Diana Lamplugh could
allow the press to believe what she wanted.

Had it not been for the impeccable records McGredy-Hunt
had kept – copies of letters from the police, from Diana,
details of phone calls – we could not have unmasked him as
the source of the thesis. Alas we had. But now it wasn't just
the weaponisation of the press by Diana that was troubling

me. Now that we knew *he* was the anonymous source, some of the official letters that McGredy-Hunt had received from the police troubled me as much as knowing that Diana had misled the press.

To anyone looking backward at the case now, as we were, the letters from the police, thanking McGredy-Hunt for agreeing not to speak to the press, were hard not to interpret as a deliberate attempt to cover up and play along with Diana in her deliberate attempt to weaponise the press against John Cannan. Indeed it looked positively complicit from that position.

Following Cannan's conviction for the murder of Shirley Banks, various lurid and salacious newspaper stories were published focusing on a woman called Gilly Paige, an ice dancer from Birmingham and a former girlfriend of Cannan.

Gilly had had a sexual relationship with Cannan in the summer of 1987, just before he was arrested. Like many of Cannan's sexual relationships at the time, there was nothing untoward or particularly unusual about his relationship with Gilly. She'd been interviewed extensively by the police at the time of his arrest, and she'd provided nothing of any real evidential value.

But following Cannan's conviction in 1989, newspaper stories began to suggest that Gilly was in receipt of rather more information than she had shared with the police, particularly with regard to what Cannan knew about Suzy Lamplugh.

Two years later, in 1991, on the fifth anniversary of Suzy's disappearance, the press once again suggested that Cannan had revealed lurid details to Gilly about how and where Suzy might have been raped and killed. The media alleged that this communication between the two had happened during a drive through the West Midlands in 1987, a year after Suzy's disappearance, when they had visited a notorious 'lovers' lane spot' at the disused Norton Brickworks, near to the former Norton Barracks and close to where McGredy-Hunt lived.

None of these very specific allegations were to be found in Gilly's original police statement.

It's not entirely clear whether Gilly sold these lurid tales to the media, or whether the information was attributed to her dishonestly by persons unknown or the media itself. But it was here, from the newspapers, the idea that Suzy might be buried at Norton Barracks began.

Of course, in 1991, the allegations in the newspaper caused quite a stir, re-emerging as they did on the fifth anniversary of Suzy's disappearance. As a direct result of these wild stories, the police were forced to establish what the facts actually were.

This fell to Det. Supt Brian Edwards of the Met, the man who, by 1991, was the officer in charge of Suzy's case. Gilly Paige was tracked down and the pair spoke at length on the phone about what was being claimed in the press. During the call, Gilly retracted everything in the articles, saying that none of it had ever happened. She specifically quashed all suggestions and innuendo that Cannan had ever confessed to raping and murdering Suzy Lamplugh.

Scotland Yard moved immediately to stop the rumours from spreading further, releasing a statement to the press denying that there was any evidence linking Cannan to Suzy's disappearance, a stance they had maintained ever since the media had first tried to link Cannan to Suzy's case.

On Gilly Paige's dealings with them in 1991, the police announced in a statement: 'She has not repeated some of the statements attributed to her by the media and she stands by the statement she made to Avon and Somerset Police some considerable time ago.'

Publicly, and following the police intervention, Gilly firmly denied that Cannan had ever confessed to her that he was responsible for Suzy's disappearance, saying that she was not prepared to discuss the circumstances surrounding it and that she had told the police all she knew at the time.

With regards to the former Norton Barracks as a possible burial site, the police included in their official statement that there was 'clearly insufficient evidence'. Edwards confirmed that although detectives had visited the site, there was never any suggestion that Suzy had been concealed there. With such vague and imprecise information, the police stated they had considered it unworthy of further investigation.

The matter was dropped, and nothing more was said about Cannan or Norton Barracks – at least not until 1999, when Diana Lamplugh placed the stories of the anonymous 'prison education system' source in the newspapers and the same gossip began to do the rounds all over again.

Even the idea that the information had come from the 'prison education system' was in itself a twisting of the truth. As a freelance industrial trainer with a background in electronic engineering, Graham McGredy-Hunt had spent time during the summer of 1999 running evening classes for prospective prison staff at the Prison Service College on how to maintain the hydraulically operated gates, how to run the prison control systems and closed-circuit TV systems. He could be loosely classed as part of the prison education system, but only just. He certainly had nothing to do with the prisoners, which was the implication circulating across much of the media as a result of what Diana was saying.

But the worst thing about knowing McGredy-Hunt was the anonymous source who had rekindled the urban myth that Suzy was buried at Norton Barracks was that he hadn't *ever* suggested it was Cannan that had killed Suzy or put her there. In fact, at the point McGredy-Hunt had spoken to Diana Lamplugh, he didn't even know who Cannan was.

On our visit to meet McGredy-Hunt and his free-running house ferrets, we'd discovered that he was somewhat of a local obsessive regarding the infamous West family of Cromwell Street. It was McGredy-Hunt's fanatical belief that Suzy's killers were Fred West and his younger brother John, who'd both lived in Gloucestershire, just twenty miles from McGredy-Hunt's cottage. According to McGredy-Hunt, Suzy had chosen to write the fish-related name 'Kipper' in her work diary because John West shared his name with a brand of tinned tuna.

He'd explained to us that the 'anonymous information' he'd passed to Diana Lamplugh in November 1999 wasn't exactly new either. It all stemmed from an incident that had taken place in October 1986, though he'd done nothing with it until 1999.

McGredy-Hunt told us that one night in October 1986, he'd picked up a hitchhiker at an M5 service station. During a conversation, the hitchhiker – for whom he had no name or contact details – said he'd heard a rumour that a builder from Gloucester had killed 'a missing woman from London' and that this builder had then buried her in a make-shift grave at Norton Barracks in Worcestershire.

Although her name was never mentioned, McGredy-Hunt concluded that the missing woman to whom the rumour referred must have been Suzy Lamplugh.

He chose not to inform the police about the information. In fact, he told no one.

Several years later, in 1992, when Fred West was arrested, and the horrors of his Cromwell Street home were revealed, McGredy-Hunt made the connection to Fred West and the story the hitchhiker had given him, because Fred West was a builder. But again, in 1992, McGredy-Hunt decided not to contact the police. He did, however, begin making his own enquiries locally.

After the Ministry of Defence sold Norton Barracks, McGredy-Hunt said he'd heard it had needed remedial building work to make it safe, and that serial killer Fred West had possibly once been a building contractor working there – all reinforcing the idea to him that Fred and John West were responsible for Suzy's murder.

But even then, McGredy-Hunt kept this all to himself, until he told it to Diana Lamplugh on the phone in late 1999, nearly fourteen years after his alleged meeting with the hitchhiker.

'I can see you're disappointed.' Caroline smiled across at me as I tried to reconcile what we'd just discovered.

'Only because that's *not* how murder investigations should be run. What if the family of every murder victim got to direct their own police investigation, deciding who was and who wasn't to be investigated? It would be chaos!' I was still struggling to believe it.

Diana Lamplugh had repeatedly pushed the idea that John Cannan was *the* suspect in Suzy's disappearance. It was Diana's unrelenting obsession that he *was* Suzy's killer. After all, when the newspapers began linking Shirley Banks' disappearance to that of Suzy's, and then Cannan to it, it was on Diana's insistence that the Met sent officers to investigate it, not because there was any evidence of any linkages.

The police, for their part, had interviewed Cannan several times between 1987 and 1990 about Suzy, all at Diana's behest, and again not because there was any evidence. He had denied any involvement in the case every single time the police spoke to him. And in support of his denials, they found no evidence to link him to the case either.

But neither Diana Lamplugh nor the media thought that this was sufficient. They simply were not satisfied that there was no evidence, and his denials only made it worse. In their eyes, he simply *had* to have known Suzy, and there was constant pressure for there to be further investigative work to prove it. Diana ensured this, of course, by publicly linking him to Suzy's disappearance whenever she could, and the myth was reinforced and continued in the press, the media happy to sell papers off the back of it.

'It's pretty shocking, to be honest,' I added.

'Well, if you thought that was iffy, it gets worse. I've got some more very bad news for you,' Caroline said, shaking her head.

48

'What? That can't be true. It *can't* be,' I exclaimed.

'It is. I've double-checked it – twice.' Caroline slid a diagram of a family tree across the table to me. 'There is an irrefutable link between Diana Lamplugh and John Cannan.'

I studied the family tree Caroline had drawn.

'You're saying that Diana's legal counsel is related to John Cannan's married lover?' I asked.

'Yes, it's unbelievable,' Caroline said, not looking up from her notes. 'I only came across it by chance when I was going through the court reporting on the Shirley Banks murder trial. One of the reporters mentioned that Annabel Rose, John Cannan's girlfriend and solicitor, who testified in his murder trial, and whom he was in a bitter dispute with, was related to the eminent solicitor Sir David Napley.'

'The same David Napley who was giving Paul and Diana advice on how to keep Suzy's case open? Wow!' was all I could think of saying.

'I didn't believe it myself until I double-checked it,' Caroline continued as I tried to understand how no one had ever seen this link before.

Sir David Napley, the founder of Kingsley Napley Solicitors was an eminent defence solicitor of the 1970s and 1980s. He was perhaps best known, at the time, for his defence of politicians, celebrities and minor royals, all of which made him something of a minor celebrity himself. But more recently, there had been questions about his ethical conduct after it was revealed he had lobbied the then director of public prosecutions, in person, to ensure a paedophile, Sir Peter Hayman, escaped prosecution in 1978.

Sir Peter Hayman, once a distinguished British diplomat and intelligence operative came to the notice of police after a bag full of child-abuse images and obscene diary entries involving sex with children was found on a London bus in March 1978. A few weeks later, a second bag containing more of the same material was found in St James's Park by an officer of the Royal Parks Police. As police began their investigation and searched a flat Hayman was using, they found he was a member of the now infamous Paedophile Information Exchange. David Napley intervened, negotiating directly with the Director of Public Prosecutions, and literally bypassed any police investigation. The police were ordered to issue a caution for the matter.

But there appeared to be something darker in Napley's involvement with Hayman. In 1981, when Hayman was named in Parliament as a paedophile, Napley appeared to be involved in helping to manage Hayman's reputation – criticising those who had named him; expressing opinion on the conventions of Parliament. It seemed to go much further than mere legal advice.

David Napley was knighted for his role with the Law Society, somewhere he likely came into contact with the likes of the Director of Public Prosecutions and formed friendships. During the seventies he is also thought to have become acquainted with Paul Lamplugh. And, perhaps rather oddly, it was to Sir David Napley that Paul and Diana Lamplugh turned for legal advice following Suzy's disappearance.

'It was Napley who the Lamplughs talked to about using private detectives, to bolster and comb through the police investigation in the first days of Suzy's disappearance, if I remember rightly?' I asked.

Caroline nodded.

During our research, we'd discovered that there had been a lunchtime meeting in Soho on Wednesday, 30 July 1986, between the Lamplughs and Napley. There, they'd discussed the possibility of engaging a private detective to shadow the police investigation. This documented meeting was the reason we knew who Sir David Napley was.

The suggestion that the Lamplughs needed legal advice, and that they'd discussed using a private detective, was an unconventional event, especially so early in the police investigation. Caroline and I had thought Napley a strange addition but benign. Yet now, with his direct familial connection to John Cannan's murder trial, Napley's involvement in Suzy's case appeared to be much more malignant, perhaps even aggressively invasive?

49

'It's just not normal for the mother of a murder victim to be planting stories about suspects in the media.'

'No,' Caroline agreed.

'But when you find out that the mother's solicitor is linked to a dispute with the suspect she's planting stories about, that a member of *his* family had a failed relationship with the suspect and then testifies in his murder case – a trial which ultimately culminated in the suspect ending up behind bars…' I was talking to myself mostly.

Caroline didn't need to hear any of this – she understood what an outrage this all was.

John Cannan and Annabel Rose allegedly first met when he'd asked her to act as his solicitor in a legal bid to gain access to his estranged daughter following his divorce. The meetings had taken place while Cannan was a serving prisoner in HMP Horfield (now HMP Bristol) in 1983 and part way through his sentence for a rape committed in 1981.

After leaving Wormwood Scrubs in 1986, there was said to have been a chance meeting between the two, again in Bristol. After this, Cannan embarked on a sexual relationship with married Annabel, becoming so infatuated with her that he then moved to Bristol simply to be close to her. He would later describe her as the biggest thing to happen in his life.

It wasn't clear exactly what had gone wrong between them, but by the end of summer 1987, something had indeed gone awry. Cannan had hired a private detective to look into Annabel's life, to establish information about her parents, and he had begun making official complaints about her professional and ethical conduct as a solicitor. It led to Annabel having to confess the adulterous affair to her husband and resigning from her law firm.

It wasn't, therefore, that Cannan had just appeared from nowhere when he was arrested for the Shirley Banks murder. For several weeks leading up to Banks' disappearance, he had been a thorn in Annabel's side.

Was Sir David Napley aware of all of this going on in the background, well before Banks disappeared? After all, as the former head of the Law Society, one would expect Annabel Rose to have sought Napley's advice about the complaints and the ethical problems created by her adulterous and unprofessional affair with Cannan?

After becoming aware of Cannan, his criminal history and his proximity to Suzy at the time of his release from prison, was it Sir David Napley who had deliberately planted the idea in Diana Lamplugh's head that Cannan was Suzy's killer?

Even at Cannan's trial for the murder of Shirley Banks, things seemed slightly odd. There were two key pieces of evidence which linked Cannan to Banks. He had possession of her car, but arguably the most damaging was that Banks' thumbprint was found on intel inside his home. Despite Cannan saying he'd never met this woman, her fingerprint was discovered on the private eye's dossier into Annabel Rose and her parents.

Something seemed very amiss.

'Maybe we'll need to specifically ask Det. Supt Shaun Sawyer about John Cannan? About the circumstances of his Lamplugh reinvestigation, and why the police named him as their one and only suspect in 2002? Maybe we *are* missing something?' asked Caroline.

'Shaun Sawyer's no longer a detective superintendent; he's a chief constable, and I'm not sure we'd get that sort of interview with the serving chief constable of Devon and Cornwall Police,' I said, laughing.

Caroline checked her notes. 'Someone else then?'

Given all of these very bizarre occurrences and coincidences, it was imperative we found someone.

50

The sun was shining, the sky was blue and the traffic on the motorway seemed remarkably light as Caroline and I headed out on another very long car journey.

I'd managed to contact Albert Clyne, and he'd kindly agreed to talk to us about John Cannan and the CPS refusal to prosecute him. Albert was a former senior member of the reinvestigation team and had been one of Det. Supt Shaun Sawyer's men.

Now in his sixties, former officer Albert Clyne had long since retired from the Met. He had become acquainted with Suzy's case in 2000, when it became known as Operation Phoebus, after Diana had forced the police to reopen the investigation by misusing McGredy-Hunt's intelligence about Fred and John West. Albert was a leading proponent of John Cannan's involvement in Suzy's disappearance.

'On the way to meet Albert, you can tell me about what you found in the photographs you took under the Prince of Wales dining-room floor – as long as it isn't top secret,' Caroline teased me from the passenger seat as we glided down the motorway in the sun.

'It's not a secret. But…' I hesitated. 'Well, I've turned into a bit of an anorak about the evolution of the Guinness harp logo.'

'What?'

'The Guinness family adopted the harp symbol as the trade-mark for their brewery. The harp, which serves as the central emblem of Guinness, is based on a famous fourteenth-century

Irish harp known as the "O'Neill" or "Brian Boru" harp, which is now preserved in the library of Trinity College, Dublin,' I explained, sounding exactly like a Guinness anorak.

'That's all very interesting, but what on earth does it have to do with the photographs you took?'

'Under the dining-room floor there's a very odd-shaped pile of rubbish. I would expect rubbish to be scattered evenly. But this mound is all in one place. I wanted to know how old this pile of rubbish might be. Was it there at the time Suzy went missing, or is it more recent?'

Caroline stayed quiet. I could sense her trying not to take the mickey out of me as I drove.

'This rubbish pile is made up of all sorts of things – building rubble, paint cans and pieces of wood. But one of the items you can see among this odd-shaped mound is a Harp Lager can. You remember the slogan – "Harp stays sharp until the bottom of the glass"?'

Caroline started laughing. 'I do remember it. They still sell Harp Lager?'

'They do, but not in the type of can that's in the pile of rubbish under the floor of the pub. The design of that particular Harp logo, and colours on that particular can, mean that it's been under the floor since the 1980s. And what's more, it was never sold in the pub, because Harp is a Guinness product, and Imperial Inns & Taverns didn't sell it in their pubs…'

'How do you know that?'

'Because I spoke to Michael Hutchings about it, and he said his pub never sold Harp on draft, and they certainly never sold it in tin cans.'

Caroline shrugged. 'So what does this all mean?'

'So we can date this pile of rubbish, or at least one of the items in it, to around the time Suzy went missing.'

During 1984, when the kitchens had been installed at the pub and the billiard room converted to a dining room, the raised 'stage' section installed for diners had created a cavernous void consisting of several thousand cubic feet of empty space underneath. But in good old British navvy style, the builders had emptied rubble, rubbish and refuse from the building works into the void before sealing it with floorboards and finishing it with ceramic tiles on top. The Harp can was among the rubbish put underneath the floor.

In 2007, during a purely cosmetic makeover, the stage area had been lowered from above, and the floor put back to its original height, before being tiled over again. But the pile of rubbish remained untouched beneath the floor; the now vintage Harp can and the odd-shaped pile of rubbish left undisturbed.

'So you're saying that we need to look underneath that pile of rubbish because it's about the right age and it's been undisturbed since the 1980s?'

'I'm saying it's a very solid, viable line of enquiry considering we have evidence that Suzy might have been going to the pub the afternoon she went missing, yes. When we consider that there was a huge space under that floor in 1986, that it was easily accessed, that Michael had problems with blow-flies down there on a couple of occasions, and that there's an odd-shaped pile of rubbish and the right vintage of Harp can in there, one that wasn't sold at the pub – it makes me very suspicious of what's underneath.'

'I quite like your anorak-ness.'

'I spent a whole weekend learning this stuff.'

'It seems to have been worth it,' she replied, smiling. 'Can't we just climb in there and search through this eighties mound of rubbish?'

'We could, if the pub let us, but I have reservations…'

'Why?'

'Let's find out what Albert Clyne has to say about John Cannan first.'

51

'It's a big story and very complicated, lots of twists and turns. I'm actually not sure you're going to get it all covered today, to be fair,' Albert Clyne said as he looked over my shoulder, squinting into the harbour behind me.

The afternoon sunlight reflected off the glassy waves, casting dazzling flashes of light like sparkling diamonds onto his face.

Albert had told me that this restaurant had a great view, and he wasn't wrong – it did, although he'd positioned himself so he faced it and I got to stare at the other diners sitting inside the glass extension.

After an all-day drive, Caroline and I had finally made it to the refurbished Victorian pier where Albert had suggested we meet. The blue skies and fabulous coastal scenery had made for a pleasant journey, so I wasn't overly bothered about looking at the view. I just hoped Albert was a man who could actually tell us exactly what was what.

I'd seen Albert's gangly frame approaching from the town, immaculately dressed in a pair of beige chinos and a blue shirt. We'd agreed to shout him lunch and he'd wasted no time with banter or repartee before sitting down. Instead, he'd ordered a drink then began to explain his thoughts.

With the sun's glitter from the waves on his face and white mop of hair, his angular features made him look a lot older than his years.

'If you're going to do anything on John Cannan, you've got to start with his offending history. He started off, which is typical for a sex offender, with stealing underwear from clothes lines and indecent assaults as a minor, half of them I imagine he got away with, probably schoolkids and what have you. And then he progressed to stalking women, kidnapping them, sexually assaulting them, raping them, to murder...'

Caroline grabbed a pen, taking copious notes as Albert rattled off his thoughts.

The smell of the sea and the sound of the herring gulls squabbling pier side behind me felt incongruous alongside Albert's monologue.

'Mummy's boy, I think,' he carried on. 'I think he was definitely a mummy's boy, went to private school, his parents were quite well-to-do, and he was a big disappointment to them. Apart from the offences, he's one of these people who just couldn't knuckle down, or couldn't get a decent job...'

Albert explained that, in the months before Suzy's disappearance, Cannan was on day release from a hostel at Wormwood Scrubs prison. According to Albert, Cannan had purchased a red Ford Sierra or Cortina with another member of the prison hostel, for them to use as transport during the six-month period they were on day release – this being the six-month period that had led up to Suzy's disappearance.

'And that red car, we actually seized that car. We found it after many years and forensicated it,' Albert said.

Out of the corner of my eye, I could see Caroline's ears prick up at the mention of forensics.

'But, you know,' Albert continued, 'apart from saying Cannan had been in the car, there was nothing else...'

'Oh. Okay. So you didn't find any DNA from Suzy in it, nothing like that?' I asked.

'No. No.' Albert shook his head.

So the car the police knew Cannan was using in the months that led up to Suzy's disappearance contained no evidence of her presence in it?

Albert agreed. He explained that in fact there was *no* forensic evidence worthy of any mention at all in the entire case. It had been like that since 1986 when Suzy disappeared, and their reinvestigation in 2000 had failed to find anything of significance.

'There's been all sorts of people who've had a go at this case since then, and none of them have ever contacted me, which I find outrageous,' Albert continued as the herring gulls quietened down slightly.

I wondered if Albert was referring to the police's most recent digs.

Albert explained to us that the reinvestigation team had considered searching the garden themselves back in 2002, though they had decided it was unlikely that Cannan would have transported Suzy's body 125 miles to his mother's home in Sutton Coldfield.

He opined that the dig was in some way linked to the finding of Police VHS cassettes of Cannan's police interviews, which were made public by *The Sun* newspaper shortly after the dig started. *The Sun* claimed that the tapes had been found in a skip in Merton, but Albert disputed this.

'I don't believe that for a minute. Someone's either nicked them, or it's a copy, and they've sold them to *The Sun*.'

I agreed that it was an implausible story. Whoever released the videos was vindictive, wanting to further smear Cannan, to reinforce the police narrative – the narrative that had been consistently pushed, despite a lack of evidence to support it.

It seemed to me that even after all these years, the press and media were the preferred weapons of choice for those wanting to paint Cannan as responsible for Suzy's disappearance. Due process, the rule of law, the idea that one is innocent until proven guilty, was for others, not for Cannan?

'Well, there was another bit as well,' Albert continued. 'There was another bit that came to light with *The Sun* as well. They had the videos, which they sort of drip-fed out in the days of the… But the first thing that came out, there was something else. But certainly something else – they recovered some document or something.'

'The Phoebus Report?' Caroline asked.

'That's it.' Albert smiled. 'Now, I've read that report. This was the review report that Barry Webb was the author of. I've read it because I had to read it to put into context why they wanted the review done. So I've read that, and it was very scathing of the original inquiry under Hackett and all that. *The Sun* had a copy of that. I haven't got a copy of it! I wish I'd kept a load of stuff, but we did it the way you're supposed to do it. It was all put away on the file.'

Aside from his animosity toward Det. Supt Malcolm Hackett, Albert's statement seemed important for another reason. The Phoebus Report had been written by DCI Barry Webb in early 2000, immediately after McGredy-Hunt had come forward at the end of 1999 with his 'secret and anonymous information' about Fred and John West.

Was Albert suggesting that the report was provided to give the investigation team parameters and boundaries; areas of the investigation that were to be focused on and others not? Surely this wasn't how they conducted themselves in the reinvestigation, by assuming that some parts of the case were out of bounds and that the only evidence that would be subject to scrutiny in the reinvestigation would be anything that they could pin on John Cannan? Albert confirmed that in essence, the main term of reference was to eliminate or implicate Cannan.

'The 2000 reinvestigation, how did that come about?' I asked, hoping to get to the bottom of why McGredy-Hunt's 'Fred and John West story' had never been revealed as the precursor information that had caused the Met to undertake a review.

'Right… Greater Manchester Police had just done a pilot, which was reinvestigating cold cases. It was quite successful and ACPO [the Association of Chief Police Officers] all over the country said let's have a go at that. They did it in the Met – they set up a unit headed by DCS Barry Webb. They picked some very high-profile cases, and Suzy Lamplugh was one of them.'

Had Det. Supt Shaun Sawyer not told Albert about McGredy-Hunt and Diana's misinformation in the press, or was Albert trying to bluff us?

I studied Albert's expression, hoping he'd give away the answer, but I honestly couldn't tell if he was just totally ignorant of what had actually happened, or if he was trying to protect McGredy-Hunt as a source.

As Albert continued, it became clear that something had likely happened between him and Hackett. He kept referring everything back to him, as if all the failures in Suzy's case should be laid at Hackett's door. According to Albert, Hackett was chief among the reasons that the entire original investigation had failed. The police's Phoebus Report, he claimed, 'castigated' Hackett.

Yet we knew that the original inquiry work in 1986 had not actually been conducted under Hackett at all. He'd inherited the case at the beginning of 1987, following Carter's retirement, more than five months after the investigation had started, and after all the investigative decisions and lines of enquiry had been put in place.

Albert then explained to us that he had previous experience of Hackett from around the time of the original Lamplugh investigation, because the pair had worked together. When Albert was a detective sergeant, he'd been seconded onto a murder investigation at Notting Hill where Hackett had been his SIO.

Albert explained, 'I could have been on the Lamplugh enquiry but there was a murder at Notting Hill and I'd been seconded to that instead. That was run in tandem… He was the SIO. And he was as good as gold.'

But something had clearly happened in the relationship between Albert Clyne and Malcolm Hackett, because by the time Albert came to talk about Hackett's work on the Lamplugh case, he described him as 'away with the fairies'. Albert felt Hackett hadn't followed lines of enquiry and couldn't understand why he'd refused to believe John Cannan was a credible suspect.

Albert alleged that, eventually, Hackett had ordered two detective sergeants to visit Cannan in prison but had specifically advised them not to interview him under caution. It seemed that Cannan was treated by police as someone that might be able to assist the investigation but did not have his rights read to him as a suspect might have.

However, Albert's allegations seemed rather pointless. This strategy had been used by Hackett simply to get Cannan talking. If required, everything said in that conversation could ultimately still be used in evidence and eventually submitted to the CPS.

Albert was also scathing of Hackett's belief that Diana and Paul were responsible for pushing Cannan forward as a suspect. Hackett had believed someone was trying to steer the police investigation through the media and felt there wasn't a shred of evidence to support Cannan as a suspect. But this, Albert concluded, was laughable.

I wondered if Albert was completely ignorant of what had actually happened? This was exactly what we had found taking place both in 1987 and in 1999. Someone had been supplying information to the press and media, seemingly to keep the case open and put pressure on the police to act on intel received.

As the sun reflected off the waves and danced across his face, Albert scoffed at this idea, claiming he had no idea why Hackett could ever believe such a thing. According to him, the original police team had missed vital clues and evidence because the manual, handwritten card indexing system had been insufficient and cumbersome. Albert believed the thousands of cards brought with them a risk due to the sheer volume of material that had to be searched by hand.

He told us that one of his jobs had been to convert this handwritten, paper-based card index into an electronic one, by putting it on HOLMES, a computerised system designed for large and complex investigations. This, he said, is what had taken the bulk of the time in the second investigation, because everything had to be manually typed into the HOLMES system.

'It's very labour intensive,' I agreed. Just how long would it have taken to convert every single one of the 26,000 entries on the original card index system into computerised records with no errors contained within?

But as Albert spoke of the number of entries on the cards and not the number of statements or witnesses in the case, I started to wonder why. In major incident room police speak, the number of witnesses and number of statements was the metric we used. It was always how we gauged the size of the case. But when asked, Albert couldn't give us an idea as to how many witnesses or statements there were, only the number of entries on the original cards.

'That was a huge task, and while we were doing that, we were following lines of enquiry and interviewing *new* witnesses. We had quite a lot of people come forward, erm, with the new press release and the *Crimewatch* TV coverage,' he continued.

Albert explained to us that the evidence that pointed to Cannan being Suzy's killer was collected by the police in 2000, and that there wasn't any in the original investigation of 1986 and 1987. But, due to new appeals in the press and on the television in 2000, he said four new eyewitnesses had come forward. All of the eyewitnesses claimed to have seen Cannan in the Fulham area in the days that led up to Suzy's disappearance.

One witness claimed to have been persistently asked out by Cannan after he saw her in a shop. Another claimed that they'd seen Cannan looking through the window of Sturgis estate agency. A taxi driver claimed that he'd dropped Cannan off in Fulham near to Shorrolds Road on the day of Suzy going missing. And the last witness claimed that Cannan had looked round her house for sale, in Shorrolds Road, without booking an appointment. Albert told us she claimed that Cannan had been scared off when he became aware of her husband's presence in the house.

I asked Albert about the reliability of this witness testimony and ID evidence when it was a decade and a half after the events had allegedly taken place. Why were *new* witnesses coming forward so many years later, *only* after numerous appeals in the media during 2000?

On this point, Albert conceded, 'I'll be the first to admit, we built up a circumstantial case. The real clincher clearly would have been having some direct evidence, which we never really got,' he agreed.

Albert's belief, as he explained it, was that when he coupled these *new* sightings with Cannan's denial of knowing where Fulham was, alongside claims that Cannan was known by the nickname 'Kipper' in prison, it *had* to mean that Cannan was Suzy's killer.

I said nothing. The case sounded more like idle gossip at the school gates between parents who'd watched a little too many television crime dramas, rather than an actual criminal allegation the police would have been bold enough to put in front of the CPS.

We'd been sitting with Albert for two hours, enjoying coffee and local crab cakes. He was a likable chap, and I could see why people enjoyed having him talk about the case to them. But the reality was, grasping the actual evidence against Cannan in this case was like trying to hold on to a handful of sand as it slipped through your fingers. You were left with evidence of absolutely nothing, exactly as the CPS had been when they'd declined to proceed with a case against Cannan in 2002.

Perhaps sensing my exasperation, Albert began his persuasion offensive all over again.

'What you've got to keep at the back of your mind is the photofit of "Mr Kipper". That *is* John Cannan without any shadow of a doubt. If you look at a photograph or you've met John Cannan, as I have, and you look at that photofit, that is him to a T,' he said, trying to convince us of something, anything.

'When you talk about the photofit,' I interrupted, 'that's the artist's impression from the next-door neighbour, Harry Riglin, who saw *a woman* and, potentially, John Cannan, standing outside 37 Shorrolds Road?'

Albert appeared not to know who Harry Riglin was and went off on a tangent again with another monologue. So I asked him why the police, in 2000, hadn't asked Harry to try and identify Cannan as the man he had seen standing outside Shorrolds Road? This, after all, would have been necessary to prove the case? But Albert's reply was that he thought Harry was dead when they were reinvestigating the case in 2000.

This was incorrect, Harry had been very much alive when they'd arrested Cannan during the 2000–02 reinvestigation.

The police hadn't even bothered to check?

It seemed that the new police team had had little or no contact with the original core witnesses from 1986; those that had provided the foundations of the police narrative at the start.

What the new police team had wanted, and what Albert's focus seemed to have been, was to find those people who hadn't given witness statements in the original case, by appealing for them to come forward anew – or perhaps by cherry-picking old names from the original card index that they didn't have statements for?

It was like they were panning for gold in a murky river of information, and everything else was a waste of their time. Only information about Cannan would sparkle and stick to the bottom of the pan?

I then asked Albert if there had been suspects eliminated in the original 1986–87 case.

'No, no, no, no, no. There wasn't even a matrix about possible suspects. That was drawn up subsequently… and we did it, in the reinvestigation, and it all kept coming back to Cannan. We eliminated every other suspect. There was only Cannan; Cannan was the only one still standing…'

'You had a matrix of suspects?' Caroline piped up. 'Who was on it?'

'The people who came into the inquiry originally, and a few that we thought there's some intelligence or evidence to put them in the frame. The matrix was basically a load of boxes – why these people fall into it, why they don't. Basically trace involvement. And we eliminated every single one of them, apart from Cannan. Every way we went came back to him.'

'And you don't think there's any way that there's someone in the inquiry, previously, that's been missed?' Caroline asked.

'I don't think so. I'd be very surprised if there is. Very, very surprised. We looked at everyone that had come into the inquiry beforehand. Erm. And we eliminated the same people, again. Even though they'd been eliminated the first time.'

'On what basis? How did you eliminate them?' I asked.

'On certain criteria. Were they in Fulham at the time? Did they know Suzy? Were they in a relationship or previous relationship with her?' Albert replied.

'And did you see that as a big factor? That they'd had to have had a previous relationship with her?' I asked.

'Well, it would make sense. She had a number of boyfriends. Some had been interviewed…' Albert smiled at me.

We already had a reasonable amount of evidence suggesting Suzy wasn't even in Fulham when she went missing, because she'd gone to Putney, on the other side of the river. We also knew she'd potentially gone to the pub on a simple errand, rather than meeting up with anyone she was having a relationship with.

If our new line of enquiry was correct, the suspect matrix fell apart on just those two points alone.

'Why do you think John Cannan killed some people and not others?' I asked.

We knew Cannan had been able to build and sustain relationships with numerous people during the time of Suzy's disappearance. What had convinced Albert that he was involved with this particular offence while he was successfully maintaining these other relationships with women?

'As I said when we first started, if you look at his offending record, he starts off low and gradually gets more and more violent. And his modus operandi is to see a woman he fancies, might be in the street, might be just because he's… he's one of these people who drives around and suddenly… in car parks… just spirits them away… Shirley Banks was murdered. I believe Suzy Lamplugh was murdered because he got to the stage where he thought, *I don't want to go back inside. Best way to get rid of a victim that's seen me, knows who I am, is to top them, basically.* But we can't say when he latched on to her.'

'What about his girlfriend and solicitor, Annabel Rose?' I asked, wondering how Albert would respond.

'You see…' Albert looked thoughtfully into his glass as he formed his answer. 'We don't know how much Annabel Rose knew about Cannan. This again gets very political. You know she's a solicitor. How good she was, I don't know. Cannan definitely had an affair with her. Definitely. Her husband is a barrister on the Western Circuit. I had a screaming row with him on the phone. He made a complaint against me. So I couldn't personally go and see her to take a statement. So I delegated two officers to do it. She's in denial as well. She was no help at all. We'll never know how involved she was with him. She, for reputational reasons, would not assist the enquiry at all. I believe she probably didn't know of Cannan's background. Because he's such a Walter Mitty,' he responded, looking up at me as he finished.

I was taken aback by his answer. Why didn't the Met seem to have a fuller understanding of exactly who Annabel Rose was in John Cannan's life? Was it because they'd been dissuaded by the complaint made against Albert Clyne?

It suddenly occurred to me that during our research, we'd never seen, heard or read Diana Lamplugh ever mention Annabel Rose publicly by name. Why hadn't she made a big deal out of Cannan's surveillance of Annabel's parents? This surely would have bolstered her own claims that Cannan was stalking Suzy.

In November 2002, just after police had named Cannan as their one and only suspect, Diana did claim in the press that he had made repeated attempts to contact her at the Trust, by placing numerous phone calls from prison. Had Cannan tried to warn Mrs Lamplugh about the link between Sir David Napley and the cases? Was Cannan aware of any potentially malign influences at play?

Who was actually in control of the second investigation? Was it Det. Supt Sawyer, or was it Diana Lamplugh?

Albert talked for another hour about John Cannan, and we were happy to listen. He watched the harbour behind me, and I watched the colour of his face bleed into red as the sun got lower in the sky. We were learning a lot about the way the police had approached the case in the reinvestigation.

As we were finishing the interview, I asked Albert about his views of Suzy's Ford Fiesta being continually used by the police as a prop for witnesses to look at in reconstructions. After seizing it on the night of her disappearance, the police had transported it around and driven it themselves on at least two different occasions during the first week of its seizure. They'd even let an actress drive it during a second reconstruction.

In my eyes, this was no way to treat an exhibit. Especially not the most fundamental piece of evidence in the case – basically the only crime scene the police had ever really had.

Albert responded with, 'They never seized the car. It was sitting unlocked, close to or just outside one of the addresses that they'd viewed.'

The police *had* seized Suzy's car, but it was the last part of the sentence that really intrigued me – 'close to or just outside one of the addresses that they'd viewed'.

There had only been one supposed house viewing that lunchtime – at 37 Shorrolds Road – Suzy's car had never been parked close to or seen outside this address. Why did Albert now think that *two* house viewings had taken place that day?

Her car had been found by PC Christopher Dollery in Stevenage Road, a completely different part of Fulham – and more than a mile away from the house for sale at 37 Shorrolds Road.

Albert's statement didn't really make much sense to me.

I settled up the bill for our meal and we made our way out onto the pierside. Caroline and I both thanked Albert for his time and shook his hand.

As we parted, he called back out to us over his shoulder, 'There's more twists and turns to come in this case – watch this space!' and ambled off in the direction of the setting sun without another glance.

I had absolutely no idea what he was referring to.

52

'I don't know why they went and searched *that place*, or what the trigger was.' Graeme Gwyn sounded defensive as we talked about what had prompted the police to dig up John Cannan's mother's old garden. The dig had taken place not long after I'd met him in the pub to initially sound him out about Suzy's case.

We were in one of the rooms next to the HOLMES suite at Patrick Dunne House in Sutton, South London, the south-west base for the Met's Homicide and Serious Crime Command. The relatively new building, at the eastern end of Sutton's infamous one-way system, had been named after a police officer who'd been murdered in the early 1990s.

'But that's up to the SIO. They searched that place.' He shook his head before concluding, 'I dunno how they got the information – must have been years old.'

I'd decided that we simply couldn't risk just climbing into the space where we believed Suzy's remains might be concealed in the Prince of Wales pub and start rummaging around for confirmation of our findings. We could potentially be disturbing vital evidence that might convict Suzy's killer.

The right thing to do was to involve the police.

I'd spoken with Lizzie Lamplugh, the youngest of the four Lamplugh siblings, to explain that we had interviewed a significant number of the original witnesses in Suzy's case and that we believed we'd made some important discoveries. In the first instance I offered to share this with her family before we did anything further, if that was what the family wanted. But she'd asked me to share the evidence we had with the police, and she'd not enquired as to what it was that we knew.

I was left wondering how many people had contacted the family, claiming to know what happened to Suzy.

So here we were, with Graeme Gwyn, the former detective chief inspector who was now a civilian investigator on the Met's Murder Review Group, sharing what we knew with the police.

Constructed under a private finance initiative in 2003, Patrick Dunne House was a huge, slab-sided building with few windows. It was a far cry from Sutton's elaborate Edwardian police station next door, built in a Dutch style around 1908 and designed by John Dixon Butler.

Dixon Butler had served as the Met's surveyor from 1895 until his death in 1920, by which time he'd designed over 200 police stations and courts, some of which were still standing and had been given listed, protected status. His buildings were notable for their architectural quality, with handsome iron railings and inscribed lintels identifying the building as a police station. They literally advertised the police to the public, screaming, 'We are here – come in and talk to us.'

Soulless Patrick Dunne House was its polar opposite. A fortress, based around a central courtyard parking area to hide itself from prying eyes, it was designed to be anonymous; to keep people out.

I'd been there a few times during my years spent in the police, back when the paint was fresh, the carpet was new and the grain on the wooden doors wasn't filled with grime. As we sat listening to Graeme talk, I was struck by its current state of neglect. Barely fifteen years old, it was unloved, uncared for and falling apart at the seams.

Graeme was talking about the new police team now assigned to handle the Lamplugh case.

'I'll try and get you in touch with them,' he continued. 'I just know there's a reluctance with them to have a face to face and talk to people. If it were me, I'd want to get as much information as I could off you, but… I'm right down the bottom of the pecking order.'

We'd just handed Graeme a hundred-page evidential package which included a formal signed written statement from me, detailed architectural drawings and photos of the Prince of Wales pub. He'd thumbed through it and read several parts while we'd been sitting with him, surveying the mess of the building around us.

'This needs to be passed to the team that's dealing with it,' Graeme said, patting the package he was reading.

He then explained that he'd already spoken with the team dealing with Suzy's case, which he called the 'Special Casework Investigation Team', and I got the distinct impression he'd tried to gain control of the case but had been warned off of it.

'I think from your perspective what I'd be looking for is just the hook, to get them to do it. Have a little bite, and then they'll want more. But I think they need to get in touch,' he continued, patting the bundle of papers we'd given him as he read.

None of what I was hearing was filling me with any confidence.

Why wouldn't an investigative team want as much as they could get? Why wouldn't they want to look at our information? We'd spent years and tens of thousands of pounds tracing and interviewing the original witnesses in the case.

Who and what had caused the dig at Cannan's mother's house? Was it purely vindictive, done just to reinforce the existing police narrative because we'd been poking around and asking questions?

'I'll pass this on to the enquiry team.' Graeme smiled. 'And I'll give you details of them, if that's alright?'

'Sure,' I responded. There really didn't seem much other choice.

'Hopefully they'll get in touch,' he said unconvincingly.

'What are your thoughts on what we've got, Graeme?' I pointed at the bundle of documents we'd given him, hoping to get an understanding of what had actually gone on between him and the Special Casework Investigation Team.

'They've got to consider having a look, haven't they?'

I shrugged. 'Have they?'

'If it's new information. If they haven't done it. If they didn't know about this pub before, and it's all new. Then it's new, and you'd have thought, well, you'd want to do something with that, wouldn't you?'

'Yeah,' I agreed.

'Otherwise you'll never know. And my favourite phrase is: "If you do nothing, you get nothing."'

I looked over at Caroline. Her look said the same – she was unconvinced.

'It just needs a bit more digging…' He smiled.

I turned back to him and narrowed my eyes. Was he joking?

'Well, not literally *digging*. But, you know,' he replied, reading my expression and chuckling.

53

The radio on the car was playing Lewis Capaldi's 'Someone You Loved' as we drove toward the City to ensure that our VIP client got to their meeting safely and securely. The day was bright, with few clouds in the sky as we glided slowly along what was left of the Embankment, much of it now surrendered to cyclists.

Suddenly the radio was interrupted by a loud ringing sound. This was always rather embarrassing when there was a client in the car. My colleague, who was driving, looked across at me sternly. I'd forgotten to disconnect my phone from the car's Bluetooth. I hit the car's infotainment button to cancel the call without seeing who the caller was. Lewis's sad song about losing the love of his life returned.

'Sorry about that,' I called over my shoulder to the male client in the rear of the car. He didn't reply. Lewis began singing again.

But just as he got to the chorus, my phone began to ring again, silencing Lewis and relegating him to nothing more than a photo on the radio dashboard.

I pulled the phone from the pocket of my jacket and ended the call directly on the handset this time. The calls were from a journalist. We'd worked together previously on a story about counterterror policing.

I quickly thumbed a text to him – 'I can't talk now. I'll ring you later' – before turning the phone off.

My client was shaking his head and frowning.

Half an hour later, when I'd safely escorted him to his meeting and I was standing at the base of one of the city's tallest buildings, I switched my mobile back on. There were several texts from even more journalists and from Caroline, all asking that I contact them urgently.

I called Caroline back first.

'What's up?' I asked.

'You're not going to believe this!' She sounded really annoyed.

'Try me.'

'I was just sitting down for five minutes after picking the kids up and doing the food shopping. And a breaking news headline popped up on my phone – "New police search in Suzy Lamplugh case."'

'Oh wow, really? That was quick – we only gave our stuff to the police about ten days ago.'

'I thought the same at first. But…' She paused and sighed. 'The police aren't searching the Prince of Wales pub.'

'What? Where are they—'

'Worcestershire,' she replied, cutting me off. 'The area they're digging up isn't far from Norton Barracks, about seven miles away. It's all linked to Cannan again. The news reports say that police have received 'new information' as a result of the media coverage of the previous dig at Cannan's mother's old house.'

'I can't believe it! Not again. I'll see if I can get hold of the police on the phone; see if I can find out what the hell is going on. This is a joke.'

54

'According to climate scientists, climate change is the biggest threat to long-term human survival on the planet...' The radio was on in the car as I drove back down the motorway toward London.

I wasn't really paying much attention to it. My mind was elsewhere.

I'd been on an unsuccessful hunt for the home of former Det. Supt Malcolm Hackett. Whilst it had been a pleasant trip, all I'd netted was an ice cream and a bag of chips while I watched the seagulls bother people sunbathing at the beach.

In 1987, Malcolm Hackett had been the SIO in Suzy's case during the tail end of the original investigation. He was the man that Albert Clyne seemed intent on pinning the blame on. But my search hadn't gone according to plan as the home address I'd developed for Malcolm Hackett had turned out to be the wrong one.

I would eventually have some contact with Malcolm via email, but he would never fully respond to my questions about the relief bar worker Clive Vole and the police officers who had been sent to the north of England to take a statement from him in late 1987. I desperately wanted to understand why the police had never considered the Prince of Wales pub as a place where Suzy might have gone that lunchtime.

'And, they say, record temperatures across much of the world over the past two weeks could make this July the hottest month ever measured on Earth.' The radio presenter sounded almost excited by the idea.

It was certainly shaping up to be a very warm month.

'And in other news, police say a search of land in Pershore, Worcestershire, for Suzy Lamplugh has ended after they found no evidence.'

The presenter suddenly had my full attention again. I turned up the radio and slowed the car down.

'The estate agent who went missing from London in 1986 has never been found. Officers believe she was murdered and have been searching land in Worcestershire for the past two weeks. But the search has now ended after nothing was recovered. The Met Police thanked their counterparts in West Mercia for their assistance, together with landowners and the Pershore community for their cooperation. Police say that they remain committed to securing justice for Suzy and her family and will continue to assess any new information received in connection with this case.'

55

It had been four months and fifteen days since Graeme Gwyn had told us that the Special Casework Investigation Team were reluctant to meet with anyone, and that they'd be a tricky group to deal with face to face. But even after hearing that, I hadn't fully anticipated the difficulties we would experience in actually getting them to engage with us.

But after a wait of 137 days, we were finally here, in a meeting with the balding and bespectacled Det. Supt Stuart Ryan, the man who said he was now in overall charge of Suzy's case at the Met.

As the formalities and chit-chat subsided, it was clear that Ryan was channelling his inner headmaster at me, talking to me like I was a schoolboy.

'I feel like I'm on the naughty step,' I jested with him.

'Ohhh, yes,' he responded with a chuckle.

Our meeting was taking place inside Cobalt Square, a weird, triangular-shaped premises that belonged to the Met and lived in the shadow of MI6's headquarters at Vauxhall. In recent years it had been used by the Met as backfill following their decision to dispose of the Broadway's New Scotland Yard tower block in 2012.

While several million pounds had been lavished on the place, neither the building nor the down-at-heel location were very popular among staff. The surrounding area held little allure to senior management figures who had been unceremoniously uprooted from the Yard and replanted here because they weren't important enough to be given offices in Westminster.

It was late on a Friday afternoon and it seemed everyone in the building was observing dress-down Friday here. Even Ryan was joining in. He wore an open-necked shirt that hung loose at the back from his suit trousers. On his feet he had red, woven-knit trainers.

But no one had told us that we could have come in jeans; I was wearing a suit and tie, and Caroline had on a trouser suit and silk blouse.

Over the months that we'd been in limbo, we'd established, through frequent prodding via email, that the Special Casework Team was led by a DCI, who had an acting DI and a couple of DCs working for her. Above all of them, Ryan was their overall boss.

During the toing and froing, Ryan had accidentally copied us into one of his internal emails, revealing some of the police's thinking on how they intended on dealing with us. So we already had a good idea, prior to the meeting, that the police were simply going to offer us information that rebutted what we'd sent them.

To this end, Caroline and I had agreed a strategy before going into the meeting. She would take the lead and ask the majority of the questions, using the opportunity to establish what we could about the evidence the police believed rebutted the idea that Suzy's body might be below the dining room at the Prince of Wales pub.

We hoped that this would throw Ryan off balance, as he'd probably treat me as if I were still a member of the police service – a naughty schoolboy.

Caroline began by disputing the numerous false eyewitness accounts which claimed to have seen Suzy at 37 Shorrolds Road on the day she had gone missing.

'They haven't named her…' Ryan agreed, hesitating momentarily. 'Nobody's named her as being the person outside that address, in Shorrolds Road. But in terms of the fact that it *looked* like an estate agent showing that location at the time, which fitted in with what was in her diary, her car just round the corner… But she's not been named, because she was never named.'

It was an important statement, an important admission by the police, that none of the three eyewitnesses the police had interviewed in 1986 had ever positively identified a woman they claimed to have seen as being Suzy.

But there was something else, something just as important in Ryan's answer – 'her car just around the corner' – this was exactly what Albert Clyne had claimed to us as well.

Albert had said, 'It was sitting unlocked, close to or just outside one of the addresses that they'd viewed.'

One of the addresses that they'd viewed.

Both Stuart Ryan and Albert Clyne believed there was a second house viewing the day Suzy had gone missing, and that this viewing had been where Suzy's car had been abandoned?

I let it pass as Caroline pressed on with her questioning.

'And what about identifying her from a photo?' Caroline sought clarification of Ryan's earlier answer, asking if any of the witnesses had identified the woman they'd seen from a photo of Suzy.

'No,' Ryan agreed. 'And she was never named.'

'And Suzy didn't have the key for the house showing either, did she?' Caroline pushed on as she smiled at him, recognisably happy with her progress so far.

'Well, we assumed she did have the keys.' Ryan let out a sigh before continuing. 'Because her manager went round to 37 Shorrolds Road and knocked on the door on the day to see if she was there.'

Ryan was referring to Mark Gurdon, who had originally said in his witness statement that he had gone to 37 Shorrolds Road looking for Suzy when he'd discovered the entry in her diary after she'd gone missing. Gurdon's assumption had been, at the time, that the key was missing, and that Suzy must have had it with her.

But our investigation had revealed something entirely different.

'So how did the police's own scenes of crime officer get inside 37 Shorrolds Road to forensicate the property the next day with the key, if Suzy had disappeared, taking that key with her?' Caroline asked.

'We, er, don't know where those keys came from,' Ryan admitted awkwardly.

'They came from the estate agent's,' Caroline stated.

We knew there was only one key. Mark Gurdon had told us so.

'So,' Ryan started, sounding a little defeated, 'you've got that bit too. We don't know where the keys came from,' he conceded. 'So yeah, the... so we don't know where the... so...' Ryan stumbled over the end of his sentence, seemingly unsure how to finish it.

These admissions from the police were truly breathtaking but also heartbreaking at the same time.

During the four months we'd waited for this meeting, I'd regretted involving the police. I was certain that we could have searched the void underneath the dining-room floor at the Prince of Wales ourselves by now. We could simply have employed exactly the same forensic archaeological team that the Met outsourced their specialist searches to. But with Suzy's sister asking that we share the information we had uncovered with the police, we wanted to respect these wishes.

Yet despite our frustrations, this meeting had also been worth waiting for. With the police accepting we were right about the witnesses, and right about the key, this meant that the 'Mr Kipper' diary entry and the Shorrolds Road appointment were fictitious. And we were most of the way there in proving that Suzy must have been going somewhere else that lunchtime.

'But the key, just, the keys themselves – they don't undermine that part of it, as far as we're concerned...' Ryan's words tailed off again as he tried to convince himself that the police narrative around the 'Mr Kipper' viewing still had some credibility.

Did this belief stem from the idea that there was a second house viewing, one that *hadn't* been written in Suzy's work desk diary? Was this a property viewing that had been withheld from the public?

It seemed to be the only explanation.

But as we tried to seek an explanation for this, Ryan's tone changed. He began to suggest that our investigation had fallen short of achieving anything, despite his admissions so far to the contrary.

It simply wasn't good enough, he said, that we were suggesting that Suzy's remains could be under the dining-room floor of the Prince of Wales. In order to be able to say this, he claimed, we'd have to provide him with a motive for why whoever had killed her there had chosen to do it.

'There are certain key bits which you cannot answer in your hypothesis,' he chided. 'There are key bits within our *investigation*, which is public record, which you cannot account for in your *hypothesis*' – he smiled – 'which knocks your hypothesis down completely.'

'It's not a hypothesis,' I mumbled. A hypothesis is something more than a wild guess but less than a well-established theory.

'Bits which you have failed to account for in your hypothesis, which if you accounted for, it could actually say why it's occurred,' Ryan bumbled on, oblivious to my point about the terminology he was using.

'What bits are they?' asked Caroline curiously.

'So being blunt… The car. It's moved,' replied Ryan.

'From the pub?' Caroline sought to clarify his point.

'One point seven miles, yes.'

'Yeah. Because it would have been outside the pub when Suzy parked it there,' Caroline replied logically.

It seemed obvious that if Suzy had driven to the pub to collect her lost property and gone missing in suspicious circumstances there, her car would be a huge red flag, sitting right outside a potential crime scene. Wouldn't someone connected to the pub have moved it, to avoid any police interest, dumped it somewhere within walking distance and then walked back to the pub?

This seemed pretty straightforward to us.

'But they've moved it to the location just near the place where she was due to meet "Mr Kipper"?' Ryan asked.

'No,' Caroline replied, frowning.

'Well it was! Actually it was!' Ryan raised his voice at Caroline as if she were now the naughty schoolchild.

Caroline started to explain that this was incorrect. Suzy's car had been found in Stevenage Road, in a completely different part of Fulham, nowhere near Shorrolds Road. Her car was nowhere near the fake house viewing that had been written in her work desk diary.

But we were back at this stumbling block again, with him believing Suzy had done a second house viewing and that this was in Stevenage Road, or that she had arranged to meet 'Mr Kipper' there. I was sure that Ryan was fundamentally wrong about what he was saying, but watching him argue the facts with Caroline was entertaining, nonetheless.

Albert Clyne had said something almost identical to us.

Yet we hadn't missed a piece of evidence of this magnitude. There was never any mention of a second appointment that day by anyone. While it had been lightly suggested as a possibility in the newspapers, because of a 'For Sale' sign in Stevenage Road, there was never any actual evidence of it.

Caroline continued to badger Ryan, trying to get to the bottom of it.

'Alright! Enough!' Ryan shouted over Caroline to cut her off. 'I'm not getting into an argument about it!' he shouted. 'We are not investigating it any further! It is closed!'

I could tell from the look on Caroline's face that she was surprised at the rude and disrespectful way Ryan had shouted at her, yet she kept her cool.

Our meeting strategy had been largely successful.

But Ryan wasn't done. He grabbed a piece of paper from a folder in front of him.

'This letter makes it clear exactly,' Ryan said, channelling his inner headmaster at me again, 'that we are not opening the investigation in terms of your hypothesis. If you identify the Prince of Wales pub as a possible location,' Ryan continued imperiously as I scanned the letter he'd handed me, 'we will make it quite clear, from the police point of view that is, that it's inaccurate and unfounded.'

'Unfounded?' I raised an eyebrow at him.

'Look, reality is,' Ryan responded, his tone now softening slightly, 'we cannot do anything further, at this stage.'

Caroline and I stayed silent.

'But if, coz I don't think you're going to let it go,' he sighed, 'because of the amount of time and effort you've put into it. As I said to you at the start, the amount of information you've actually collated and recorded has been really good. But if you get the golden thread, which suddenly changes everything...'

So it wasn't unfounded, it was incomplete – and Ryan was now offering us some investigative advice.

'What would be the golden thread for you to look at it then?' I asked, wondering where this was going.

'The golden thread would be something like: Was she seen going into the pub at three o'clock that day?' he replied. 'Was she actually seen going into that pub? Because we know for a fact, for a *fact*, from Clive and Karen, that pub was busy.'

'That's what they've told you?' Caroline asked.

'We know that for a fact, from them... So reality is – we know—'

'That's what they've told you, yes,' Caroline said, conscious of the anomalies in all of the witness accounts.

'The reality is this,' I began when he fell quiet, 'there are a lot of discrepancies in the accounts given by the witnesses. You should be using those discrepancies as evidence that there's something clearly wrong with your investigations, something clearly amiss at the pub, and going to search it.'

There was a long pause before Ryan spent a further several minutes trying to justify why the police were not going to. 'You would need to get a proper motive for the actual incident,' he said, appearing to round off his answer, 'rather than just was it because there was something *salacious* in her diary and she didn't want someone to take it, and therefore she's tried to get it back and there's been an argument and someone killed her.'

It was a bizarre comment – 'something salacious in her diary and she didn't want someone to take it'.

In all our witness statements, evidential packages and written submissions to the police, we had never once speculated about the content of Suzy's personal pocket diary found at the pub. Neither Caroline nor I had seen the content of Suzy's 1986 personal diary. In fact, we'd not found a single witness who remembered ever seeing her with this personal pocket diary.

The police, and whoever *had* seen Suzy's personal diary while it had been at the pub, were the only people who knew of its content.

'You've got to come up with a motive,' Ryan continued. 'Why has this woman gone into a pub when she's told everybody she's not going to the pub until later that evening?'

Ryan's statement confirmed that the police held evidence that once again agreed with our investigation – that Suzy had planned to go to the pub on the day of her disappearance. The only point of contention was that Ryan claimed she was going there that *evening* and not in the *afternoon*.

We knew that the police had somehow come into possession of Suzy's lost property from the pub after her disappearance. But who amongst Suzy's friends, family and colleagues had known that Suzy was going to the pub that day to pick up her stuff?

Apart from the police and those at the pub, we hadn't spoken to anyone who really knew she'd even lost her items, let alone that those items were waiting at the Prince of Wales for her.

'But how could Suzy be in two places at once? *You're* saying she's going to the pub, but later on. Yet she had a house viewing at 6 p.m.?' Caroline asked, flushed with frustration at the way Ryan was speaking to her.

And this was an important point. Some of Suzy's Monday evening was already spoken for. She had recorded another appointment in her work diary to show a house at 6 p.m. to a client called Joanna Wright in Waldemar Road. We knew that Suzy's colleagues had become particularly worried when she'd missed that specific evening appointment.

'You've really got to work on your motive,' Ryan tried again with his investigative advice. 'In terms of saying, this young girl, she's gone into a pub and for some reason someone has killed her, dumped her body and then moved her car, very close to where she's actually got a work appointment with "Mr Kipper" at the same time.'

'It wasn't dumped at the "Mr Kipper" appointment!' Caroline interjected, trying to explain this to him for the second time. 'The car was dumped in a different road – it just happened to be near another house that was for sale with Sturgis, one that had a Sturgis sign outside it. It wasn't anything to do with the alleged "Kipper" diary appointment.'

'And then the killer carried on with their day and worked normally?' Ryan asked sarcastically, ignoring Caroline's attempts to correct his misunderstanding of the facts around where the car was found.

'Why not?' I asked. 'Why isn't that possible?'

Ryan was laughing, shaking his head. 'You've got to be a certain type of person in the first place. A killer doesn't just walk down the road acting normally – there'd be something in the background, either previously or post, in terms of violence. You're saying this person's done that? Dumped the body? Driven the car up? Come back down? End of story. Rubbish! Absolute rubbish!' he shouted.

As he shouted, I thought back to my police colleagues who had interviewed fifteen-year-old Liam Tovell in his living room, hours after he'd killed Joanne Eddison; her body concealed under his bed just one floor above them. I thought about my own interview with Liam, with Joanne's body buried in the waste ground behind his house, as his mother served us tea and biscuits and fussed around us, Liam sitting there cool as ice.

None of these telltale signs were apparent in a fifteen-year-old who had never killed before and never killed again. There was no such thing as an archetypal killer, no typical telltale signs of a killer, and there was certainly no loss of cognitive function.

And what if Suzy hadn't been murdered *at all*? Why did there have to be a serial killer, or a murder, or even a motive? What if there had been some sort of terrible accident at the pub and someone had simply covered it up?

I decided not to share any of these thoughts with Ryan. It seemed as if we were just going round in circles. 'What we're saying to you is that it's a massive mistake for you *not* to look for Suzy's body in that pub,' I stated.

'Nope! So we're not!' Ryan barked.

I remained silent.

'If you provide more information, we will reassess it. I've got no issues reassessing it. But you need a proper motive. You need a proper identification that she actually attended the pub that day.' Ryan lowered his voice. 'You've got to prove that actually there's something salacious in her diary.'

Again, he seemed to be claiming the content of Suzy's pocket diary had made her a target. For some reason, the police seemed obsessed with the content of this secret diary.

I thought back to Clive Vole's comments. About the urgency he seemed to place on Suzy wanting her diary back from him. The way he'd recited back to us Suzy's fervent words on the phone that lunchtime: 'Have you got my diary? Have you got my diary? You have got my diary, haven't you?'

56

It had been three days since our meeting with the Met at Cobalt Square. I was at home looking through our early research files on Suzy's case.

Det. Supt Ryan's persistent suggestion that it was the content of Suzy's secret pocket diary that might have been the motive for the attack on her at the pub was stabbing at my insides.

During our research into the case, we'd noticed that there was a steady stream of news stories which attempted to paint a picture of Suzy as being sexually promiscuous. The basis for these stories had been Suzy's older personal diaries.

According to her mother, Suzy was dyslexic, but this didn't hold her back from being an avid writer. And this inclination to write seemed to run in the family. Even before her daughter's disappearance, Diana had co-authored a number of books and pamphlets on health, well-being and fitness. In addition to this, she would also regularly write long family newsletters, with no detail too small or too trivial to leave out.

Diana was a self-confessed self-publicist; she wanted as many people as possible to read what she had to say. But for Suzy, the writing was of a more private nature and took a different form. She kept detailed, personal, daily diaries, and given the amount of risqué content shared in the media from Suzy's diary aboard the QE2, it seemed that no detail had been too small or too trivial for Suzy to leave out either.

Following Suzy's disappearance, many of her old personal diaries were handed over to the police, who naturally pored over them in minute detail. These older diaries became a source of investigative leads, as officers traced and spoke to the men who appeared in their pages.

We had mostly ignored the rumours we'd seen in the newspapers but had found it difficult to escape when confronted with the feelings of former police officers who'd worked on the case. There were countless examples and comments we'd heard which betrayed their inner voice; that they too had seen the content of these personal diaries, content which, as Ryan had said, was 'salacious'.

I'd wanted to ignore them because I recognised that attitudes toward one-night stands and frequency of sexual partners had all changed considerably in the decades that had passed since Suzy disappeared. And we weren't finding any evidence that the number of Suzy's sexual partners appeared to be a factor in this investigation.

As we interviewed people away from the police, it was rarely even mentioned. Suzy was well liked, hard-working, good fun and professionally successful. And her private life was private. People accepted Suzy for who she was.

But while Diana Lamplugh would claim in public, 'There were no grey areas in her life. She was exactly what she seemed to be and exactly how other parents would like their daughters to be,' the truth, for her parents, was rather different.

Suzy was a chameleon.

Suzy's personal diaries laid bare to all those who read them, including her grieving parents, what was really going on in her life. And this must have been incredibly difficult to come to terms with, especially for parents with strict Wesleyan Methodist views such as those of Diana and Paul Lamplugh.

I don't think any parent wants to understand their adult child's most intimate secrets, especially while trying to deal with the idea that they've been murdered – though this was the situation the Lamplughs found themselves in as they trawled through Suzy's private life independently of the police, in their desperate search for clues.

During our meeting with Ryan, he had touched on something that we hadn't fully considered.

What if, as he had said, the contents of Suzy's secret pocket diary – possibly just jotted down so it could be transcribed in detail later to a bigger ledger at home – were so 'salacious' that they were at the centre of everything that had gone wrong?

There were two parts to this. Firstly it would have shaped the way Diana and Paul Lamplugh behaved toward the police investigation.

With their strict Wesleyan Methodist views, might it have meant that there was something in those secrets that offended them? Were there things that struck them as so concerning that they'd questioned everything they held dear about their daughter? Might this have motivated them to do things to ensure that those secrets remained confidential, such as taking the initiative in the media strategy, meaning the police couldn't lead it?

There was evidence that Paul and Diana had furiously attacked anyone publishing lurid details about Suzy's sexual history, despite sometimes, inadvertently, being the source of the stories themselves.

As with anything of the size and magnitude of Suzy's disappearance in the British media, some parts of the press were less gracious and less well behaved than others. As some of the stories deteriorated and moved into Suzy's private life, Paul and Diana took an unprecedented step for the parents of someone who was missing. They involved one of the country's top libel lawyers, Peter Carter-Ruck, in efforts to rein in what the press could and couldn't say about Suzy.

Libel cannot be applied to the dead – and although Suzy wasn't declared dead for several years, there was a general assumption, within a few weeks, that she was never going to be found alive – thus some believed she'd never make a libel claim against them.

Paul and Diana, however, engaged Carter-Ruck and targeted with legal threats anyone who dared to print stories they didn't like, hounding them with complaints and menacing them with the promise of hostile court action unless they withdrew them. More than that, during our research, we had discovered that Paul and Diana Lamplugh had also made a number of Suzy's boyfriends sign non-disclosure agreements, legally gagging them to prevent them from speaking about the intimate details of their relationships with Suzy to anyone.

Suzy's posthumous reputation was managed just as if she were alive. Her desperate parents even lobbied the Home Secretary, albeit unsuccessfully, to change the law, so that libel could be applied to the dead in the same way as it did the living.

Did Suzy's parents feel that any negative press was some form of personal attack on them, an infringement of their believed rights to exclusivity in the media, and on their ability to fundraise for their trust? Did all of this point in support of them knowing that the content of Suzy's personal diary was indeed 'salacious', as Ryan was claiming?

At one stage the Lamplughs even involved the police, helping to ensure that the correct narrative was adhered to. In September of 1988, Paul Condon, the Met's Assistant Commissioner, had been forced to say publicly:

> It is not the policy of the force to make moral judgements about the lifestyle of victims of crime. However, in view of intense publicity about Suzy Lamplugh and her family, we feel honour-bound to say that our investigations revealed nothing more than that Suzy was a modern young woman.

In other words, the secrets in Suzy's personal diaries were not to be talked about.

But thirty-one years later, in our meeting with Det. Supt Ryan, the officer now in charge of the case, all the furore about this had been forgotten. It was clear Ryan had missed any memorandum that Condon might have left in the file, telling everyone *not* to talk about the secret diary's 'salacious' content.

It was that very discrepancy that was niggling away at me.

Had Paul and Diana been so thorough in their management of what could be said about Suzy, and by whom, that they had either intentionally or inadvertently pushed the police away from considering the content of Suzy's secret diary as the motive for an attack on their daughter?

Was this why the 'Mr Kipper' narrative had happily been pushed by all from the outset? I began to feel some sympathy for the situation that Det. Supt Carter might have found himself in those first few days. Were parameters and boundaries already being put in place on day one of the investigation in terms of where the police should and shouldn't be looking?

And did this explain why Paul and Diana, in their torment, had involved Sir David Napley within forty-eight hours of Suzy going missing, to help manage all this, to avoid any damage to the family's reputation?

Napley certainly had pedigree in this department after all.

Had Ryan inadvertently shared with us a crucial part of the puzzle?

57

20 December 2019
33 years, 4 months, 22 days missing

'How well did you know Suzy?'

'Not that well really. At the end of the day, I employed her. She was a bubbly young lady,' he said, his voice deep, gruff and confident.

The police were still placing considerable weight on the 'Mr Kipper' entry Suzy had put in her desk diary for the day she'd gone missing. Despite police admissions that Suzy hadn't had the key to do the viewing at 37 Shorrolds Road, nor had she even been positively identified by any of the witnesses near to the address that day, they still believed Suzy was actually meeting someone she believed to be a prospective house buyer. Though now they were suggesting she'd met him somewhere else, not at Shorrolds Road – but at the 'other house viewing'.

It was a fallacy. If the entry in Suzy's diary was bonafide, why was the address wrong? Why hadn't she taken any house keys *at all*?

With all of our recent discoveries about secret diary entries, we really needed to dig deeper, to understand not just that the entry was false but *why* it was false. Everybody we'd spoken to had said that Suzy followed the rules at work. She wasn't someone who stepped out of line.

But for Suzy, secrets were something wholly different to telling lies and breaking rules. Growing up with strict Wesleyan Methodist parents, some things she just preferred to keep to herself.

During one of our interviews with Mark Gurdon, Suzy's branch manager, he'd admitted to us that he thought she was going to Putney the day she'd gone missing, perhaps to do a spot of shopping. But then it was somewhat baffling to me that if Mark Gurdon knew this, why would Suzy need to put a fake entry in her desk diary? Perhaps there *was* a second house viewing somewhere that lunchtime.

The deep, gruff and confident-sounding man on the other end of the telephone was Keith Perry, another former employee of Sturgis estate agency. His name had been mentioned during my interview with Martin Sturgis. Martin had said Keith might have been one of those that had been lunching with Mark Gurdon in the Crocodile Tears wine bar on the afternoon Suzy had gone missing.

Sitting in my car, not far from the Palace of Westminster, I listened to Keith on the phone as I waited for a VIP to arrive. The Christmas decorations were up, and some of the roads were closed.

The State Opening of Parliament was about to take place – the second in two months. The Conservatives had just won a landslide victory in a snap general election, and Boris Johnson had been crowned the country's Prime Minister. The Queen was once again on her way to Parliament to repeat the rigmarole she'd only just completed back in October, but this time she would be wearing a day dress and hat rather than her ceremonial robes, and travelling by car rather than horse-drawn carriage.

During our telephone conversation, Keith explained to me that while he'd had a couple of brief phone calls with the police, they'd never bothered to take a written statement from him. Our research had uncovered that the police in 1986 had been operating under the general impression that Keith was 'just another manager'.

But as I soon discovered, Keith Perry wasn't just *another manager*, which is exactly how he'd been described to the police. The luncheon that day was said to be *just some* managers meeting for lunch. But Keith was a man who did not take kindly to mistakes and errors.

'I was *a partner*!' Keith rebuked me sternly, after I'd mistakenly suggested he'd been *just* a manager. 'I was in charge of all the Sturgis offices. I was the residential sales partner – I basically employed everyone that worked there! Hire and fire, as they say,' he barked back, sounding a little as if he were shouting at me on a military parade ground.

I apologised for my mistake, and he wasted no time in telling me all about Sturgis and that he'd been the person responsible for giving Suzy a job with the company.

'We did lots of things to do with property. We had different elements – chartered surveyors, commercial, overseas – but essentially the largest element of the business was the residential side. I had my private offices in Barnes. That's where I was based, which actually wasn't attached to a sales office. It was basically executive offices. My immediate thought, when Suzy came for the interview, was that she would probably do well in sales. And I think she did. But as soon as I'd employed her, and once she had an agreed date to start working, she was despatched to Fulham, where she worked. And she was under Mark Gurdon's command on a day-to-day basis there.'

This was very helpful. We'd been trying to establish who had interviewed Suzy and given her the job at Sturgis. Keith's answer seemed to dispel an old story that Suzy had simply waltzed into the Fulham branch one day, as the fancy took her, and brazenly bagged a negotiator job on the spot.

I asked him about the day Suzy had gone missing, and if he could remember it.

'I can, for the simple reason that I, on a regular basis, used to go to the branches to see what was going on and impose my will on them, if you like. And that particular day I went to Fulham, and I had lunch with Mark Gurdon. And when I went into the office, prior to going out to lunch with him, I obviously saw all the staff in the Fulham office and I – I can't remember what I said, but er, I probably had a brief chat with all of them as I usually did.'

This was most enlightening. The man who'd interviewed Suzy for her job, the man who'd enforced the rules and policies in the branches, had seen Suzy shortly before she'd left the office that Monday.

This added a whole new dimension to the 'Kipper' diary entry that day.

Suzy wasn't worried about what her line manager, Mark Gurdon, thought. As he'd already told us, he thought Suzy was going to Putney to do some shopping. But with Keith Perry, the company 'enforcer', hovering around Fulham that day, would Suzy really have left the office without something being recorded in her diary?

It was more likely Keith Perry that she had feared?

Keith said that he couldn't remember if he'd popped back into the Fulham branch again after lunch. He believed he'd been formally notified that Suzy was missing later that evening.

'You were the strongman around policy and all that sort of thing?' I clarified.

'Yes, basically I was the OC,' Keith responded, even referring to himself in military terms – officer commanding (OC) was someone in charge of platoons, troops and sections in the military. All of his terminology was military based.

Keith clarified that it was Mark who ran the Fulham branch on a day-to-day basis, and that he would have known what Suzy would have been up to.

'I was their employer, but the only thing I found out about them was if – if they were out of order or misbehaved.'

He said that he'd never had any cause for concern about Suzy, and that he knew little about what she did outside the office.

'I didn't know much about her private life. That was down to them. I was only interested in what they actually did for me,' he said matter-of-factly.

I thanked Keith for his time and ended the call. I almost felt like saluting him in recognition of his help.

It was easy to imagine Suzy being intimidated by this gruff, confident-sounding, military-style manager who just happened to have been visiting her office on the very day she needed to get out to collect the secret pocket diary she didn't want anyone to see.

Keith Perry wasn't just a manager. He was Suzy's boss's boss, and he wasn't one to be messed around with. He had both the ability and clout to cause a lot of trouble for both Suzy and Mark Gurdon, if she'd been found to have been out of the office, on a personal errand, on the day she'd gone missing.

58

'I'm gonna make us a nice cup of tea,' Wendy Jones said with a cheeky smile in a broad Estuary English accent, before darting off toward the kitchen at the back of the house.

It had taken me two and a half years to track the diminutive Wendy Jones down. After months and months of research and eliminating hundreds of people with the same name, I was delighted that I'd eventually found her. And even more so now that she was offering me a cuppa.

Back in 1986, Wendy, her husband Barry, their two young children and their Rottweiler puppy had all lived at 123 Stevenage Road. It was a newly built, yellow-brick terraced house located on the north bank of the River Thames, in the same road as Fulham Football Club's Craven Cottage ground.

Just after 10 p.m. on the day of Suzy's disappearance, her white Ford Fiesta had been discovered by PC Christopher Dollery. It had been abandoned opposite Wendy's home in Stevenage Road. The location was more than a mile away from the fake Shorrolds Road house viewing written in Suzy's desk diary.

In her role as a negotiator at Sturgis estate agency, Suzy had been entrusted with a company car. During the spring and summer of 1986, she could regularly be seen zipping around South West London in the nearly new, 1.1-litre white Ford Fiesta, registration number: B396 GAN. It was a model from the lower end of the Fiesta range with few of the mod cons, but it was small and easy to park. What made it even more of a boon was that her employer allowed her to drive it for personal use in the evenings and at weekends too. With no markings on it to distinguish it from any other car in the area, it helped give Suzy the look of the upwardly mobile, girl about town that many at the time craved.

The discovery of Suzy's car represented one of the few things that the police could ever prove beyond doubt in their investigation – something they really could actually call a fact.

When PC Dollery found the car, he radioed in to report it. His call was logged into the Metropolitan Police Call and Despatch system, and the Police National Computer was updated and a report placed on it. All were indelible, undisputable records created at the exact time they happened.

As the radio call came in, Fulham CID mustered as many men as the small, divisional police station could find. Forensic teams were called; search teams were assembled. Even Paul Lamplugh himself became involved with the car because he was with DCs Mick Jones and Steve Hill at the time of PC Dollery's radio call. All of this meant that the finding of the car couldn't be disputed; it was a fact that PC Christopher Dollery had found the car parked opposite Wendy's Stevenage Road home, just after 10 p.m. on the night of Monday, 28 July 1986.

By the time the CID arrived at the vehicle, it was agreed that it was unlocked and the driver's seat – pushed right back as far as it would go – was much further back than five-foot-six Suzy would have needed it. Although it was unclear who had actually pushed the seat back, this suggested to investigators that her company car had been driven and abandoned there by her abductor, and not parked there by Suzy herself.

But while it was fact that PC Dollery had *discovered* the car in Stevenage Road at 10 p.m., there was plenty of dispute about the time it had actually been *abandoned* there, opposite Wendy's house – and part of this dispute involved Wendy herself.

There were a number of witnesses who claimed to have seen a car similar to Suzy's parked at differing times in Stevenage Road on the day Suzy had gone missing. Other witnesses

in the road that day had seen nothing at all. Wendy Jones'
original 1986 account suggested that she'd seen it parked
directly opposite her house at some time around 12.30 p.m. to
12.45 p.m. and that it hadn't moved all day, which was one of
the things we'd come to talk to her about.

After returning from her kitchen with a tray full of mugs
of tea and packets of biscuits for Caroline and me, Wendy,
in a blue floral dress, settled down in the chair next to me
and explained what she remembered. Her husband, Barry, also
joined us.

'If it *wasn't* school holidays, I probably would have been
in the kitchen doing something, because I didn't work at that
time. But because it *was* school holidays, the kids were in the
house, I was probably out the back, in the little garden.' She
sipped her tea as she spoke. 'I probably would have seen more
than I did, if it wasn't school holidays.'

Despite the lapse of time, Wendy sounded slightly disappointed that she hadn't seen someone parking the car and
getting out of it. She realised the importance of the car in the
case.

Wendy was correct on the dates. At the time of Suzy's disappearance, it was the long school summer holidays. For many
schools in the area, the last day of term had been Friday, 18
July 1986. From Saturday, 19 July onwards, the local school-
children would be free to run wild for six whole weeks.

Wendy explained that at the time of Suzy's disappearance,
she was looking after her four-year-old son and her daughter,
who had just turned eight. The children had previously attended the Rainbow Playhouse, a playgroup in nearby Bishop's
Park. Through the playgroup, she'd become friends with Ann
Mahon who worked there. Ann happened to live on an adja-
cent road, close to Wendy.

'I was quite friendly with Ann. Her boys were a bit more
grown up. That day, the day Suzy went missing, I'd arranged
with Ann to go and get a bit of shopping and then take the kids
to the cinema to see *Pinocchio*. We were going at lunchtime to
get the two, half-two matinee. I remember my kids had saved

up their pennies. This is how I know it to the day. So we were going to go to the bank, which was on Fulham Cross, to cash all the pennies up for them, so they could have a little spend,' Wendy explained.

But before they'd set off to the bank, Wendy had had to walk her Rottweiler on a circuit of the local area, with her two young children in tow. They left the house via the back garden, which had a gate into an alleyway at the rear leading into Millshot Close. From there, they reached the River Thames and walked the puppy north along the towpath and up to a nearby green. They'd then turned south toward the house, along Stevenage Road, approaching this time via the front door. And it is then that Wendy claims to have first seen Suzy's car parked opposite her house, partly obscuring the entrance to Ann Mahon's garage. The fact that it was obscuring the garage was why Wendy claimed to have noticed it.

After placing the puppy back in the house, collecting the pennies for the bank and the items the kids needed for the day out, Wendy and Ann set off in the car for NatWest bank at Fulham Cross.

In 1986, police decided to check what time Wendy and Ann had been in the bank, so that they could then work backward from that to work out what time Wendy might have first seen the car opposite her house. When they checked, they found Wendy and Ann had been in the bank at 12.49 p.m. that day. But working backward, this meant that Wendy's sighting of a car parked opposite her house had likely taken place before Suzy had even left the office.

Wendy's account, while it sounded convincing, baffled the police. How could Suzy's car have been in Stevenage Road before 12.40 p.m. when witnesses in Suzy's office claimed that she hadn't even left the office by that point? It had to be a different car Wendy had seen. But Wendy was insistent that she wasn't mistaken – the same car was there all day, parked opposite her house.

When she'd returned from watching *Pinocchio* at the cinema with her children at around 5 p.m., she was certain that the car was still in the same position. Later that night, at around 10.30 p.m., she claimed it had been this same car that she'd seen the police swarming all over as she drove back into the road with her husband Barry, after picking him up from a late shift at Earls Court Exhibition Centre, where he worked at that time.

But when police checked with other witnesses, who also claimed to have seen a white car parked near Wendy's house that day, some were saying they'd seen a vehicle parked in Stevenage Road as early as midday. Police believed it could have been one that had just been parked in a similar location, and not Suzy's car at all.

Two workmen digging in Stevenage Road that day even disputed that there had been a car there at all before 4 p.m. They told police they'd been on site from 9 a.m. until 4 p.m. that day, just yards from where Suzy's car was eventually discovered. Both stated that they hadn't seen her vehicle nor had they seen anything untoward or suspicious at all.

Given that it was impossible for Suzy to have been abducted, then her car driven by the abductor and abandoned outside Wendy's house *all before* Suzy had even left the Sturgis office that day – and given the other conflicting eyewitness accounts – it should have been a straightforward exercise for the police to say that it wasn't Suzy's car that Wendy had seen at lunchtime that day in Stevenage Road.

However, rather bizarrely, despite being perplexed by Wendy's account, and despite it being completely implausible, the police spent several weeks trying to bend their narrative around what Wendy had told them, desperately trying to make her account fit.

At one point, police even shifted the time Suzy had left her office – claiming that perhaps it had been at 12.30 p.m. rather than 12.40 p.m., enabling, at a push, the car to arrive in time for Wendy Jones to be right. It seemed somewhat strange that the police had gone to such trouble to try and accommodate an impossible sighting of Suzy's car into their narrative.

'I remember it like it was yesterday. They came and took her car late, I remember that…' Wendy explained how she'd come home that night after picking up Barry and found the police next to Suzy's vehicle. 'And I remember, we came back, and we came in and someone knocked at the door and they said, "Do you know whose car that is? Did you see anything?" And I said no.'

Wendy paused before adding, 'Because I remember her mum coming...'

'Her mum came and saw you, did she?' I asked, surprised.

'Yeah. Her mum came that night, yeah. It was late, as well...' Wendy frowned.

I had known that Paul and Diana had done their own enquiries; they spoke at length many times of conducting their own investigation in the Fulham area and of taking their dogs out along the Thames that night in an attempt to find their daughter – but it had never been revealed that they had gone door to door interrogating witnesses themselves.

Paul knew the location of Suzy's abandoned vehicle because he'd been with DC Mick Jones and DC Steve Hill when they'd all heard the news over the radio that the white Ford Fiesta had been found.

Paul and Diana were likely just anxious to help, but at the time, their involvement had been much more of a hindrance, and police had had to warn them off, requesting that they vacate the area with their dogs and leave the investigation to them.

Diana's involvement with the witnesses in the case troubled me.

Despite their initial attempts to bend the narrative to fit Wendy's alleged sighting of Suzy's car, around three weeks later, things had all changed. By 20 August, the police publicly conceded that the white car spotted parked at 12.45 p.m. in Stevenage Road may not have belonged to Suzy, as first thought, and they put out an appeal for any driver who had parked a white car in Stevenage Road that day to contact them.

Nevertheless, there was something decidedly odd about the efforts that the police had gone to in order to try to incorporate Wendy's account into their narrative in 1986.

Even more confusing was that despite that very public declaration in August 1986, that Wendy was mistaken about her earliest sighting, more than thirty years later, Det. Supt Ryan was attempting to say to us that Wendy's statement, at least in part, was something which should be relied upon.

When I asked Wendy about the type of car Suzy had owned, Wendy seemed convinced that the car she'd seen was silver and not white. And more interestingly she suggested something else:

'I remember her number plate: GAN – it ended in GAN. I remember that. But I don't know the other bit.'

'Could there have been a couple of different cars with similar number plates around that day?' I pondered.

'I don't know if estate agents have a fleet of maybe three or four cars they all use?' Wendy suggested.

'Was it possible that there'd been two different cars?' I asked.

'Personally, I don't think it moved…' She shook her head. 'Because there was a conflict with the police saying to me, she was *not* going to yours in Stevenage Road, but to Shorrolds Road.'

There was conflict with the police about where Suzy was going that day?

This was an interesting statement, especially given that Stuart Ryan and Albert Clyne had both suggested that Suzy's car was found near another house that she was showing to a client.

In August 1986, someone had indeed tried to push the idea into the public arena that Suzy had done another house viewing in Stevenage Road, at Wendy's home.

Certain media outlets reported that Suzy had taken 'Mr Kipper' to see a second property on sale in Stevenage Road through Sturgis estate agency. It was alleged that the car had been parked outside the property at lunchtime and indeed was there for much of the day, but nobody had called on the female house seller.

The question was, who had *revealed* this to the press?

'Why was her car there? I don't know,' Wendy continued. 'It wouldn't have been the fact that she'd parked it there and walked, because it was too far to Shorrolds Road. And I was adamant, I was adamant that the car was there. And it didn't move.'

'Your house was on sale with Sturgis, wasn't it?' I asked, trying to understand what Wendy meant about conflict with the police.

'It was,' she agreed, 'for a short time.'

'Were there any other Sturgis "For Sale" signs on your road? Did anyone else have a "For Sale" sign up?'

'No, I don't think so…'

'And Suzy wasn't coming to your house that day?'

Wendy shook her head and explained that, despite this, the police had still thoroughly searched her house and looked in her garden.

As Wendy sipped her tea, her husband, Barry added, 'Yeah, the main question, from the police's perspective, was whether Suzy was due to show anyone around our house. But we weren't due a viewing that day.'

'No,' Wendy agreed.

'Our contact was Mark Gurdon. We never had contact with her personally – we always dealt with Mark in the office,' Barry confirmed.

'It was really difficult because there was a lot of coming and goings. And Suzy's mum, she actually brought a medium round. Do you remember?' Wendy added, turning to Barry.

'Yeah,' he sighed.

'She knocked. And I just said to her, "Look, I wish it wasn't the school holidays and I'd have seen something more, and then I could have helped." She was trying everything, so she said, "Could I bring a medium to your house?" And I said, "If it helps, bring anybody you can." I remember it scared me a bit, because she said the medium kept saying, "Go back to Wendy's house! Go back to Wendy's house!" And I was thinking, oh my God. But you'd do anything to help the lady if you could have…'

As we finished our tea, listening to Wendy and Barry talk about their family, I began to worry about exactly how much influence Diana and Paul Lamplugh had had on the police investigation right from the start – right from the word go.

Why were the police now claiming that Suzy was due to do a viewing at Wendy's house the day she went missing when that was incorrect? And who had been propagating this idea in the press?

Wendy was likely one of the very first witnesses that the police traced themselves, yet Diana Lamplugh had interrogated her on her doorstep before she'd even given a formal written statement to the police. In fact, Wendy would tell me that it would be more than two weeks before police would actually take a full written statement from her.

'I probably didn't pay much attention to the car when I was coming back from the dog walk. Just like, there's a car there, and it's a little bit across Richard's drive. But I quite like cars, don't I?' Wendy rounded off our meeting as we finished the last of her biscuits.

'Yeah, yeah…' Barry agreed with her.

'I'm really into cars. And I think I would have known it was a Ford Fiesta.' Wendy paused and then motioned toward her front window. 'Like now, if there was a car parked across my drive, like yours is, and I'd gone out for four or five hours and come back, I would remember.'

I had parked my car across Wendy's drive. Wendy had seen me get out of it and she'd seen it over my shoulder as we entered her house. But she hadn't seen it for the past fifty minutes we'd been talking, and neither could she see it from where she was sitting. Any description would be from memory.

'What car have I got, Wendy?' I asked, keen to put her to her own test.

'Well, I would know it was silver, and a Jaguar…' She smiled.

We all laughed.

My German car was blue.

59

'Did my ex-husband tell you where I was?' Zoe Hutchings said, raising her voice as I introduced myself. 'I didn't want to be found!'

'I know, I'm sorry. I *am* sorry,' I tried to placate her.

I was both sorry and elated at the same time. I'd finally come face to face with the most elusive witness in Suzy's case.

Zoe was now in her sixties, considerably younger than Michael Hutchings, her ex-husband with whom she'd run the Prince of Wales pub in 1986. Her immaculate blonde bobbed hair made her look ten years younger than that though.

I knew that Zoe didn't want to be found – I didn't need her to tell me this. I'd travelled hundreds of miles looking for her, leaving messages with friends, her ex-husband and previous places of work. I'd called at address after address hoping that she still lived at one of them. But Zoe remained distant, uncontactable, out of sight and responded to none of my overtures.

Despite her suspicions, no one I'd spoken with had actually told me where I might find her, where she worked, or even the city she lived in; they'd all kept shtum. I'd tracked her down using good old detective work. But 2020 was shaping up to be a year of complete surprises, and here I was, face to face with Zoe.

We were, however, both wearing face masks.

Oddly, the reason for the masks was also the reason that I'd been able to eventually track her down. A pneumonia outbreak in Wuhan, China had led the Chinese to discover a novel strain of coronavirus causing mild to severe respiratory infection. A pandemic had swept from China and quickly across the globe, hospitalising and killing thousands in its wake. It had been nearly five months since the UK Prime Minister had announced unprecedented laws locking people in their homes, banning them from seeing family or friends and closing businesses, all in the hope of stemming the spread which had infiltrated our National Health Service and care homes, causing all sorts of problems.

My security work, largely dependent on the travel and hospitality sectors, had taken a huge nosedive, leaving me with much more time on my hands. Time I'd used to redouble my efforts to find the ever elusive Zoe. Eventually I'd managed to narrow down where she lived and worked, and landed on two places.

The second of the two places, many hours' drive from London, had brought me mask to mask with her.

'Has anyone told you what I want to talk to you about?' I asked, trying to calm my own nerves as well as hers.

Zoe shook her head. 'Nope.'

'You worked in London, at the Prince of Wales pub...'

Zoe nodded.

'I'm writing a book about Suzy Lamplugh. I'm trying to find out what happened to her. And I believe it could be something to do with her lost property at the Prince of Wales.'

There was a long pause. Zoe frowned, looking past me, as if trying to remember the details.

'I believe *something happened*,' she said. 'We were actually on holiday.'

'Yes,' I responded enthusiastically.

'I think we went to Rhodes? But, erm, who was running the pub?

'Was it a couple called Clive and Karen?'

'Yes!'

'I've spoken to both of them. There's some confusion about why the police became involved, and that's one of the things I'm trying to get to grips with. Why were the police called in the first place about this lost property? Is that something that would usually have happened with lost property?'

'No.' Zoe shook her head again, her brow still furrowed.

'Your ex-husband, Michael, seems to think he was present when Suzy's property was actually found. I wanted to check that *you* hadn't found her items or had anything to do with the lost property at all?'

'No, I don't remember that,' Zoe replied.

'No? You never gave a statement to the police at all?' I enquired.

'Nope,' she said, shrugging.

It was crazy. Despite Zoe and Michael Hutchings being the permanent, full-time managers of the pub, the police had barely had any interaction with either of them. Neither of them had been asked for formal written statements. It was testament to how little the police understood about the inner workings of the pub on the very day Suzy had gone missing, the day she was due to go there and collect her lost property.

It was one of the fundamental flaws of the police investigation. A gaping void in which anyone could say anything they liked about what had happened at the Prince of Wales and it be left completely unchallenged.

Everything the police knew about the pub and what did or didn't happen there on the day Suzy had gone missing had come from the stand-in staff; from Clive Vole and Karen Furness – two relief workers who were only there for a short space of time.

'Surely the police have records – you don't need my help on this?' she asked.

I explained that I was trying to piece together what had happened on Sunday, 27 and Monday, 28 July 1986 at the Prince of Wales. I wanted to know how Suzy's property came to have been lost there, who came into contact with it and exactly who was at the pub during those two days. I needed Zoe's help precisely because the police had made absolutely no effort to understand any of this at the time, and there were no real records aside from what Clive Vole, and perhaps Karen Furness, his ex, had told the police.

We talked briefly about Brendon, the cellar boy, though Zoe couldn't remember his surname, only that his family had a bric-a-brac shop on the same part of Upper Richmond Road as the pub.

Despite her original reluctance to speak with me, Zoe agreed that we could speak again. She pledged to search her personal records as well as her old passports for entry and exit visas to establish where she and Michael had been on holiday at the time of Suzy's disappearance.

I left for my long drive home a little happier than when I'd arrived.

We were still making progress, despite the problems we now faced with the Prince of Wales pub – Food & Fuel, the lease-holders of the pub who we'd previously been dealing with, had gone into administration due to the coronavirus pandemic.

60

'Hey!' I greeted Caroline at the front door of my South London home. Now that lockdown rules were being relaxed in many places across England, Caroline wanted to make the most of the weather. She'd insisted on walking from the station and wouldn't let me collect her.

Southern England was experiencing a significant heatwave. Temperatures had exceeded 36°C across parts of the south-east while I'd travelled back in the car yesterday. The weather men and women were predicting several more scorching days with 'tropical night-time temperatures'.

'Good to see you,' she responded with a big, bright-eyed smile as she walked in. 'Your garden's grown since I was last here,' she quipped, looking out onto the messy lawn.

'Yeah, right,' I said, chuckling. Household chores like cutting the front lawn were a long way down my list of priorities. While my paid work had taken a hit during the pandemic, I'd filled the time going through Suzy's case again, piece by piece, making sure we hadn't missed anything.

Caroline walked out into the garden, sat down at the large table on the decking and put her bag on the seat next to her. The table was already laid out with various photos and pieces of paper for our meeting.

'You look nice today,' I said, looking at her bright yellow summer dress. But it wasn't just her outfit. She looked happy – the happiest I'd seen her for more than a year. They say the eyes are the windows to the soul, and that seemed very true today – her blue eyes sparkled.

She smiled. 'Thank you.'

'How was the trip down?' I asked, sitting down opposite her.

She frowned. 'It was surprisingly busy – hard to believe we're in the middle of a pandemic.'

'Yeah, I wondered if it would be. It's the State Opening of Parliament; the Queen is welcoming in the new MPs – I'm guessing the whole world is in London today?'

'Oh, yes, that would explain it,' she replied, beaming.

'What's up with you? You look pleased with yourself. What's with the dress?'

'You're taking me out for a socially distanced lunch after our garden meeting.'

'Am I?'

'You are. We're really getting somewhere with this case. You've found Zoe, and hopefully she's going to call and we can move this on. But I've found something too...' She beamed.

I laughed. 'Let's have it then.'

'Put these in.' Caroline passed me a set of Bluetooth headphones while she fiddled with the screen of her smartphone.

I placed the headphones in my ears.

'Listen to this.' Caroline hit the play button on her phone.

'There's such a gap at the moment. Er... There's ga... The gap between... wh... wh... where Suzy was last seen, coming out of the car, er, house, to the car... And where the car was found...' My ears were filled with the sound of Diana Lamplugh's voice.

'What is this?' I spoke over the talking in my ears.

Caroline paused the interview; Diana was silent.

'After our meeting with the police, with Det. Supt Stuart Ryan, you asked me to go back over everything we had.'

I nodded.

'It's from a batch of old interviews. I listened to them months ago and told you there was nothing particularly useful in them.'

I frowned. 'Okay...'

Caroline was smiling so much it looked like she'd won the lottery. 'Well, I relistened to those radio interviews again.'

'Okay.' I couldn't think what she might have found.

'This one is an interview with Diana, recorded on 30 July 1986 – Diana's fiftieth birthday.[2] It's a Wednesday. Suzy hasn't even been missing for forty-eight hours yet. So everything is still fresh in everyone's mind, right?'

'Yes,' I agreed.

'Listen.' Caroline hit the play button again.

Diana's voice, as if from the dead, again filled my ears.

'And nobody,' Diana sighed, 'has come forward… I gather there may be a few leads, which would be fantastic, but we just want to hear something. If we could hear something positive… I – we…' Diana paused. She sounded absolutely heartbroken, not the polished performer that many would come to know in later years.

She continued: 'We're absolutely convinced that she's alright, but it's an awful long time and if… if she is shut up in a house, anywhere, erm… By now she's going to be very tired and very hungry and very lonely… And I so badly want her to get free.'

It was heart-wrenching to listen to, more than three decades later, knowing that Suzy had never been found, and that both Diana and Paul were now dead. Although Diana sounded like a broken mother, at points during the interview there were also snatches of hope that Suzy was still alive. The events were so new and raw, and it was so soon after Suzy's disappearance, that Diana's voice still conveyed some last vestiges of optimism in places.

'Certainly we've met a lot of Suzy's – most of Suzy's friends,' Diana continued, 'and they're very good friends, and they've all been rallying round us like mad, and helping. And I am sure we'd know, if she had a friend…'

Diana paused, as if the words eluded her.

The male interviewer cut in with a question in reference to 'Mr Kipper': 'So you're ruling out the possibility that she's actually run away with this fellow, whoever it may be?'

---

2. Source: LBC/IRN, 30 July 1986, Copyright Global Radio UK Ltd. Reproduced with permission.

'There's absolutely no way that Suzy would have gone off and left her job. It would be totally out of character. She wouldn't have left,' Diana replied, pausing again. 'She was looking forward to my fiftieth birthday, which is today… and we were looking forward to celebrating together. We're very much a family. She'd given us a lovely present at the weekend. They'd all got together, all four children, and paid for a hotel for us to stay in. She'd arranged tickets for us to go to the theatre, and that's why she came round on Sunday evening to find out how we'd enjoyed it. She'd been windsurfing and she was in very good form. And she was looking forward to going out with Adam on Tuesday. And playing tennis on Monday, and, erm, there was absolutely no reason, there was no indication. And she's not that sort of person—'

'Monday!' I shouted. 'Rewind, and play that again!'

Caroline fiddled with her phone screen. Diana was silent for a moment before continuing. '… she was looking forward to going out with Adam on Tuesday. And playing tennis on Monday…'

'Bloody hell!' I pulled the headphones from my ears.

'You heard it?' Caroline asked excitedly.

'Diana said that Suzy was due to play tennis the night she went missing.'

'Yes, that's exactly what she said.'

'Suzy must have told Diana when she saw her on Sunday?'

'Yes!'

'That's never been mentioned?'

'No, nowhere, never. I've done a keyword search for tennis in everything we've got, and there's nothing – other than some references to her being an occasional tennis player, it's never mentioned anywhere. It's been completely missed.'

'There was no tennis kit in Suzy's car when it was found at 10 p.m. that Monday night?'

'Nope.' Caroline shook her head excitedly.

'Which means… her original intention, when she left for work on that Monday morning was to go home after work that evening and collect it?' I asked rhetorically.

'But?' Caroline pushed a piece of paper across the table to me. It was a black-and-white photo of Suzy's work diary the day she went missing.

'But she couldn't,' I responded, looking down at the photo before pausing.

I could feel the excitement building inside me, and now understood exactly why Caroline was looking so pleased with herself.

'Tennis matches typically last a couple of hours, sometimes three? Civil twilight on the day Suzy went missing began at around 8.55 p.m. and we know from the cricket reports just how overcast and gloomy the day was. There wouldn't be enough light to play tennis *after* sunset, assuming she's playing outside,' Caroline explained.

Mark Gurdon had told us that he sometimes played tennis at Clapham Common on the public courts there, near his home, close to where Adam Leegood lived. He hadn't ever mentioned playing tennis with Suzy, but it was possible that they all used public outdoor courts.

'She had a 6 p.m. appointment in her diary that day,' I said, reading from the photo of Suzy's diary, 'to meet a Joanna Wright outside number 43 Waldermar.'

'She did,' Caroline agreed. 'We know her colleagues got worried when she missed that meeting. And the police have previously confirmed they'd traced every other appointment in Suzy's diary. They were all bonafide. The only appointment they couldn't trace was the *Kipper* one.'

I nodded. 'Yes, which suggests the Joanna Wright appointment was bonafide.'

'If that 6 p.m. Joanna Wright appointment were to run over, there wouldn't have been enough time for her to go home and collect her tennis kit, let alone go to the pub and collect her chequebook and diary before her game?'

'No...' I agreed. The 6 p.m. Joanna Wright house appointment was potentially the spanner in the works for Suzy's plans the day she went missing; the reason why she *had* to go to Putney that lunchtime.

301

'There's some reporting around a tennis racquet found out on display in her flat. That might mean that she never reached home to pick her tennis stuff up?' Caroline suggested.

One of the things Det. Supt Stuart Ryan had insisted we needed, in order to convince him that our version of events was viable, was to prove why Suzy had gone to the Prince of Wales *in the afternoon*, when according to the police 'she's told everybody she's not going to the pub until later that evening'.

It was implicit in what Ryan was saying that, according to the police, Suzy's entire Monday evening after work was free, that she could simply go and collect her property from the pub at any point that evening. They didn't seem to know that the Sturgis office wouldn't be closing until 6 p.m. or about the 6 p.m. Joanna Wright appointment. And they certainly hadn't been aware that Suzy was playing tennis that night and needed to grab her kit in advance.

'There was simply no free time in Suzy's evening to fit all this in, was there?' I asked, though we both already knew the answer.

Caroline shook her head. 'I think she's had a last-minute change of schedule and tried to cram her errands in at lunchtime to free up her evening.'

I joked that there was something slightly surreal that the information about Suzy playing tennis was provided by Diana Lamplugh, almost as if she was giving us the evidence from beyond the grave.

'That's not all she's provided us with,' added Caroline excitedly. 'I've got more...'

She explained that when she'd gone back through our research, she'd noticed something else that Diana had told the press and it impacted upon the location of Suzy's abandoned car.

She pulled out a copy of an old newspaper article from August 1986 and began summarizing it. 'It's the first fortnight of the investigation, everything is fresh in people's minds. Suzy's parents are appealing to the public, not only to look out for the keys to 37 Shorrolds Road but also to keep an eye out for Suzy's keys to her company car and flat. It's actually the description of her company car keys that is the crucial bit,' Caroline said, beaming.

We'd been agonising over the issue of Suzy's car being abandoned opposite a house for sale for a long time. I'd repeatedly suggested that Suzy's car left close to a Sturgis 'For Sale' sign was *not* a coincidence, and that the driver had done so with the knowledge of where Suzy worked. But how had the driver found this out?

Nick Bryant, Suzy's flatmate, had suggested that as Suzy was very talkative and fairly forthcoming, it wouldn't have been difficult for anyone who spoke with her to find out that she worked for Sturgis.

But now we had another answer.

'Suzy's car key was on a yellow key fob belonging to Sturgis estate agency,' Caroline stated.

'So whoever had Suzy's car keys *knew* that she worked for Sturgis because of the branded key ring?' I suggested.

Caroline nodded, showing me two more photos. One showed an image of a yellow plastic Sturgis key fob and the other a shot of the Sturgis 'For Sale' board located outside 123 Stevenage Road. The company name, distinct keyhole logo and bright yellow corporate colour were evident on both the car key fob and the estate agent's sign.

The key ring also listed many of the Sturgis branches across London: Mayfair, Knightsbridge, Kensington, Fulham, Barnes Chiswick, Clapham, Putney, Richmond, Sheen and Wimbledon. We knew from our dealings with the Sturgis staff how busy they were. It was one of the largest estate agents in South West London, shifting at least 1,500 properties a year with £200 million in sales. Their sale boards were absolutely everywhere.

'Whoever had possession of her car keys could have driven around *any* part of South West London and found a yellow 'For Sale' sign to match that fob, then dumped her car next to it,' Caroline added grimly.

'This is dynamite! Well done, really well done.' I smiled across at her.

'Not bad for a housewife in the Home Counties, eh?'

'You're the best detective I never had on my team, Caroline.'

61

The former landlady of the pub, Zoe Hutchings, called me back on the phone, and we spoke at length about her summer holidays during the eighties as we tried to work out where she and Michael had been at the end of July 1986, instead of running the Prince of Wales pub.

She kindly dug out her old passports and sent me scanned copies. We concluded, from looking at the passport stamps in 1986, that she and Michael had not left the country to holiday in Rhodes or any other part of Greece. In fact, the reason they had taken time out from the pub was not due to a foreign holiday at all.

After many hours of racking her brain, Zoe had realised why she and her husband Michael had taken a short period of leave. On the morning of Thursday, 24 July 1986, as Britain nursed its hangover following the royal wedding between Prince Andrew and Sarah Ferguson, Zoe's sister had given birth to her third child at a hospital in South Wales. Zoe and Michael subsequently took a week off work for a visit to see her and the newborn.

But as Michael Hutchings explained to me, booking and taking a holiday from the Prince of Wales pub, indeed any Imperial Inns & Taverns pub, wasn't just a simple case of getting someone to cover for you and then rushing off. The process was far more painstaking and laborious than that – and involved more people than I had realised.

The area manager would have to be contacted; the holiday would have to be agreed and signed off; the company would have to organise a stocktake. A stocktaker would then have to come in and audit the product on the premises, before a handover to any caretaker staff could take place.

I tracked down Patrick Beatt who had been a stocktaker for Courage and then Imperial Inns & Taverns for five years during the late eighties. He had worked north of the Thames mostly, but occasionally had ventured south too.

He talked me through the process of stocktaking and handovers: 'There was a process for licensees to request holidays. You'd approach the area manager with a holiday request. The area manager would organise the reliefs to be present and a stocktaker to do a handover. All that took a few days to organise…'

He explained that the stocktake and handover was a formal process and both the licensee and the relief would be expected to be present. All of the money and stock in the building had to be checked and accounted for, then both the licensee and the relief were expected to sign the stocktake forms and agree what was being handed over. If there was any money or stock missing during a stocktake, this would be deducted from individuals' wages, so it was something everyone wanted to get right.

Stocktakers would arrive early in the mornings, at 8 a.m. or 8.30 a.m. The stocktake and money count, which was done right down to individual packets of crisps, would take a maximum of four hours but could be faster than that. Once the forms were signed, the licensee would be released, free to go on their holiday or wherever they were going, and the relief would then be in control of the building, and the stocktaker would leave. At the end of the relief period, the process would then be repeated again, and the stock and money handed back to the licensee.

The working week in Imperial Inns & Taverns pubs ran Sunday to Sunday, so it made sense for holidays to start on Monday mornings. Patrick said he would normally be finished by midday each day.

The stocktake would only have happened Monday to Friday and couldn't have taken place at the weekend, so, with the baby not being born until the Thursday morning before Suzy's disappearance, the earliest that the stocktaker could have arrived was by Monday morning to do the changeover on the very day that Suzy had gone missing.

Zoe and Michael had travelled by car from the Prince of Wales pub to see Zoe's sister in hospital during the latter part of the morning on Monday, 28 July 1986. Neither Zoe nor Michael could remember who their stocktaker that day was.

I called Zoe back and explained what Patrick had told me.

'It was my sister's third baby, so I don't think we would have been in any rush to get there, and with Michael being so conscientious at work and being the brewery's training manager, he would have waited until Monday morning.'

She concluded that Clive and Karen had likely arrived on Sunday, 27 July 1986, and all four of them had been at the Prince of Wales pub on Sunday night together.

It now made sense why Michael had some recollection of the lost property, because he had been there when it had been found. Zoe agreed it was possible the normal activities in the pub might have been curtailed that Monday morning – there might have been no food served, and the pub could even have been closed because of the handover and the stocktake.

Did Suzy visit the pub to collect her lost property during a period when the venue was closed to the general public?

62

'Well, episodic memory is the memory for your personal experiences. So if you're asking someone, "What were you doing on this day in 1986?" And they're trying to remember...'

Elizabeth Loftus is a cognitive psychologist, an expert on human memory. As one of the world's foremost experts on the malleability of human memory, she has written countless books and research papers on the subject, and was ranked amongst the most influential psychological researchers of the twentieth century. I was extremely fortunate to have been able to speak with her.

Loftus was more than an academic, she had taken her research and applied it to the real world, in legal settings, consulting or providing expert witness testimony for hundreds of very well-known cases, including those of Ted Bundy, the American serial killer; Timothy McVeigh, the Oklahoma bomber; and OJ Simpson.

I wanted Loftus's advice on the content of Wendy Jones' and Clive Vole's interviews, given the age of the memories and that both interviews contained a level of detail that we hadn't seen from anyone else in our case.

The police appeared to want to disregard what many of our witnesses had told us during their interviews. It was as if they disbelieved their testimony.

In Clive Vole's case, there were indications that the police simply didn't accept that Suzy's property was found by him on the Sunday night, or that he'd then spoken to Suzy on the phone the day she'd gone missing. And that he was somehow mistaken when he indicated Suzy was going to the pub in the afternoon, rather than the evening.

In Wendy's case, the police disputed that no house viewing was arranged at her property at 123 Stevenage Road on the day Suzy had gone missing.

Somehow both were wrong, according to the police, so I'd asked Elizabeth Loftus for assistance in understanding long-term memory.

The rain hammered against my office window as I thought back to our conversation. Outside in the road there was a sea of stationary red tail lights, traffic caught in the rain as people tried to make their way home in the darkness. The red lights made the darkness seem even darker. The weather forecasters were suggesting that today was going to be the wettest day since records began in 1891. It was slightly odd, prophetic even, that the previous record had been set on 25 August 1986, less than a month after Suzy had gone missing.

As I read through my notes, Elizabeth Loftus's voice filtered back into my head, her glamorous-sounding American accent brightening the dark, wet British night like Californian sunshine.

'It's obviously such a long time ago, witnesses are not going to have much of a memory except for probably some of the details that they would have rehearsed in subsequent interviews… and maybe thereafter, because for them to try to dig up something fresh, that they haven't already committed to a verbal report, is not going to be easy or particularly reliable.'

I'd explained the situation, particularly with Clive Vole's interviews, that we had been able to corroborate parts of what he was saying, and that it felt like a lucid and real memory as he explained the events to us, but that the police were suggesting it was unreliable and couldn't be trusted.

'When you press people for details and they don't have details,' Loftus had explained, 'are they feeling maybe some pressure to produce them? And people do try all kinds of different things, whether they're guilty or innocent, to respond to that pressure.'

'And they make things up? Is that perhaps your suggestion?' I'd asked.

'Well, they can fill in details with inferences or speculation that then can somehow become or start to feel like a memory. That's what people sometimes do when they're under pressure. And by pressure, I don't necessarily mean overly coercive, I mean just a feeling, like, "I need to produce more details. That's what's being asked for here."'

This perhaps explained Wendy's account – why she remembered part of the car's registration number but got the colour of the car wrong – because her memory had been populated with information from different sources?

Wendy had remembered that Suzy's number plate ended in 'GAN' but had suggested to us that Sturgis estate agency might have had a fleet of perhaps three or four cars they all used.

This was an important point. What if there had been a couple of different cars with similar number plates around that day?

On checking with Martin Sturgis, we'd discovered that it was a lot more than just three or four vehicles. His estate agency had more than 150 company cars, many purchased as a job lot.

To follow this up, we'd checked with the Driver and Vehicle Licensing Agency (DVLA) to find out how many other vehicles had shared a similar number plate to Suzy's and discovered that at the time, 900 vehicles had a registration starting with the letter B and ending with the letters GAN. Among this number were another thirty-three Ford Fiestas that were either white, silver, grey, beige or cream.

But if Wendy *wasn't* able to correctly identify the type of car she claimed to have seen early that lunchtime, and the colour was only slightly wrong in her recall, it wasn't just the thirty-three Ford Fiestas in that group we needed to consider. We found there were actually a total of 313 vehicles with a similar-shaped body design and a B-GAN registration that were white, silver, grey, beige or cream.

There would have been a number of different police officers who spoke to Wendy Jones, even in those first few precious hours after finding the car. But as Wendy had told us when we met – in the days that followed, even after the police had removed Suzy's car, a mobile police office was put in its place. The searches of the area, the drains and the waterways were coordinated from the mobile unit. But there was no toilet nearby, and Wendy's facilities were used by those manning the police office. She also became a police resource for cups of tea and coffee too.

Wendy's formal written police statement wasn't taken from her until some weeks later. This was after she'd had all of this contact with the police, after Suzy's parents had become involved with her, and after the spiritual medium had been at her home at Diana Lamplugh's behest. All of those influences would surely have applied pressure to her to add more and more detail to her account?

Had she actually seen a car earlier in the day at all? Or was the testimony of the two workmen – who'd said there'd been no car there earlier in the day, and there still wasn't one there when they'd left at 4 p.m. – more reliable?

And in Clive Vole's case too, his police statement hadn't been taken until a year after he'd found Suzy's chequebook.

Loftus recommended that I speak with Professor Ray Bull, an English academic, best known for his work on investigative interviewing of criminal suspects, witnesses and victims. As a professor of forensic psychology, his main expertise related to the conducting of investigations. He'd written several books and co-authored research papers on deception detection.

He was one of the world's leading experts in his field, meaning he was in great demand across the globe. But such was the allure of Suzy's case it wasn't too difficult getting him involved. On the contrary, he'd instantly been interested in reviewing our information in between his globetrotting schedule.

The question of whether Suzy was visiting Wendy Jones' house that day, at 123 Stevenage Road, wasn't up for debate. Wendy and her husband had never ever dealt with Suzy as their estate agent, had confirmed to us that they had no viewings booked and that Suzy was not coming that day. Again, Suzy had taken no door key for their property. Their house sold successfully some time later. One had to conclude that the police were wrong here.

But with Clive Vole's information, Professor Bull had spent several weeks assessing and reviewing it. We had met to discuss his findings when his schedule permitted.

He'd told us: 'One of the crucial points you also wished me to address was could a person have the recall he had, with some prompting from you, across so many years? In my view, yes, he could recall things. Partly some of what he talked about was relatively routine, like – let's assume he's telling the truth at the moment – where they would put lost belongings that people had left in or around the pub. On the way down to the cellar, on the electricity box. So it's not surprising that he gave that detail.'

The professor reminded me of a science teacher from my school days – bespectacled, with bushy white hair to the sides of his head and a matching handlebar moustache. But it wasn't just his appearance – he had that instantly likable, calm manner about him too; the type that could give you scathing criticism but still somehow keep it positive. There was a type of unshakable integrity about him.

When I'd asked about the finding of the lost property at the pub, Professor Bull had said: 'Clive's recall of where he found the stuff, that seems reasonable, because it was relatively unusual. And when he talks about that, you'll know, from your expertise, that when people are lying, what they want to do is avoid giving you detail, particularly detail you can check up on. Now, we can't check up where he found it, but by and large, I personally find it acceptable what he says about finding her stuff. And going to the Chinese takeaway, he didn't need to say that if he was lying.'

We talked about the phone calls to the pub the day Suzy had gone missing, and Professor Bull had remarked: 'So Suzy called the pub, and at the end of your first meeting with him,

Clive finally admitted to you that he did speak to her on the phone. You had to push him a bit, to be a bit clearer, and then he admits that he did speak to her. Suzy did phone. He admits to that. So then we move forward to later in the afternoon, when allegedly she said she was going to come, but then she never turned up, according to him… And then he says some other person, which he later says is a woman, allegedly phoned up and the gist of it was "keep her there". And crucially, one of the queries I have about his story, he says, "This woman said keep her there, and phone me," but he never says what he did about that message, does he? Because if that message were true, think about how long ago it was, thirty-three years? He would have had to have asked that person for her phone number in order to call her back, because there's no automatic way in those days on your phone of knowing who's calling you. So you didn't ask him about that. Fair enough. But he didn't volunteer, "I took her number."'

Detecting lies wasn't an exact science, and with some people being much better at lying than others, it was often a very subjective test. This was the same from a psychological point of view too. The polygraph, often referred to as a lie detector test in popular culture, is a misnomer. The polygraph doesn't actually detect lies – it monitors heart rate, blood pressure and skin conductance to detect the increased anxiety that often accompanies a lie. But one of the reasons that polygraph results are inadmissible in court is that they fail with people who don't get anxious about lying. And these are the same liars who can most easily fool you in a real-life scenario too. You had to be clever to catch them out.

The crucial point on the interviews for me was that the accounts mainly held water – they were to be believed and seemed to be telling the truth.

A professor of criminal investigation, Professor Bull had even rounded off one of our meetings by asking, 'Why haven't you dug up the pub yet?'

It was something that I'd felt the police should be doing, not us. But with the pub lease having changed hands because of the coronavirus pandemic, gaining access to the premises had become a problem. The new leaseholder had not replied to my communications.

And there was already talk in the media of a second national lockdown to control a surge in new COVID-19 infections.

63

'What? That can't be right.' I was shocked.

'It is, and that's exactly what they're going to do,' Dean Kingham explained.

Dean Kingham was John Cannan's current lawyer. Cannan had recently suffered a debilitating stroke at the age of sixty-seven and, having already served more than thirty-two years of his minimum thirty-five-year sentence for the murder of Shirley Banks, it had left him unable to function as he once would have. He had asked Kingham to make an application to the Parole Board to either be recategorised as a lower risk prisoner or released – as he could no longer possibly be a risk to the public after the stroke.

My feelings about Cannan were juxtaposed. Staring me in the face was a convicted rapist and murderer. But someone I wholeheartedly believed to be completely innocent of any involvement in Suzy's disappearance. And moreover, what Kingham was telling me was incomprehensible to anyone that had been around the British criminal justice system for any length of time.

We'd previously established that throughout the duration of Cannan's 1989 trial for the murder of Shirley Banks, Suzy's name had never once been mentioned in Exeter Crown Court. This was the trial that had led to Cannan's conviction for which he had initially received a whole-life prison term. Nor was Suzy's name mentioned during his appeal in 2008, where the whole-life term was changed, and he was given a thirty-five-year minimum tariff.

314

But now, all these years later, the Parole Board was asking Kingham about Cannan's involvement in Suzy's disappearance. The Parole Board was the statutory body that would decide on the recategorisation or release of Cannan from custody. But as Kingham was explaining to me, the laws governing his release had all changed due to the John Worboys case.

The Parole Board would investigate whether Cannan still posed a risk to the public. They'd make an assessment of his risk, their assessment based on a written dossier. The dossier would contain previous convictions, pre-sentence, psychiatric and psychological reports. There would be evidence from the prison and probation service about his behaviour at HMP Full Sutton. But under the new rules, consideration would also now be given to mere allegations, allegations that had never been charged by the police, let alone placed before a court.

Alarmingly, under the new laws, the Parole Board had the ability to make a finding of fact. They could decide, without any criminal trial whatsoever, on a much lower burden of proof, that John Cannan had indeed murdered Suzy Lamplugh.

Moreover, Parole Board panels could be presented with allegations that have been made against the prisoner or those that were under active investigation by the police, enabling the board to adjudicate on them as if they were true.

Suddenly, after the changes to the laws and regulatory framework by the Parole Board, all the recent digs, rumours and the wild allegations we'd seen in the press over the past two years about Cannan took on a clarity all of their own.

I'd made overtures to Cannan's solicitors in an attempt to understand how he had become so entangled and ensnared in Suzy's case. The answer, I was sure, could be found at the meeting in London's Chinatown, just forty-eight hours after Suzy had disappeared – the meeting between Paul and Diana Lamplugh and Sir David Napley. From this point onwards, Sir David Napley became involved in the investigation and began pulling strings in the background.

But with the people at that meeting now dead, I would have to turn to Cannan to try to understand, at least from his perspective, how this had all happened. Was there something of value amongst the correspondence between the police and Cannan over the past thirty-four years that would be of use? Something that might topple their house of cards against him?

64

The traffic was a nightmare as I tried to make my way into Central London to reach a client. Most of the nation was still in the midst of a full lockdown due to the COVID-19 outbreak, yet sitting alone in my car on a cold and windy Albert Bridge, the roads seemed to be gridlocked, almost as if there were no lockdown at all.

I turned on the radio, hunting for some travel news.

'In the capital today, thousands have marched in defiance of the controversial Police, Crime, Sentencing and Courts Bill, a new piece of government legislation that would curtail public protest. Scuffles broke out and parts of the demonstration descended into ugly scenes. Some protesters threw cans, bottles and flares at police. Thirty-three arrests were made. It comes just a week after violence between police and protesters at the Sarah Everard vigil in Clapham,' a female newsreader explained.

Protests were currently banned under lockdown legislation, preventing large gatherings from taking place. But following the abduction and murder of 33-year-old marketing executive Sarah Everard, and due to the ongoing draconian laws, many people were unhappy about what they called 'heavy-handed police tactics' and potential changes to their rights to demonstrate. This public unrest appeared to be the reason why I was stuck halfway across the Thames on a Saturday afternoon.

Just like Suzy, Sarah Everard had gone missing from South West London, her disappearance resonating in the media and with the public alike. Her abduction had reignited the debate around women's safety, and parallels had been drawn between Sarah and Suzy's cases. Due to the renewed media interest, the police had been forced into issuing a statement on Suzy's case:

> The Metropolitan Police Service's investigation into the disappearance and murder of Suzy Lamplugh is ongoing, and detectives remain committed to securing justice for her family.
>
> We will continue to ensure that no stone is unturned, as we know that one piece of information could provide the breakthrough for detectives.

Could it be that the Met was quite happy to ignore anything that didn't fit their preferred narrative in Suzy's case?

Coincidentally, on the day the police had discovered Sarah Everard's remains in a wood near Ashford, Kent, I'd received some correspondence from Dean Kingham, John Cannan's solicitor. We'd sent a series of questions to Full Sutton Prison where Cannan was now serving life imprisonment and his replies had come back.

Cannan described to us how he'd ended up at Wormwood Scrubs prison hostel at the end of his initial prison term: 'I was transferred from HMP The Verne on 25 January 1986 (under the Pre Release Employment Scheme) and arrived at the Scrubs hostel P.M. on the same date.'

At the beginning of 1986, Cannan had been moved from a Category C men's prison located within the historic Verne Citadel, on the Isle of Portland in Dorset. At the time, it was an open-style prison with very low levels of violence, good staff–prisoner relationships and a considerable training programme for prisoners.

In order to reintegrate Cannan back into society, he'd been moved to London, to a pre-release hostel at Wormwood Scrubs. Cannan's letter explained that he'd been a resident there for six months until 25 July 1986, but at certain points in his reply, he sounded exasperated that we'd sought answers to such basic questions.

We'd asked Cannan a series of rudimentary questions because we hadn't wanted to assume anything. Assumptions had been the cause of most of the problems we'd encountered in the Lamplugh case. And, like everyone else we'd contacted, we'd wanted to get the answers first-hand, directly from the interviewee. Like much of our investigation, the hard part was getting to the facts.

Despite his outward annoyance, Cannan had dutifully answered what we'd asked. He said he first became aware of Suzy's disappearance through the media in 1986 – around the time of her disappearance, just like everyone else had. However, following his arrest for the murder of Shirley Banks in autumn 1987, he began to see that he was also being personally linked to the Lamplugh case:

> The Avon and Somerset Police, at interview in Filton [Police Station] in 1987, were sometimes asking me Lamplugh-inclined questions. Moreover, the Avon and Somerset Police were using news conferences to suggest that I could be involved in the Lamplugh case. [See the press Oct 1987 onwards]. As for the Met, I think the first they interviewed me was in the autumn of 1989.

We'd asked Cannan if he had ever been known as 'Kipper' whilst in prison.

His response to this was unequivocal:

> Nobody, I repeat nobody, has ever called me Mr Kipper. This only arose as an accusation *after* my name was linked to the Lamplugh case by the Met and the media.

We were particularly interested in Cannan's whereabouts around the time Suzy had gone missing. We asked Cannan about his alibi and what he said next was rather interesting:

> My mother and I provided the Met with my simple alibi for 28 July 1986. We were in Birmingham nearly all day on Monday, 28 July. Had the Met acted quicker, my sister and brother-in-law would have provided 100 per cent water-tight corroboration. Both, sadly, are now dead. What I do

remember well is how frustrated and surprised we felt by the pedestrian pace of the Met to interview us all.

So not only did the Met *not* have any direct evidence against Cannan, he had also provided an alibi for the day that Suzy had gone missing. Whether one wants to believe an alibi or not, it can't simply be dismissed out of hand by the police – it's a matter for a court to test.

I knew from our research that this part of Cannan's letter did have a ring of truth to it too. Back in the summer of 1990, following renewed media pressure about the case, the police had gone back to Cannan again and interviewed him at length over the summer months. They'd spoken with several people in the Birmingham area who'd confirmed that they had seen Cannan in the West Midlands on the day Suzy went missing. By September 1990, police said that no further questioning was planned, and by October 1990, police were adamant that there was no evidence to support a charge. John's older sister Heather and her husband, Anthony Proctor, had both died shortly after these interviews – Heather in 1991; Anthony a year later in 1992.

At the bottom of his letter to us, Cannan had tried to provide some corroboration that he'd left London three days before Suzy had gone missing:

> Please find enclosed my job references from Superhire where I worked. Please note the date they were made out and given to me, 25 July 1986. That day was the last day I spent in the hostel and Superhire. I think it was a Friday. I said goodbye to all the staff, got my references and then caught a train from Euston to New Street, Birmingham. I got home to my mother's at about 5 p.m. that night. I spent Saturday and Sunday at home with my mom. I spent Monday in Birmingham with my mom [sic] so as to do some shopping.

What he'd sent us purported to be a signed reference from Superhire, a company where he'd worked for six months on day release from the Wormwood Scrubs hostel. At the time,

Superhire had been based in Acton, West London. It was a furniture-and-prop-hire company well known within the film and TV industry.

John Cannan's job reference read:

25 July 1986

TO WHOM IT MAY CONCERN

Mr John Cannon [sic] having worked for this company as a Bookman for the past 6 months has proved himself to be a reliable, honest & most conscientious worker.

I have no hesitation in recommending him for any position he may apply for, if however you should need any further information, please contact the undersigned.

Yours Faithfully,
R.C. BURGESS

It raised the question: was this a real job reference? And if the date on it was correct, did this help corroborate Cannan's insistence he had left London that Friday?

Turning off the radio and my car engine, I grabbed some notes I'd made over the past few days about Superhire. If I was going to be stuck on the windy Albert Bridge for some time, I would at least try to make the most of it.

I'd spent several days trying to find out who the signee R. C. Burgess was and whether they were still alive. I'd tracked down a number of previous employees of the company and asked them for help, but most had refused to talk to me.

One had inadvertently pointed me in the right direction though, and I'd located a telephone number for a possible match to the name on the bottom of Cannan's reference. As the wind buffeted my car from side to side, I dialled the number from my notes.

After just a few rings the phone was answered.

'Hello, is that Richard?' I asked

'Yes, speaking,' a voice at the other end of the line responded.

After introducing myself, and explaining the purpose of my call, Richard Burgess confirmed that it was indeed his signature on Cannan's job reference and that he remembered him well.

'Cannan came for an interview – we had a position, and I interviewed him. He was a very intelligent chap. And subsequently got the job. And then stayed there for a while,' Richard explained, recalling the events of thirty-five years ago. 'I worked for a company in the TV business, a prop-hire company, and that had loads of valuable stuff.'

'Was Cannan's job set up by the prison?' I asked.

I'd read up on the pre-release employment programme. It was quite special, and Cannan was lucky to have got onto it – testament to how well behaved and trusted he was by prison authorities. At the time, there were just eight pre-release employment scheme hostels in England and Wales, providing the opportunity for just 200 long-term prisoners a year to spend the last six months of their sentence in ordinary employment.

At the Wormwood Scrubs hostel, around twenty-five to thirty men were involved in the scheme at any one time, returning to the hostel each evening. The scheme helped prisoners prepare for their return to society in a practical way by providing guidance on how to find employment, covering aspects such as registration, income tax and national insurance and teaching the prisoners how to live on a restricted budget. The cost of their board and lodgings at the hostel were deducted from their wages before it was paid to them.

Before any prisoner could take part in the scheme, he had to go before a selection board which looked at his background, the crime he had committed and his prison record – and the board decided whether he was suitable or whether he would be a danger to the public. If a prisoner was selected to take part in the scheme, his case had to go before the regional prison director before it was finally approved. Even those previously involved in violent crime, such as murder, were eligible for the scheme, as long as they were deemed suitable, were nearing the end of their sentence and had passed all the stringent prison checks. It was hard to believe that Superhire was not aware that Cannan had previously been convicted for the theft of a car and for rape.

'Well, I'm not sure...' Richard hesitated. 'I told him that I needed a letter from the prison. And I said, "Can you get me anything to substantiate that?" And he managed to get that. He subsequently brought me a letter, all on prison headed paper. So I imagine he had to tell them he had a job, otherwise they wouldn't have let him come and go during the day. Originally he had to sign out in the morning before he left for work, and sign back in before six o'clock in the evening.'

'The job reference that Cannan has provided to me with your signature on is dated 25 July 1986, which is the Friday that he left the hostel,' I explained. 'And his recollection is that the date he left the hostel is the day he left Superhire. He collected the reference and then went where he was going from there. I wonder if you have any recollection about that final meeting at all?'

'At the time I was sorry to see him go, because he was a good worker,' Richard responded.

'I can show the reference to you if we can meet at some stage. Obviously this lockdown makes that difficult, but the date on the reference is Friday, 25 July 1986. If you'd dated it 25 July, would that be the same date you gave it to him?'

'I would have thought so. I mean it's so long ago, I can't remember.'

'Can you remember anything about where he said he was going afterwards? Did he say he was going to stay somewhere?'

'Only that he was planning to have a fresh start in Bristol. That's as much as I knew.'

'Do you know why he was going to Bristol?'

'No, as I say. He just said he wanted a fresh start and he'd decided it was going to be there. He didn't give me any reason. Or if he did, I can't remember. But I don't recall him saying anything.'

'And there were never any problems with him at Superhire?'

'No, as I said to you, I was sad to lose him as an employee at the time, because he was so very well liked by all the other staff.'

I thanked Richard for his time and bade him farewell.

It wasn't conclusive, but the man who'd provided the job reference to John Cannan three days before Suzy had gone missing did give some support to Cannan's intent to leave London that day – Friday, 25 July 1986. And for the three days that followed it, Cannan had an alibi, including the day Suzy had gone missing. Yet the police had eventually ignored his alibi evidence or chosen to disregard it.

'We will continue to ensure that no stone is unturned,' I repeated the line from the police statement on Suzy's case.

The steel bridge known as the Trembling Lady shook beneath me as the wind howled and the traffic began to flow.

65

The dark side of human nature, of what one person can do to another, and how we behave when confronted with most unspeakable situations both frighten and fascinate us in equal measure. It's why crime fiction is so popular as a genre. But when a mystery actually plays out in real life, as Suzy's has for more than thirty years, it occupies a special place in our imagination.

When I started this journey, my original intention was to find where Suzy had ended up on that fateful day in July 1986; to discover how she could have vanished without a single trace, as her mother once said, *as if she had been erased by a rubber.*

Along the way, I have learned a great deal about the way my fellow humans treat others in unspeakable situations.

From the very first witness I spoke with in this investigation, Adam Leegood, a former boyfriend of Suzy's, it was clear that there was much more to this story than most understood And his abnormal reaction to our questions – storming out of the meeting and leaving his coffee to go cold on the table in front of us as we wondered what we'd said to upset him – set a pattern for the entire investigation.

Everyone we spoke with, without question, would say or do something that was totally unexpected. Each of the characters in the case would divulge to us another miniature revelation that reset the narrative by a fraction of a millimetre, the cumulative difference building all the time.

Why was it that Adam was so upset with our questions around what had or had not happened at the Prince of Wales pub when Suzy was said to have simply lost her chequebook and secret pocket diary?

I was never able to understand that. I still don't. Adam has not replied to my subsequent communications.

When we first spoke with Suzy's work colleagues at Sturgis estate agency, apart from the strange argument with Nigel Hindle, life in the Fulham Road branch seemed unremarkable on that last morning there for Suzy. But a mere scratching of the surface revealed that it was anything but. It was clear that on that fateful day, a whole host of unique dynamics played out for her in the most tragic way.

Mark Gurdon, Suzy's immediate line manager, eventually admitted that he thought she was going home to Putney that lunchtime. Why would he think this with an appointment written in her work desk diary to meet a 'Mr Kipper'? Why had Mark made the subconscious decision to call her friends and family *before* he considered visiting 37 Shorrolds Road? And why had the police decided to break into Suzy's flat but not visit Shorrolds Road that night?

While he would never actually say it explicitly, it seemed likely that in the intervening years, any faith Mark Gurdon had put in the 'Mr Kipper' diary entry had dwindled away.

When we looked further below the surface, beyond what the police had ever tried to do, to understand what was really going on amongst the other Sturgis personnel, we uncovered that the office was not only short of staff that day, but that the company rule enforcer, its militaristic hirer and firer, Keith Perry, was also present.

His presence at Sturgis' Fulham Road branch at exactly the same time Suzy desperately needed to get out of the office on a personal errand hadn't factored into any of the police inquiries. The police didn't even take a statement from him. They'd never asked about the company branch staffing policies, set by Martin Sturgis the owner and enforced by Keith Perry. They had failed to understand how this would have impacted upon the way Suzy behaved that day.

Mark would explain to us that it was his management style to run 'a pretty relaxed ship' in his own branch, and so long as there was 'no disappearing off for hours and hours on end', he was fairly relaxed about where his staff were during the day. Though of course, when I interviewed the owner, Martin

Sturgis, I found that there were policies and procedures that he expected his enforcer to ensure the staff adhered to. When I spoke with Keith, I was given the impression that anyone would take what he said as an order or instruction, not just a piece of friendly advice.

In the moments before she left the office, it was this conundrum that Suzy found herself up against on that fateful day. Was it surprising that I had been able to find this out more than thirty years later? Or was it more surprising that the police had never bothered to look for these nuances and understand the unique office circumstances Suzy had found herself in?

Every investigation is always full of stories or 'subplots', as Nigel Hindle had called his inter-office relationship with Stephanie Flower – and it's the job of the investigator to understand how the subplot intersects with the main narrative.

But, as I found out, none of what was going on in the office and who was present there that day seemed of any concern to the police, because none of it helped them tell the story they wanted to share with the public.

It was the police themselves, perhaps with the help of Suzy's parents, who, within hours, decided on a narrative and the most likely scenario of Suzy's disappearance, thus setting investigative lines of enquiry and closing their minds to anything else before they'd barely interviewed a single witness.

Everyone loves a mystery after all. And 'Mr Kipper', the shadowy house buyer, was a much better story than Suzy placing a false entry in her desk diary to comply with the company's policies just because the company enforcer was present that day?

The 'Mr Kipper' narrative seemed to suit and fascinate everyone in equal amounts, even the police. There was a bogeyman to follow; someone the investigation team and the media could visualise, and a story that would unnerve yet entertain the public, all at the same time. It would go on to sell a lot of newspapers and make Suzy's case infamous.

So as the police concocted the narrative around the 'Mr Kipper' diary entry, they completely ignored the fact that Suzy didn't have the door key for 37 Shorrolds Road with her. And they seemingly also ignored those work colleagues that might have had an inkling, deep down, that the mysterious 'Mr Kipper' likely didn't exist.

It simply wasn't possible for Suzy to do that viewing at 37 Shorrolds Road that day – not without the key. And the key still being at the Sturgis office would have proved that. Yet somehow this fact was ignored, despite the police themselves eventually coming into possession of the only key that Sturgis had. The key the police would use to let their own scenes of crime officer into 37 Shorrolds Road, less than twenty-four hours after Suzy had gone missing. The key the police would admit to us they had in their possession when we challenged them about it many decades later.

Who at Sturgis handed that key over to the police? I have my suspicions as to who that was, and I believe it was a genuine oversight at the time, but I shan't name them here. Mistakes happen, of course. It's a fact of life, especially in emotive, fast-moving situations.

I then uncovered that the police had deliberately misled the press about what their chief witness, Harry Riglin, had said to them, right from the very outset. And it was clear, from Det. Supt Nick Carter's police appeals, from the very words that he had used in those first few days, that Suzy was never identified by Harry Riglin as being outside 37 Shorrolds Road. Harry's statement described only 'a fair-haired lady', yet whilst quoting these exact words, Carter would in his very next breath claim that this was the last time Suzy had been seen alive.

Why would the senior investigating officer mislead everyone like this?

How would it have looked if the police had admitted that Suzy had made a false entry in her diary and hadn't taken the key with her to do the viewing? What would that have done to the initial press coverage, something that was important to both Carter and the Lamplughs? After all, everyone agreed that the media coverage would help in finding Suzy and could only be a good thing?

But there was something else I found too. There were people within the investigation team who believed that Harry Riglin's account, the words in his witness statement, were malleable. Instead of concluding that it *wasn't* Suzy that he had seen that day in Shorrolds Road, the police looked for excuses as to why Harry was *unable* to identify the woman he'd seen as Suzy.

By way of explanation, they told the senior investigating officer that Harry Riglin couldn't be relied upon to identify Suzy because he was so transfixed by the good-looking man. And their reasoning to explain this all away? Harry was gay.

This resulted in a deliberate, conscious decision by Carter to allow the 'Mr Kipper' narrative to lead in those early days, despite there being no evidence to support that Suzy was ever at the house in Shorrolds Road.

And when the senior investigating officer is pushing a particular narrative, was it any wonder that glaring clues – such as the house key being left in the Sturgis office and Suzy not having it with her – were overlooked, or even completely ignored?

I'd suggest not, and the individual at the Sturgis office who then handed the key over to the police is not to blame for this – the problem is, and was, with the investigation team.

Carter's main strategy was to gain as much media coverage as possible. Haunted by the failure to find out what had happened to schoolboy Martin Allen in 1979, something that he in part blamed on the lack of media coverage of the case, and under pressure to get a result because of his own fast-approaching retirement date, he may well have thought he had very little choice.

So, up against the clock and with the media braying at the door for a story, the 'Mr Kipper' narrative likely seemed to the police a prudent choice to run with as an initial line of enquiry.

In those very early stages, Carter was in the process of trying to build a relationship with the Lamplugh family. He was keen they remained onside and assisted in the investigation. He could not be seen to cast any doubt on the veracity of Suzy's work-diary entry. However, the problem was that by *not* identifying Suzy at Shorrolds Road, Harry Riglin, the chief witness, cast *huge* aspersions on the police assumption she'd gone there.

But publicly revealing this information risked upsetting Paul and Diana, as well as unfavourable press coverage.

It's difficult to know for certain why Carter decided upon the route he took in those first crucial hours and days, but when I listen to the paucity of the information provided by the police, and the questions fired at Diana and Paul Lamplugh from the media during that first press conference, it could also be argued that he wasn't completely in control. In their anguished and distressed state during those initial stages, Paul and Diana were setting the narrative which would ultimately shape the police investigation.

Again, this is something that Carter may have felt was necessary, to placate and maintain the cooperation of the family. He may have believed that it was a relationship that he could manage. He was, after all, said to be a very experienced detective. But even he couldn't possibly have anticipated how big a story it would become in the press, how much the public would love the mystery, or how Paul and Diana's growing influence and media presence might impact upon the investigation.

However, within days, the warning bells should have been ringing. Det. Supt Carter quickly lost control of any media strategy he had set, as Diana Lamplugh began organising her own press conferences in the garden of her house and bringing in mediums and spiritualists to assist in the hunt. And it was against this backdrop that Sir David Napley began operating in the shadows. Paul and Diana were encouraged to interview witnesses themselves; to conduct their own investigation; to share questionnaires about Suzy's life with her friends in order to look for clues as to who might have been lurking in the background. Much of this activity was done completely independently from the police – perhaps even using private detectives.

The police, in their own investigation, would unearth connections between Suzy and John Herring, someone that Suzy actually knew, someone that had the nickname 'Kipper' and who had lived in both of the roads listed in her work desk diary on the page for 28 July 1986. But by then it was too late. The narrative that Carter had set had taken on a life of its own.

The police were no longer able to control the avalanche they had helped create. It was now impossible to stop.

John Herring was an innocent friend with an alibi and no personal involvement in Suzy's disappearance. He was not the murderous 'Mr Kipper' that the police, the media or the Lamplughs wanted. The 'Mr Kipper' they were after *had* to have previous convictions and a penchant for kidnapping, raping or killing women.

And so, cheered on by Paul and Diana, in the pursuit of progress and answers, seven days into the investigation, with not a shred of evidence to support the 'Mr Kipper' narrative at all, the police pushed ahead and conducted a reconstruction of the *events*. Except that it wasn't a reconstruction – they had no idea what the facts were. It was a fictional mystery drama played by police officers themselves and supported by real-life props and locations from Suzy's life.

Having watched this dramatisation of the police narrative on the television, some members of the public now came forward, believing that they might have seen something similar to the fiction that had played out on their screens. The false narrative began to snowball, thus reinforcing the story that the police had themselves created.

The vast majority of the information the police generated in those first few months was worthless. It took them nowhere further in the case, whilst at the same time exhausting their resources and overwhelming their investigative capabilities.

And naturally this frustrated the Lamplughs, creating further problems between the family and more senior members of the police – especially when there was talk of closing the investigation because it wasn't coming up with any actual evidence of what had happened.

As the police stalled in their attempts to investigate their own narrative, the void of information and lack of progress was filled by the Lamplughs and Sir David Napley. Paul and Diana became more and more proactive, throwing up lines of enquiry in the media in the hope of sparking new public interest and the desperate belief that something, anything, would turn up. The narrative and control began to spiral away from the police. It was a vicious circle that no one could undo.

As Christmas of 1986 approached, and Det. Supt Nick Carter retired, the investigation was already fatally flawed, littered with falsehoods, failed strategies, assumptions, incompetence and staffed by a police team who were hopelessly out of their depth, incapable of finding the truth amongst the mountain of misinformation they'd created for themselves.

The battle was long since lost. It had been lost within twenty-four hours of Suzy going missing.

As 1986 became 1987 and Det. Supt Malcolm Hackett stepped into Nick Carter's old shoes, hairline cracks began to appear in the relationship between the police and the Lamplugh family.

Through no fault of his own, Hackett would inherit an investigation beyond redemption, along with the exasperation of a bereaved family seeking to redress the balance at the loss of their daughter.

Of course, the Lamplughs, by then, were so distressed by the inactivity on the case and failure of the police to find a single piece of evidence that would help in delivering their desire for justice that they saw the police as part of the problem. It was Hackett who would eventually inherit the lion's share of the blame in the media, as he attempted to draw a line under the police activity on the case.

The reality was he stood little to no chance of extinguishing the impassioned fires that simmered in the background. Paul and Diana, as distraught parents, had a burning desire for a result in the case. They wanted to move on with their lives and look to the future for the rest of the family's sake. But the desire for an end to the pain had perhaps become so strong that it had the potential to create the exact opposite of what everyone wanted: a miscarriage of justice.

The police had lost control of the case and the relationship with the family now plumbed new depths.

66

Following the disappearance of Shirley Banks in 1987, ostensibly during a Bristol shopping spree one dark October evening, members of the press began linking her disappearance to that of Suzy's. It wasn't the first time that links between the Lamplugh investigation and other tragic cases had been suggested in the media; it had happened frequently since Suzy's disappearance.

But this time it was different. By this point, Det. Supt Malcolm Hackett had closed the investigation into Suzy's disappearance. Despite arguments and protestations from the Lamplughs, he'd sealed the files and redeployed the staff. His decision was final. The police could go no further. Paul and Diana were devastated.

And so it was, as the first layer of dust in a Hammersmith store room settled onto the now sealed files of the Suzy investigation, the disappearance of Shirley Banks presented Paul, Diana and Sir David Napley with a huge opportunity, provided that the necessary connections could be made between the two cases.

During September 1987, in the month before Shirley Banks' disappearance, John Cannan had been involved in a bitter dispute with solicitor Annabel Rose. He was making accusations about her conduct as a solicitor and had employed a private detective to place her parents under surveillance. The dispute led to Annabel having to confess her affair with Cannan to her husband and eventually resulted in her resigning from her job with her law firm. And it was at this juncture, with the Lamplughs desperate for information on a link between the Shirley Banks case and their daughter's, that Cannan was arrested for the Banks murder.

Suddenly, Diana began making accusations against Cannan in relation to Suzy's disappearance, armed with detailed and intimate knowledge of his background and previous convictions. It was information which likely came from Sir David Napley, whose cousins (Annabel Rose's parents) had been placed under surveillance by Cannan in his dispute with Annabel. The motivations of the Lamplughs and Sir David Napley couldn't have been more different, of course, though it would lead inexorably to Cannan being named as the prime suspect in Suzy's case.

For the Lamplughs, Cannan represented someone that the police *had* to investigate, a reason they'd *have* to reopen Suzy's investigation. For Sir David Napley, Cannan was someone that was causing trouble for the whole Napley family, someone who was in the process of damaging not only Annabel Rose's career, but the professional reputations of several legal careers surrounding her. His arrest and incarceration, even if only briefly, would provide all parties involved with what they wanted?

Initially, Avon and Somerset Police had struggled to find the evidence to charge Cannan with anything other than the theft of Shirley Banks' car. Even if charged with that, it was possible he could be granted bail.

Somehow, the *News of the World* newspaper became aware of both Cannan's name, his history and previous criminal convictions and published them. This took place on the very same day that Diana Lamplugh began pleading with the Met Police's Deputy Assistant Commissioner, Paul Condon, to reopen the case. She claimed that, if he didn't reopen Suzy's case, there would be questions raised about a 'police cover-up' and the investigation would be discussed in the House of Commons. As for the *News of the World*'s actions, the paper would later be fined in the High Court for contempt.

Hackett refused to consider Cannan as a viable suspect, despite the detailed dossier that Diana and Paul had built, most likely through Sir David Napley. The Met stood firm, supported by their colleagues in Avon and Somerset Police, who also agreed that there was nothing to connect John Cannan with any involvement in the disappearance of Suzy Lamplugh.

Undeterred, Paul and Diana mounted a concerted PR

campaign to convince anyone that would listen that they were right – ably supported, I'm sure, by Sir David Napley. Their drive at that time was likely just to have Suzy's case reopened. The news media assisted whenever they could – this was, after all, exactly the type of 'Mr Kipper' they could really get behind and the public were fascinated with.

Over the next decade, Diana and Paul seem to have convinced themselves that their PR was actually evidence, and that they were right. They believed that the artist's impression of the man Harry Riglin described at 37 Shorrolds Road was a good likeness of Cannan. They coupled this with Cannan's previous criminal convictions, his rough proximity in time and space to the area they believed Suzy went missing in, the seeming non-existence of other suspects and the idea that whoever killed Suzy didn't abduct any more estate agents after Cannan was arrested. Surely they couldn't be wrong?

During the nineties, the police repeatedly rebuffed all of these allegations *and* the lurid suggestions that circulated in the press supporting them. At one point, in 1991, the police spoke at length to Cannan's former girlfriend, Gilly Paige, for a second time. She disassociated herself from sensationalist press headlines surrounding her sexual relationship with Cannan and publicly stood by her original police statement.

Again, the Met held their ground. They were content with Cannan's alibi and that he had been eliminated from their inquiry. They were adamant: the case would remain closed. Cannan was not a suspect.

But by 1999, things had changed. Diana Lamplugh had become one of the most powerful voices for female victims of crime that the country had ever seen. Through the Suzy Lamplugh Trust, she campaigned for new laws and regulations which were unprecedented in their nature, helping to support thousands of people through her work. She was awarded the Order of the British Empire (OBE) in 1992, in recognition of her achievements through the trust. As a sitting member of several parliamentary committees, she could count home secretaries among her friends.

So when Graham McGredy-Hunt came forward in late 1999, Paul and Diana might have believed that this could help bring things to a close – a final throw of the dice they'd thrown countless times over the past decade without success.

For the police, it happened as the political landscape was rapidly shifting beneath them. The Macpherson Report, detailing the failings in the Stephen Lawrence case published earlier that year (1999), had left the police vulnerable to accusations from bereaved families. There simply wasn't an option for them to avoid relooking at the allegations the Lamplughs were making, especially not with the Met about to get a brand new commissioner, one that couldn't afford the missteps of his predecessor.

Moreover, by 1999, everything the police had previously learned about Suzy's disappearance, and the numerous previous attempts by the Lamplughs to have the case reopened, had long since been forgotten. Most of the original investigators had retired or left the Met, and the handwritten card indexing system used in the antiquated 1986 incident room was far too cumbersome for the new investigators to fully search.

So it was much easier for the new police team to just listen to the instructions and indications given by Paul and Diana, and to appease them.

In 2000, the power thus reverted to the Lamplughs again, much as it seems to have done in that first week after Suzy's disappearance.

In Paul and Diana's desperation to have the case reopened, information was reinserted back into the investigation that had been previously discounted, taken out of context or was outright media myth. And with nobody able to successfully search through the 26,000 card entries, little, if any, challenge could be made as to the veracity of the information the Lamplughs now provided the police with.

By 2000, the Lamplughs also pushed a long line of grievances. They claimed that the police had released the wrong photos of Suzy with dark hair, that Suzy was doing a second viewing at Wendy Jones' house in Stevenage Road on the day she went missing, that the married 38-year-old Bristol businessman mentioned by a former beauty client in 1984 was Cannan and that the family had very quickly fallen out with the original police investigation team. But more than a decade on from Suzy's disappearance, seemingly none of this was fact-checked or challenged by the replacement police team. It filtered into the case and took root.

As a result, police went on what was best described as a fishing expedition through the media for confirmation of these grievances, asking members of the public to come forward with information about Cannan, which some did.

The police then populated their new computerised files with anything that pointed in Cannan's direction, eventually convincing themselves that the Lamplughs must have been right after all.

Why didn't the police go back to the original witnesses?

It's more than likely that Det. Supt Shaun Sawyer and his team thought that Suzy's case was unsolvable; that it was in such a mess, the only course of action was to use the only witnesses they had – Paul and Diana.

None of the police teams have ever understood what started Diana and Paul on the path of accusing Cannan of Suzy's murder; nor were they ever challenged about it. They failed to see the malignant interests of Sir David Napley in the background and the connections that lurked beneath the surface, which are revealed for the first time here. It's probably right to assume that Diana and Paul had no idea that their trusted solicitor had links to the suspect they would insist was responsible for Suzy's murder.

And there was an added complication; another dimension that few could see from the outside.

Diana was ill.

Paul Lamplugh would later explain that by the turn of the millennium, Diana had begun to make nonsensical announcements. When the police agreed to reopen Suzy's case in May 2000, Diana had been seen behaving oddly. She spoke fitfully about part of her body dying and being murdered. By the end of 2002, journalists were beginning to comment on how short and sharp she could be with them.

In March 2003, not long after the police had named Cannan as their one and only suspect, Diana was to suffer a major stroke. Paul Lamplugh revealed that during brain surgery, doctors had found plaques on Diana's brain, showing that she already had Alzheimer's and had done for some time. It would tragically strip her of her remaining faculties, which would result in her requiring round-the-clock care in a nursing home for the rest of her life.

Paul would explain that, in hindsight, he'd noted Diana wasn't well some time before her diagnosis. He wrote about how her personality had changed – that she'd become obsessed with certain ideas, how she could be argumentative and hostile, and that she had become very absent-minded.

A contact of the family would later publicly state that Diana had been diagnosed with early onset dementia, a condition that can affect those of working age, between the ages of thirty and sixty-five. Celebrating her fiftieth birthday in the week of Suzy's disappearance, it is possible that Diana could have suffered from dementia for many years without her knowledge. During her mid-fifties, she would be injured falling from a horse whilst out riding in Wales. The fall, in the early 1990s, left her out of action and in pain for a significant length of time. Indeed, studies show that fall-related, traumatic brain injury predicts earlier onset of dementia. Could it have been this horse-riding fall which potentially triggered Diana's illness?

It was perhaps against this background that there was a strong desire on the part of the police, indeed even from DAC Bill Griffiths himself, to placate and satisfy Suzy's ailing mother that day in the auditorium?

Was there any evidence against Cannan, or was it simply that the police, against the advice of the CPS, were trying to appease an ailing mother by saying she had been right all along?

Some years later, Paul Lamplugh would admit that it was Diana who'd insisted Cannan was named at the press conference, and as a result the family found closure that day in the auditorium.

Yet, despite many decades of insistence that Suzy was doing a house viewing with 'Mr Kipper' on the day she went missing, and the numerous attempts to connect the crime to Cannan, does the evidence collected here point to something entirely different?

I would suggest it does.

67

On the morning of 28 July 1986, Suzy arrives at work promptly and normally. Nick Bryant, her flatmate, made no mention of any problems or anything untoward about their time together at breakfast in the flat they shared in Putney. However, at some point that morning, it appears that Suzy discovered her chequebook and secret pocket diary were missing from her bag. Suzy perhaps makes contact with her bank to cancel her lost chequebook. Just one person has any vague recollection of this. Stephanie Flower, the office secretary, isn't sure if she remembers someone losing a chequebook at work on this occasion or on a previous occasion. But it's possible she does, and it's possible she heard Suzy talking on the phone to the bank, just as the police believe.

South of the River Thames, in Putney, at the Prince of Wales pub, there is a stocktake going on. There are at least five people in the pub. The full-time landlords, Michael and Zoe Hutchings, are getting ready for their drive to Wales to see Zoe's sister and her new baby. The Imperial Inns & Taverns stocktaker is listing everything on the premises and counting the money so that the premises can be handed over to the soon-to-be relief workers, who are also present – Clive Vole and his partner Karen Furness.

Suzy's lost chequebook and secret pocket diary are on the premises. According to the relief barman, Clive, he'd found them outside the pub the night before, as he'd gone to pick up a Chinese takeaway.

On Monday morning, likely acting on the conscientious instructions given by Michael to reunite this lost property with its owner, Clive is also on the phone to the very same bank as Suzy, at around the same time, with Suzy's chequebook in his possession.

That Monday morning, Suzy is made aware, potentially by the bank, that her lost property and prized secret diary are at the Prince of Wales pub in Putney.

For the staff in Suzy's office, an unusual luncheon is about to take place. The firm's enforcer, and the man that hired Suzy for her role, Keith Perry, is hanging around the office prior to going to a wine bar a few doors down. While Suzy knows Keith is going to lunch with her branch manager, Mark Gurdon, at Crocodile Tears, no one knows if Keith plans to come back into the office *after* lunch.

Suzy is likely on tenterhooks. There's a conversation between Suzy and Mark where she explains that she needs to go to Putney that lunchtime. It's her only chance that day to retrieve her lost property and perhaps pick up her tennis kit. She has an appointment at 6 p.m. with Joanna Wright and intends on playing tennis straight after, which scuppers any chance of running these errands later. There's simply no other time she can go to grab her things.

Mark appears to have made the assumption that Suzy is doing some shopping in Putney. Today, he claims to remember nothing about a lost chequebook and pocket diary.

At around midday, Mark and Keith leave the Sturgis office and go to the Crocodile Tears wine bar. At around the same time, the stocktake is coming to an end at the Prince of Wales pub. The paperwork is being signed off, and Zoe and Michael leave the premises on their long drive to see the new baby. The Prince of Wales is left in the hands of Clive and Karen.

With Keith gone, Suzy decides to nip out to Putney and collect her lost property while her managers are out at lunch. She calls the pub and there is a conversation between Suzy and Clive where she arranges to pick the items up.

Suzy disguises the personal errand with a work appointment, by placing the 'Mr Kipper' entry in her diary, just in case Keith the enforcer comes back while she is out. She doesn't touch the key to the house for sale at 37 Shorrolds Road because she has no intention of going to that property. The diary entry is fictitious but has subconscious connections to Suzy's personal

341

associations with the road names on the page. The house key remains on the rack, undisturbed, at the back of the office. She leaves her handbag, with the overt implication that she will not be away from her desk for long, but grabs her company car key on its bright yellow Sturgis fob.

All of the evidence points toward Suzy then getting into her car and driving straight to the pub to collect her lost property. What happens when she gets there is currently unknown.

According to the police, the 'salacious' content of Suzy's personal diary might have singled her out for some form of target. As the police subsequently retrieved Suzy's secret pocket diary from the pub later that week, had full sight of it and possibly still do, let's assume that they are right.

On arrival at the pub, which is potentially closed due to the stocktake and changeover of personnel, Suzy bumps into someone who has browsed the contents of her secret pocket diary. That person, likely motivated by the content of the diary, perhaps targets Suzy for some form of attack, blackmail attempt or retribution?

How would Suzy have reacted in these circumstances?

Suzy was fit, strong and confident. She was described by a number of people that I spoke with as 'able to handle herself'. She may well have tried to fight off any form of physical attack or sexual assault. However, according to her mother, Suzy also suffered from claustrophobia. And this introduces a different dynamic into what her behaviour might have been.

Suzy's lost property was described as being in the basement area that day. If Suzy was enticed down into the basement to collect the lost property, she may have suffered a panic attack. There could have been shortness of breath, difficulty breathing or a choking sensation. Rather than Suzy being the victim of a murder, there could, of course, have been some sort of terrible accident at the pub that afternoon. Could someone have simply covered this up for fear of the repercussions?

What supports the idea that something befell Suzy at the Prince of Wales pub and she remains there to this day?

All of the evidence suggests that the pub was her intended destination after she left the office that day. The relief barman,

Clive Vole, says he spoke to her on the phone, confirming with us that she was due to collect her items and that she was particularly agitated about the whereabouts of her secret pocket diary. The police also agree that she was due to collect her items from the pub that day. The alleged odd phone call to the pub, potentially from the unidentified neighbour looking for her, also supports that she might have told someone else that was where she was heading that lunchtime.

The fact that no trace of Suzy has ever been discovered and that her remains have never been found points to her current resting place being in a location that has been undisturbed for more than three decades – a secure and protected site.

The Prince of Wales pub had a large, readily accessible void underneath the stage area of the dining-room floor. This void is accessed just feet from where her lost property was said to have been awaiting her collection. The void, though now considerably reduced in height and volume, contains an odd mound of rubbish that remains untouched. The mound of rubbish under the dining-room floor can be dated as being from around the period that Suzy went missing by the items of refuse upon it.

Michael Hutchings, the full-time landlord, reports a problem with blowflies in the basement at the Prince of Wales at certain points. Blowfly larvae are carrions. As soon as blowflies find a cadaver, sometimes within minutes of death, they begin to lay eggs on it. Each fly deposits about 250 eggs in the natural openings of the body or its open wounds. The eggs hatch into first-stage maggots within twenty-four hours and begin to feed. Within seven to nine days the larvae go through various stages and eventually metamorphose into adult flies, and the cycle starts again. It's possible that Michael provides the most reliable evidence there is of a cadaver nearby.

The soil in the void underneath the dining-room floor is loamy with a high sand content. Despite the pub's proximity to the Thames, and the rain that drips in through the barrel drop doors, the space underneath the dining-room floor is separate and provides a completely different environment that is surprisingly dry and lacks moisture. In this dry environment, desiccation, the process of the body drying out after death, would likely have inhibited any smell. We also collected evidence of a drain to the sewer near to this area, which again would mask any odour there would have been. All of this points to an ideal environment for Suzy's remains to be concealed in.

If this is all correct, why was Suzy's car abandoned in Stevenage Road?

If Suzy's final destination was the Prince of Wales pub, as all of the evidence suggests it was, it would have been incumbent upon whoever knew what had befallen her there to move her car. The white Ford Fiesta belonging to Sturgis would have been, after all, a huge red flag as to her final destination. In 1986, yellow lines, road signs and kerb markings all restricted vehicles parking on the roads around the pub.

So using the car keys they've taken from Suzy, they drive the white Ford Fiesta north over the river, placing a psychological barrier between the pub and Suzy. Her car is abandoned on the north side of the river, away from the pub and away from her flat.

The effect of moving the car had a huge impact on the subsequent police investigations. By leaving the car in Fulham, in the same police area that would investigate Suzy's disappearance, the police confined all of their efforts to that area. They didn't think to look further afield. And even years later, in 2002, the police suspect matrix would be confined to only those in the Fulham area.

Whoever moved the car was thinking on their feet. As they drove Suzy's car along the most famous street in the Fulham area, where Fulham's Craven Cottage football stadium is located, looking for somewhere to abandon it, they happened across a house with a Sturgis board outside. Something that would further confuse investigators, especially in the modern day, with the idea Suzy was due to do a viewing at this second house for sale, with the completely fictitious 'Mr Kipper'.

But whoever moved Suzy's car, and dumped it opposite *another* Sturgis house for sale, *knew* she worked for Sturgis because her car key, taken from her and used to move her vehicle, was attached to a bright yellow Sturgis key fob listing many of their London branches. This vivid key fob matched the yellow Sturgis 'For Sale' boards to be found in every part of South and West London at the time.

So where is Suzy?

When I first considered investigating Suzy's mysterious disappearance it was because I believed if I found what had happened to her, where she was and could help lay her to rest somehow, I could undo all the mistakes we made in Joanne Eddison's case. Central to this belief was that it had been our failure as a police service back then to find the evidence of a murder and not *just* manslaughter, for Joanne's family. The feeling of injustice was at the heart of everything I did.

What I thought I'd find, if I could get to the bottom of what had happened to Suzy, was peace. A chance to lay the demons which plague me about Joanne's case to rest, and to move on.

Alas, the demons are still present, though now joined by others.

Suzy's tortured parents never gave up fighting for her to be found. They were driven to the point of despair, never knowing the truth because of the repeated failures of the police, enraged by it. While I was never able to meet Paul or Diana Lamplugh, it is easy for me to imagine their inner feelings just by visualising Joanne's anguished father and his spittle on my face.

Their frustration now lives on, in me, as does the anger of Joanne's father.

Paradoxically, it has made me much more aware of the plight of prisoners languishing in jails, accused of crimes they did not commit, but denied the opportunity of real justice, delivered through the courts in the correct way. It was something I never had much appreciation for as a police officer. I was always of the view there was no smoke without fire. But Suzy's case has shown me how easily smoke and mirrors can be created, sometimes unwittingly, by the police, media and public themselves. Some prisoners stand absolutely no chance of defending the allegations against them. And for as long as they remain accused, the real perpetrator gets off scot-free.

When judges swear their judicial oath in the UK, they swear they, 'Will do right to all manner of people after the laws and usages of this realm, without fear or favour, affection or ill will.' Those same judges can often be heard telling jurors in criminal trials to 'set aside their emotions' when listening to evidence, and to only make decisions on the evidence they hear and see during the trial. It's completely unnatural, of course, as we are all human, and emotions play such a central role in our decision-making.

But one of the things the British justice system has always done very well, through the lawyers, the courts, the juries, and the law itself, is to be dispassionate, for this very reason, in order for it to be fair. To rule on the evidence, and only the evidence in the case, not the emotions of those involved.

The police's role in this system is to investigate and collect the evidence, impartially; evidence that would show guilt or innocence, and then to present that evidence through the necessary channels, to ensure that anyone accused of a crime can properly challenge it.

Trials by media, where the police infer someone is guilty without ever releasing or revealing publicly what the evidence is, by holding a kangaroo court, and then allowing public opinion to be the chief judge of who is guilty and who is not, are the preserve of failed states, not the UK.

Suzy's disappearance was an unbearable tragedy which continues to affect her family to this day. The police were never able to find any evidence of what happened to her. They still haven't, yet they continue to try to persuade the world at large that they have.

Suzy's heartbroken parents felt they had no choice but to progress the investigation themselves. When they too were unable to find any evidence, they were left with only their emotions, the emotions that the justice system tries to suppress. Eventually, and facilitated by the police themselves, Diana and Paul were led to believe they could find some sort of closure, and move on with their lives, by pointing the finger of blame at a man who is never likely to see the outside of a prison cell.

For me, this fallacy makes the tragedy of Suzy's disappearance much, much worse. How can it be a victory if Suzy's killer or the person responsible for covering up her death is never identified in a courtroom? The evidence has to be tested in a courtroom. And if that evidence isn't even strong enough to support a charge, let alone bring that person before a court, how on earth can the police claim to have solved the case?

Some will say, and I would agree, that the refusal to consider other avenues of investigation – because it exposes the collective organisational incompetence of the past and opens the police up to litigation should they do so – does more than compound the problems of the previous four decades.

There can be no victory, for anyone, of any type, all the time Suzy remains absent from her poor parents' side. All the time she is missing, that she is lost, and never properly laid to rest in a location of her family's choice – no one should be patting themselves on the back and believing they've done a good job.

This should be the single and only goal of the police at this stage.

My own journey to find Suzy led me to all four corners of the UK and everywhere in between. I interviewed people in Australia, New Zealand and the US. And all along, she was in a cold, dark void under the dining-room floor of a pub, less than 200 metres from her own front door in Putney.

It is a dereliction of duty on the part of the police not to search underneath that dining-room floor for Suzy's remains. We don't know what happened at the pub and we don't know who was present, but murder or accident, that's where she is waiting, along with the rest of the answers about what actually happened in the pub that afternoon on the last Monday of July in 1986.

How much longer must Suzy wait?

For the latest updates on Suzy's case or more information about the author's other books, please visit:

www.davidvidecette.com